Libraries and Homelessness

Libraries and Homelessness

An Action Guide

Julie Ann Winkelstein

LIBRARIES
UNLIMITED®

An Imprint of ABC-CLIO, LLC
Santa Barbara, California • Denver, Colorado

Library of Congress Cataloging-in-Publication Data

Names: Winkelstein, Julie Ann, author.
Title: Libraries and homelessness : an action guide / Julie Ann
    Winkelstein.
Description: Santa Barbara, California : Libraries Unlimited, [2021] |
    Includes bibliographical references and index.
Identifiers: LCCN 2020052576 (print) | LCCN 2020052577 (ebook) |
    ISBN 9781440862786 (paperback) | ISBN 9781440862793 (ebook)
Subjects: LCSH: Libraries and the homeless—United States. | Libraries and
    community—United States. | Homelessness—United States. | Public
    services (Libraries)—United States. | Homeless persons—Services
    for—United States.
Classification: LCC Z711.92.H66 W56 2021 (print) | LCC Z711.92.H66
    (ebook) | DDC 027.6—dc23
LC record available at https://lccn.loc.gov/2020052576
LC ebook record available at https://lccn.loc.gov/2020052577

ISBN: 978-1-4408-6278-6 (print)
       978-1-4408-6279-3 (ebook)

25 24 23 22 21   1 2 3 4 5

This book is also available as an eBook.

Libraries Unlimited
An Imprint of ABC-CLIO, LLC

ABC-CLIO, LLC
147 Castilian Drive
Santa Barbara, California 93117
www.abc-clio.com

This book is printed on acid-free paper ∞

Manufactured in the United States of America

To my husband, David Boyce Danby.
Your support has meant everything.

Contents

Acknowledgments

As I worked on this book, I drew on information and resources from a wide range of sources. I'm particularly grateful for the work being done by the National Alliance to End Homelessness (NAEH), the National Low Income Housing Coalition (NLIHC), Point Source Youth, True Colors United, the National Homelessness Law Center, the Homeless Hub, ACEs Connection, the Western Regional Advocacy Project (WRAP), the National LGBTQ Task Force, the Institute for the Study of Societal Issues (ISSI), the Othering and Belonging Institute at the University of California (UC) Berkeley, the UC Berkeley Center for Race & Gender, the National Coalition for the Homeless, the National Center for Homeless Education, Larkin Street Youth Services in San Francisco, the Human Rights Campaign, the National Runaway Safeline, Lavamae[x], VoteRiders, TurboVote, abcVote, and all the other organizations that work so hard to address the intersections of homelessness, poverty, and people's lives. Your conferences, webinars, resources, and publications continue to provide me with relevant information and inspirational support.

I'd also like to thank Edwin Cortez, who first introduced me to the idea of looking at homelessness through the lens of libraries. His death was a loss to the profession.

I'm grateful to my students in the class I've been teaching annually for the School of Information Sciences (SIS) at the University of Tennessee, Knoxville. Titled "The Role of Libraries in Addressing Homelessness and Poverty," the class has been a pleasure to teach and has provided me with so many opportunities to see the wonderful work being done in libraries by those, like my students, who are committed to addressing social justice issues such as homelessness and poverty. My thanks, too, to the many class guest speakers who have offered their time and knowledge and have contributed to my ongoing commitment to collect relevant information related to this topic. I'd also like to acknowledge Diane Kelly, past director of UTK SIS, who provided me with a venue for this particular class.

Thank you, too, to Infopeople, the information and training branch of CALIFA, a California nonprofit library membership consortium, and especially Mary Augugliaro and Lisa Barnhart. Your input and support in creating the continuing education class on homelessness and libraries that I taught for Infopeople was invaluable.

A special thanks to my first editor, Barbara Ittner, who initially reached out to me about writing this book for Libraries Unlimited/ABC-CLIO and who nudged and enthusiastically supported me. Without her initial contact, I'm not sure this book would exist.

I also want to acknowledge and thank Jessica Gribble, my current editor, who has been warmly encouraging, patient, and helpful as this book has evolved. And, of course, thank you to ABC-CLIO for providing the opportunity to publish a book about libraries and homelessness.

Thanks, too, to the members of the Whole Person Librarianship (WPL) listserv, whose postings and generosity in answering my questions have made a difference. A particular thank you to Elissa Hardy—your honesty and in-depth knowledge have contributed greatly to my understanding of what libraries can do.

I want to thank members of the International Federation of Library Associations and Institutions (IFLA) section "Library Services to People with Special Needs (LSN)," in particular, Nancy Bolt, Misako Nomura, and Sanja Bunić. Working with you on the *IFLA Guidelines for Library Services to People Experiencing Homelessness* was a pleasure, and I learned so much from that experience.

My thanks, too, to my friend Vikki Terrile, who is equally engaged in this work, and to my daughters Katie Winkelstein-Duveneck and Rae Winkelstein, whose conversations and editing expertise have informed my work, and to my daughter, Chloe Bullard Gossage, whose sharp eye over the years has helped make me a better academic writer.

To my husband, David—your support, thoughts, ideas, and love have made all the difference.

Finally, I want to thank all the people I've interacted with, through focus groups, interviews, and casual conversations, who continue to offer me insights into the daily challenges of experiencing homelessness. This work is for you.

Introduction

Welcome to *Libraries and Homelessness: An Action Guide.* Whether you are working in a library, are in library school, or teaching our future librarians, I hope you are able to find relevant, applicable, and useful information that will help you gain a greater understanding of the role of libraries in addressing homelessness.

This book begins with background on homelessness, including relevant terminology, some basic statistics, and an overview of ways in which people can and do experience homelessness, including stigma and stereotypes.

It also addresses the COVID-19 pandemic of 2020–2021, reflecting on the ways in which that pandemic highlighted the societal inequities and divides that lead to homelessness.

In Chapter 2, the book moves on to look at the history of how libraries have addressed homelessness in the past, current trends, and reasons why this topic is an appropriate one for libraries to be discussing.

Details about the specific needs of those experiencing homelessness and specific actions libraries can take to address these needs are included in Chapter 3. This includes knowing your library's limits and when to ask for help.

The next section of the book, Chapter 4, focuses on creating an action plan for your library. Since each community and library is unique, you will create this action plan based on an assessment of your library and community—including assets, challenges, needs, and funding. This plan will also include making your case to stakeholders, as well as staff members, and addressing any resistance that may occur.

Chapter 5 provides information, guidance, and resources related to establishing partnerships, securing funds, and providing staff training. All of these are critical steps in carrying out your action plan.

The last chapter, Chapter 6, provides examples of actions libraries have taken and could take, both short term and long term. The stories of what libraries are doing, and the challenges and successes of their programs, can provide insights and guidance as you move forward.

The book ends with an annotated list of useful and relevant resources, as well as appendices that include samples of social worker interview questions and staff survey questions, a glossary of related terms, a sample pamphlet, tips for social workers, selecting supportive books for young people, a library self-assessment checklist, a template for the action plan as well as dream plans, an example of a grant proposal for a library social worker program, and answers from library social workers about the work they do.

This book can be used in myriad ways, depending on where you are in the process of addressing homelessness in your community. You may want to read it through or focus on the background information that relates to a particular population you are interested in serving—such as veterans or LGBTGQ+ youth. Maybe your library is ready to create an action plan, and so you begin with that chapter. Or maybe you are looking for examples of what other libraries are doing, so you can follow their model, tailoring it to your library and your community. You may find that this book informs you in different ways at different times.

However you use it, I hope this book will serve you well.

Julie Ann Winkelstein

1

About the Experience of Homelessness

INTRODUCTION

In this chapter we look at the experience of homelessness. What do we mean when we use the word "homeless"? Who is experiencing homelessness? How do we know? What are the daily realities experienced by unhoused people? We also look at related vocabulary, culture, and the privileges that accompany being housed.

HOMELESSNESS: WHAT'S IN A NAME?

What do we mean when we use the term "homeless"? What images come to mind? And how have those images changed over the years?

Elizabeth Beck and Pamela C. Twiss (2018) use these words to begin their powerful look at homelessness in the United States and how it has emerged and changed historically:

> From the late 1970s to mid-1980s, the word *homeless* shifted its function from an adjective to a noun. As an adjective, *homeless* describes people affected by such extreme social and economic hardship that they lack their own housing or a place to live. But . . . as a noun, the concept of *the home-less* became the target of academic studies, the basis for psychiatric and behavioral diagnoses, and the rationale for professional social services based on a medical model of intervention. (p. 1)

It is imperative we keep this in mind as we look at the role of libraries in addressing homelessness. This change in attitude and approach has permeated our society and libraries, and it underlies what we're willing to do and how we do it. We must always remember that homelessness and poverty are, as Canada Parliament member Adam Vaughan expressed in his remarks at the 3-day 2018 "Coming Up Together" Canadian youth homelessness conference in Ottawa, Canada, "a symptom of failure of government structure." He went on to state, "Our systems are projecting people into homelessness" (Vaughan, 2018).

These two statements provide a context for the necessity for this book and all the other programs, resources, institutions, agencies, and funds that have become a part of the story. While we are looking at what libraries can actively do, we must continue to ask ourselves: Why is this necessary? What created the need for this work?

Who?

"A great deal of what constitutes self-concept grows out of the social images that are projected about people. . . . One of the consequences of oppression is the loss of control over those projection of images. As you begin to lose control of those images, then usually the oppressor, or the power holder, creates images consistent with their objectives."

—Na'im Akbar, interview quoted in *Colored Pictures: Race & Visual Representation* by Michael D. Harris

A good place to begin is with an understanding of who is experiencing homelessness. It's easy to make assumptions about people experiencing homelessness, especially with the preponderance of visual and verbal description so common in the media and in society at large. I've included the above quote because it addresses what happens when a person's life becomes stereotyped. The idea of losing control of the images that are used to represent you is an essential factor in addressing homelessness. People who are experiencing homelessness have no control over the negative and stigmatizing images that are perpetuated in the media and elsewhere. As library staff, we need to not only be aware of this, but we also need to provide positive and supportive alternatives to these stereotypes.

One way to do this is by including the voices of those with the lived experience of homelessness. As Palestinian American scholar and author Edward Said writes in the introduction to his book *Culture and Imperialism*: "Stories are at the heart of what explorers and novelists say about strange regions of the world; they also become the method colonized people use to assert their own identity and the existence of their own history" (Said, Introduction, 1993, p. xii). We should keep this in mind as we address homelessness in our libraries.

Tone

When we talk about any group of people, we can notice how our tone may indicate our bias. If you use "homeless person" as a description of someone who is unkempt; if you assume that someone who is homeless is dangerous or unemployed or unwashed or about to attack you; if you would be mortified to be referred to as homeless because of the connotation of that term; or, if your assumptions about homelessness are that a person who is experiencing homelessness deserves it or wants it or just can't be bothered—all of those assumptions will be obvious in your tone. Each person who walks through the doors of our libraries needs us to set aside our preconceptions and to avoid using derogatory language or to employ demeaning and disrespectful attitudes.

Another reason to address vocabulary is to help you become aware of what fears you may have in relation to people experiencing homelessness. How we describe our library patrons can have a large impact on how eager we are to work with them in addressing their library and information needs. Imagine if we only talked about toddlers as smelly, messy, loud, unpredictable, and prone to falling asleep in the library. How might that affect our willingness to learn about their lives and offer excellent and appropriate library services for them?

And finally, in order to be able to navigate the system of services that may be available to them, people who are experiencing homelessness need to learn a new vocabulary. As with any group served by library staff, understanding more about their lives and these key terms can make it easier for us to communicate and understand. It's easy to get caught up in the common stereotypes and shorthand language that is used for those who don't have a permanent place to live. This approach can be misleading and can make it difficult to look beyond housing status to see a library patron who has specific needs.

In Appendix A, there's also a Glossary that provides a more extensive and detailed definition of many more related terms.

Key Terms

We'll start with homelessness. Federal and local definitions can vary, depending on the services and the funding, but for the sake of this book we'll be using the definition, adapted from the McKinney-Vento Definition of Homeless (https://nche.ed.gov/mckinney-vento-definition) offered by Patricia Popp, Virginia state coordinator for Project HOPE in her presentation to a library school class on this topic. In her presentation, she included a slide "Defining Homelessness":

An individual who lacks a *fixed*, *regular* and *adequate* nighttime residence, including children and youth who are:

- Sharing housing, due to loss of housing, economic hardship, or similar reason.
- Living in hotels, motels, trailer parks or camping grounds due to lack of alternative housing.
- Living in emergency or transitional housing.
- Living in cars, parks, public spaces, abandoned buildings, substandard housing, and bus or train stations.

Popp also defined *fixed*, *regular* and *adequate*:

Fixed: Stationary, permanent and not subject to change
Regular: Used on a predictable, routine, and regular basis (e.g., nightly)
Adequate: Sufficient for both the physical and psychological needs typically met in home environments (Popp, 2019, personal communication)

As with any population libraries serve, it's important to know the vocabulary related to their lives. For this chapter, the following key definitions are taken from the HUD (the U.S. Department of Housing and Urban Development) report: "The 2019 Annual Homeless Assessment Report (AHAR) to Congress" (Henry et al., 2020).

Point-in-Time Counts

Point-in-time (PIT) counts "[a]re unduplicated one-night estimates of both *sheltered* and *unsheltered* homeless populations. The one-night counts are conducted by CoCs [Continuum of Care] nationwide and occur during the last week in January of each year" (Henry et al., 2020).

Sheltered homelessness refers to "people who are staying in emergency shelters, transitional housing programs, or safe havens." *Unsheltered* are those people "whose primary nighttime residence is a public or private place not designated for, or ordinarily used as, a regular sleeping accommodation for people (for example, the streets, vehicles, or parks)" (Henry et al., 2020).

Homeless Management Information System

Homeless Management Information System (HMIS) data "provide an unduplicated count of people who are experiencing sheltered homelessness and information about their characteristics and service-use patterns over a one-year period of time" (Henry et al., 2020).

HUD's full definition follows:

A Homeless Management Information System (HMIS) is a local information technology system used to collect client-level data and data on the
provision of housing and services to homeless individuals and families and
persons at risk of homelessness. Each Continuum of Care (CoC) is responsible for selecting an HMIS software solution that complies with HUD's
data collection, management, and reporting standards. (U.S. Department
of Housing and Urban Development, n.d.)

Unduplicated Count

An unduplicated count means that each person is only counted once,
no matter how many times they enter and exit a system.

Continuums of Care

Continuums of Care (CoC) "[a]re local planning bodies responsible
for coordinating the full range of homelessness services in a geographic
area, which may cover a city, county, metropolitan area, or an entire
state." In the 2018 HUD report, "CoC were divided into four geographic
categories:

1. Major City CoCs (n=48) cover the CoCs that contain one of the 50
    largest cities in the United States. In two cases (Phoenix and Mesa,
    AZ, and Arlington and Fort Worth, TX), two large cities were located
    in the same CoC.

2. Other Largely Urban CoCs (n=59) are CoCs in which the population
    predominantly resides in an urbanized area within a principal city
    within the CoC (but the CoC does not include one of the nation's 50
    largest cities).

3. Largely Suburban CoCs (n=172) are CoCs in which the population
    predominantly resides in suburban areas, defined as urbanized areas
    outside of a principal city or urban clusters within 10 miles of urban-
    ized areas.

4. Largely Rural CoCs (n=114) are CoCs in which the population pre-
    dominantly resides in urban clusters that are more than 10 miles from
    an urbanized area or in Census-defined rural territories." (Henry
    et al., 2018)

It's worth noting that in rural areas it's challenging to count or identify
people experiencing homelessness. For this reason, the PIT counts are less
useful. More on this topic will be discussed when we address rural areas.

These CoCs are used as the basis for the numbers you can retrieve for your community.

Housing Inventory Count

The Housing Inventory Count (HIC) data provides an inventory of beds dedicated to serve people who are experiencing homelessness, and they are compiled by CoCs. They represent the beds in various programs, including those from all funding sources, within the services system during a particular year.

Unaccompanied Youth

These are youth/young adults under the age of 25 experiencing homelessness on their own (i.e., not with a guardian or family).

Families with Children

HUD defines people in families with children as "people who are homeless as part of a household that has at least one adult (age 18 or older) and one child (under 18)" (Henry et al., 2020, p. 2).

Parenting youth household is defined as "[a] household with at least one parenting youth and the child or children for whom the parenting youth is the parent or legal guardian" (Henry et al., 2020, p. 2)

Individual refers to "a person who is not part of a family with children during an episode of homelessness. Individuals may be homeless as single adults, unaccompanied youth, or in multiple-adult or multiple-child households" (Henry et al., 2020, p. 2).

Chronically Homeless Individual

This refers to an individual with a disability who has been continuously homeless for 1 year or more or has experienced at least four episodes of homelessness in the last 3 years where the combined length of time homeless in those occasions was at least 12 months (NAHRO, 2015).

Statistics and More

There are two major sources of statistics about homelessness in the United States: the PIT count and HMIS.

The PIT count is necessarily an undercount, because there are always going to be people of all ages who are experiencing homelessness and who aren't available to be counted for many reasons—a reluctance to engage with any kind of bureaucracy, they are not aware of the count, they are in remote areas, they don't want to draw attention to themselves (this can be particularly true for youth), and so on. There will be more discussion about this in Chapter 6, but I want to first mention that this is an active role libraries can take in addressing homelessness—being involved in the PIT count. These counts are used to determine funding and to offer a snapshot of homelessness in the United States every year, thereby being able to see any trends.

These statistics are available on the HUD website, and they are updated each year—after the PIT count and then again when HMIS data are updated. It not only can be accessed for the entire United States, but it is also broken down by CoCs, so most libraries can find specific data for their communities. For smaller, rural areas, the data may not represent the area but will offer statistics for nearby larger counties or cities. Rural homelessness can be more challenging to address, since there are fewer resources locally. We'll be talking more about this in Chapter 4, under "Assessing Your Community."

Another related and essential part of the data collected is the HIC—because those numbers represent the ability of a community to house those who are experiencing homelessness. Looking specifically at these numbers, as we'll do in Chapter 4, allows us to see who is experiencing homelessness in communities and how well their housing needs are being met.

So on to the statistics. Again, these are from the HUD report (Henry et al., 2021):

> On a single night in January 2020, roughly 580,000 people were experiencing homelessness in the United States (p. 1). Six in ten (61%) were staying in sheltered locations - emergency shelters or transitional housing programs - and nearly four in ten (39%) were in sheltered locations such as on the street, in abandoned buildings, or in other places not suitable for human habitation. Of the total number on one single night in January 2020, more than two-thirds were in households with only adults, just under 172,000 were families with children and 34,000 were unaccompanied youth.

Homelessness overall increased by about 2% from the previous year, and this reflects an increase in the number of people who were unsheltered (about a 7% increase), including unaccompanied youth who are more likely to be in this category. Black or African Americans were overrepresented in the number of people experiencing homelessness: Although representing about 12% of the U.S. population, they accounted for about 39% of all people experiencing homelessness in 2020 and 53% of people experiencing homelessness as members of families with children (Henry et al., 2021, "Key Findings," p. 1).

Other Related Statistics

USICH (United States Interagency Council on Homelessness) (2018) points out "it's estimated that about 10 to 15% of people who enter homelessness will experience chronic homelessness" (p. 2). They also indicate that there is little national demographic data related to chronic homelessness and age, ethnicity and race.

Subgroups

There are many subgroups of people experiencing homelessness, and of course there is overlap or what we refer to as intersectionality—the many ways in which a person can identify and how those multiple identities can exacerbate oppression and stigma.

These subgroups include:

- Unaccompanied youth, including youth coming from the foster system, and the juvenile carceral system, students, LGBTGQI+ (lesbian, gay, bisexual, transgender, gender-expansive, queer/questioning youth, intersex).
- Families with children.
- Veterans.
- Survivors of domestic abuse.
- Survivors of human trafficking.
- Individuals—those who are by themselves.
- Older adults.
- Persons with disabilities.
- People of color, especially those who are African American, Indigenous, or Latinx.
- Immigrants, documented or undocumented.
- Persons who have been incarcerated.

The following tables are taken from the 2020 annual HUD PIT count report. They offer some basic statistics about those experiencing homelessness in the United States, as included in the PIT count. As you can see, except for people with disabilities, persons who have been incarcerated, and students, information about these various subgroups can be found in the tables, which also offer insights into the various ways people can fall into many categories. This point is critical for libraries to keep in mind. Homelessness is a complicated story, and the more you can know about those who are experiencing homelessness, the more your library will be able to address their specific needs and the daily barriers to access they are encountering.

Table 1.1   Demographic Characteristics of People Experiencing
Homelessness, 2020

Characteristic	All Homeless People		Sheltered People		Unsheltered People	
	#	%	#	%	#	%
Total homeless	580,466	100%	354,386	100%	226,080	100%
Age						
Under 18	106,364	18.3%	95,713	27.0%	10,651	4.7%
18 to 24	45,243	7.8%	28,213	8.0%	17,030	7.5%
Over 24	428,859	73.9%	230,460	65.0%	198,399	87.8%
Gender						
Female	223,578	38.5%	156,681	44.2%	66,897	29.6%
Male	352,211	60.7%	195,798	55.2%	156,413	69.2%
Transgender	3,161	0.5%	1,412	0.4%	1,749	0.8%
Gender Non-Conforming	1,460	0.3%	439	0.1%	1,021	0.5%
Ethnicity						
Non-Hispanic/Non-Latino	450,107	77.5%	277,078	78.2%	173,029	76.5%
Hispanic/Latino	130,348	22.5%	77,297	21.8%	53,051	23.5%
Race						
White	280,612	48.3%	151,640	42.8%	128,972	57.0%
Black or African American	228,796	39.4%	167,205	47.2%	61,591	27.2%
Asian	7,638	1.3%	3,836	1.1%	3,802	1.7%
Native American	18,935	3.3%	8,106	2.3%	10,829	4.8%
Pacific Islander	8,794	1.5%	4,208	1.2%	4,586	2.0%
Multiple Races	35,680	6.1%	19,380	5.5%	16,300	7.2%

Source: US Department of Housing and Urban Development. "The 2020
Annual Homeless Assessment Report (AHAR) to Congress: Part 1: Point-in-
Time Estimates of Homelessness, January, 2021," Exhibit 1.5, p. 8.

One more fact about people experiencing homelessness: Simple statistics don't tell us the whole story, because we also need to understand
how these numbers fit into the entire populations. For example, Table 1.1
shows that African Americans/Blacks are 39.4% and Native Americans
are 3.3% of the category "All Homeless People," while Whites are
48.3% of the same population. However, in the United States, African
Americans/Blacks make up 13.4% of the population (United States
Census Bureau, 2019) and Native Americans make up 2% (World Population Review, 2021). So you can see they are disproportionately represented in the "homeless people" category. This statistic is similar to
the one in Table 1.2, which shows that African Americans make up
33.7% and Native Americans make up 3.7% of "unsheltered individuals." Jeff Olivet and Marc Dones, from the Center for Social Innovation, provide a closer look at the importance of these disparities. They
write:

> Our national conversation about homelessness has been missing a critical
> piece: an honest, open conversation about the racial dimensions of home-
> lessness. People of color—specifically Blacks and Native Americans—are
> dramatically more likely than White Americans to experience homeless-
> ness. Furthermore, pathways out of homelessness for people of color are
> complicated by ongoing discrimination in housing, employment, health
> care, and education. (Olivet & Dones, 2017)

Table 1.3 offers information about youth experiencing homelessness—in this table, we can see the statistics on youth under and over 18 who are parenting. Parenting youth may be a group of young people libraries haven't been aware of and these statistics can help understand what is happening in the lives of some young people and how libraries can support them.

Table 1.4 offers more insights into youth experiencing homelessness. As you can see, again race matters. In addition, those who are sheltered and those who are unsheltered are almost evenly split—so there are many youth who are living without shelter.

Table 1.5 looks at families with children. Besides the now obvious point that race matters when it comes to homelessness, another statistic that stands out is that a little over 60% of "homeless people in families with children" are identified as female.

Table 1.6 describes the demographic characteristics of veterans experiencing homelessness. Again, Black or African American and Native American numbers are high, as are those for males—outnumbering females by 90.9% compared to 8.4%. While this could be expected, it's important to remember there are female veterans who are unhoused.

These are all examples of considering the specific needs and barriers for your community. It is worth taking a closer look at all of these tables. We'll talk more about this in Chapter 4, when we look at assessment.

Table 1.2   Demographic Characteristics of Homeless Individuals, 2020

Characteristic	All Homeless Individuals		Sheltered Individuals		Unsheltered Individuals	
	#	%	#	%	#	%
Total homeless	408,891	100.0%	199,478	100.0%	209,413	100.0%
Age						
Under 18	3,598	0.9%	1,811	0.9%	1,787	0.9%
18 to 24	32,897	8.0%	17,232	8.6%	15,665	7.5%
Over 24	372,396	91.1%	180,435	90.5%	191,961	91.7%
Gender						
Female	120,015	29.4%	61,963	31.1%	58,052	27.7%
Male	284,599	69.6%	135,866	68.1%	148,733	71.0%
Transgender	3,067	0.8%	1,343	0.7%	1,724	0.8%
Gender Non-Conforming	1,210	0.3%	306	0.2%	904	0.4%
Ethnicity						
Non-Hispanic/Latino	328,720	80.4%	168,059	84.2%	160,661	76.7%
Hispanic/Latino	80,171	19.6%	31,419	15.8%	48,752	23.3%
Race						
White	220,572	53.9%	99,290	49.8%	121,282	57.9%
African American	137,714	33.7%	81,426	40.8%	56,288	26.9%
Asian	5,791	1.4%	2,366	1.2%	3,425	1.6%
Native American	15,074	3.7%	5,055	2.5%	10,019	4.8%
Pacific Islander	5,228	1.3%	1,974	1.0%	3,254	1.6%
Multiple Races	24,512	6.0%	9,367	4.7%	15,145	7.2%

Source: US Department of Housing and Urban Development. "The 2020 Annual Homeless Assessment Report (AHAR) to Congress: Part 1: Point-in-Time Estimates of Homelessness, January, 2021," Exhibit 2.4, p. 19.

Table 1.3   Number of People in Parenting Youth Households, 2020

	Parents in Households	Children in Households	Total People in Households
Parenting Youth (Under 18)	125	95	220
Parenting Youth Age (18 to 24)	7,230	9,400	16,630
Total Parenting Youth	7,355	9,495	16,850

Source: US Department of Housing and Urban Development. "The 2019 Annual Homeless Assessment Report (AHAR) to Congress: Part 1: Point-in-Time Estimates of Homelessness, January, 2021," Exhibit 3.4, p. 31.

Table 1.4   Demographic Characteristics of Unaccompanied Youth Experiencing Homelessness, 2020

	All Unaccompanied Youth		Sheltered Unaccompanied Youth		Unsheltered Unaccompanied Youth	
	#	%	#	%	#	%
Total	34,210	100%	17,271	100%	16,939	100%
Age						
Under 18	3,389	9.9%	1,682	9.7%	1,707	10.1%
18 to 24	30,821	90.1%	15,589	90.3%	15,232	89.9%
Gender						
Female	13,298	38.9%	7,456	43.2%	5,842	34.5%
Male	19,730	57.7%	9,350	54.1%	10,380	61.3%
Transgender	742	2.2%	315	1.8%	427	2.5%
Gender non-conforming	440	1.3%	150	0.9%	290	1.7%
Ethnicity						
Non-Hispanic/Latino	25,773	75.3%	13,757	79.7%	12,016	70.9%
Hispanic/Latino	8,437	24.7%	3,514	20.3%	4,923	29.1%
Race						
White	16,359	47.8%	7,465	43.2%	8,894	52.5%
African American	11,918	34.8%	7,496	43.4%	4,422	26.1%
Asian	471	1.4%	179	1.0%	292	1.7%
Native American	1,375	4.0%	433	2.5%	942	5.6%
Pacific Islander	478	1.4%	145	0.8%	333	2.0%
Multiple Races	3,609	10.5%	1,553	9.0%	2,056	12.1%

Source: US Department of Housing and Urban Development. "The 2020 Annual Homeless Assessment Report (AHAR) to Congress: Part 1: Point-in-Time Estimates of Homelessness, January, 2021," Exhibit 4.3, p. 43.

People with Disabilities

It's difficult to find specific statistics about people with disabilities and homelessness, except as they relate to chronic homelessness. "Priced Out in the United States" (Technical Assistance Collaborative, 2020) provides some insights into the housing for people with disabilities who rely on Supplemental Security Income (SSI) to pay their rent. As they write:

Our research reveals there was no U.S. housing market in which a person living solely on Supplemental Security Income (SSI) can afford a safe, decent unit without rental assistance. Without access to housing they can afford, too many people with disabilities are forced into segregated and costly institutional settings such as nursing facilities or state hospitals—or into homelessness."

Table 1.5   Demographic Characteristics of Homeless People in Families with Children, 2020

Characteristic	All Homeless People in Families		Sheltered People in Families		Unsheltered People in Families	
	#	%	#	%	#	%
People in families	171,575	100%	154,908	100%	16,667	100%
Age						
Under 18	102,766	59.9%	93,902	60.6%	8,864	53.2%
18 – 24	12,346	7.2%	10,981	7.1%	1,365	8.2%
Over 24	56,463	32.9%	50,025	32.3%	6,438	38.6%
Gender						
Female	103,563	60.4%	94,718	61.1%	8,845	53.1%
Male	67,612	39.4%	59,932	38.7%	7,680	46.1%
Transgender	94	0.1%	69	0.0%	25	0.1%
Gender Non-conforming	250	0.1%	133	0.1%	117	0.7%
Ethnicity						
Non-Hispanic/Latino	121,387	70.7%	109,019	70.4%	12,368	74.2%
Hispanic/Latino	50,177	29.2%	45,878	29.6%	4,299	25.8%
Race						
White	60,040	35.0%	52,350	33.8%	7,690	46.1%
Black or African American	91,082	53.1%	85,779	55.4%	5,303	31.8%
Asian	1,847	1.1%	1,470	0.9%	377	2.3%
Native American	3,861	2.3%	3,051	2.0%	810	4.9%
Pacific Islander	3,566	2.1%	2,234	1.4%	1,332	8.0%
Multiple Races	11,168	6.5%	10,013	6.5%	1,155	6.9%

Source: US Department of Housing and Urban Development. "The 2020 Annual Homeless Assessment Report (AHAR) to Congress: Part 1: Point-in-Time Estimates of Homelessness, January, 2021," Exhibit 3.3, p. 31.

Table 1.6   Demographic Characteristics of Veterans Experiencing Homelessness, 2020

Characteristic	All Veterans		Sheltered Veterans		Unsheltered Veterans	
	#	%	#	%	#	%
Total Veterans	37,252	100%	22,048	100%	15,204	100%
Gender						
Female	3,126	8.4%	1,662	7.5%	1,464	9.6%
Male	33,862	90.9%	20,324	92.2%	13,538	89.0%
Transgender	155	0.4%	49	0.2%	106	0.7%
Gender Non-conforming	109	0.3%	13	0.1%	96	0.6%
Ethnicity						
Non-Hispanic/Latino	33,190	89.1%	20,234	91.8%	12,956	85.2%
Hispanic/Latino	4,062	10.9%	1,814	8.2%	2,248	14.8%
Race						
White	21,160	56.8%	12,187	55.3%	8,973	59.0%
Black or African American	12,186	32.7%	8,380	38.0%	3,806	25.0%
Asian	450	1.2%	189	0.9%	261	1.7%
Native American	1,082	2.9%	418	1.9%	664	4.4%
Pacific Islander	370	1.0%	159	0.7%	211	1.4%
Multiple Races	2,004	5.4%	715	3.2%	1,289	8.5%

Source: US Department of Housing and Urban Development. "The 2020 Annual Homeless Assessment Report (AHAR) to Congress: Part 1: Point-in-Time Estimates of Homelessness, January, 2021," Exhibit 5.4, p. 54.

The numbers on their website are sobering:

- "There are 4,714,234 people with disabilities ages 18–64 in the United States whose sole source of income is SSI."
- SSI is only $783 per month.
- "The average monthly rent for a basic one-bedroom apartment is $1022. That is 131% of the monthly income of a disabled person in the United States, leaving no money for food, transportation, clothing, or other necessities."

The National Health Care for the Homeless Council (NHCHC) offers more statistics in their "2012 Policy Statement." As they point out: "About 15% of the non-institutionalized U.S. population is disabled, yet people with disabilities constitute 37% of people in America who are homeless." They go on to offer insights into why this number is so high:

> Diminishing affordable housing, depressed wages, higher unemployment, and decreased access to health insurance coverage over the past two decades has placed an increasing number of individuals and families with disabilities at risk of experiencing homelessness, and makes leaving homelessness more difficult as well. (NHCHC, 2012)

Experiencing homelessness with a disability is a challenge. Raising awareness about disabilities and homelessness can help libraries make a difference through actions, resources, partnerships, programs, and personal connections.

Special Circumstances

Pandemic

As this book is being written, the COVID-19 virus is active and rapidly spreading in the United States and around the world. At this point, it's impossible to know what's going to happen next: how long the virus will be active, how far it will spread, how many people will become ill, and how many will die. It's currently in all 50 states, as well as most countries around the world. As of March 26, 2021, there have been 126,702,229 reported cases worldwide and 2,779,769 people have died (Worldometer, 2021). In the United States, as of the same date, there are 30,853,032 confirmed cases and 561,142 deaths (Worldometer, 2021).

Because of the highly contagious nature of this virus, people are being asked to shelter in place, which for housed people means staying in their houses and apartments, and not interacting with others. If people are in spaces with others, they are being told to stay 6 feet away from each other, so-called "social distancing" or, a term that doesn't play down the importance of social interactions at a time like this, "physical distancing." Everyone is encouraged to wear masks, and in some U.S. counties they are required.

One population that is particularly impacted by this pandemic are people who are experiencing homelessness. People who are staying in emergency shelters are at risk, because during the day they have nowhere to go except outside, where the "hard surfaces" may well be contaminated and their access to handwashing—the most popular recommendation for protecting oneself—is small or nonexistent. At night, they are in close quarters, sharing the spaces with some who may be carrying the virus. In fact, many folks are opting to not stay in shelters at night, because of the added danger of infection. As Charles King, CEO of Housing Works, puts it, "Housing is healthcare" (Griswold, 2020).

Although people experiencing homelessness are no more likely to contract this virus, if they do, they are twice as likely to be hospitalized, two to four times as likely to require critical care, and two to four times more likely to die than the housed public (NAEH, Live Webinar, 2020a).

In addition, "Black Americans have been hospitalized or died from COVID-19 at a rate about five times that of white Americans, according to the U.S. Centers for Disease Control. Other people of color have experienced much higher hospitalization and death rates than whites as well" (Tufts, 2020). When you add this to the fact that people of color are disproportionately represented in the population experiencing homelessness, you can see that this virus is having a huge impact on unhoused people of color.

Another population particularly adversely affected by COVID-19 are older adults. As the CDC states:

> **Among adults, the risk for severe illness from COVID-19 increases with age, with older adults at highest risk**. Severe illness means that the person with COVID-19 may require hospitalization, intensive care, or a ventilator to help them breathe, or they may even die. (Centers for Disease Control and Prevention, 2020)

Shelters are taking the precautions they can. For instance, the Transitions Homeless Center in Columbia, South Carolina, provides hand sanitizer at the entrance and throughout the building. Mealtimes are being extended, and they are struggling with having their clients tested if they don't appear to qualify for testing (Scarlett, 2020). Many national organizations are coming forward to present vital information, via webinars, e-mails, and resource lists.

In addition, public libraries across the country are closing, which leaves folks without the safe space, sanctuary, resources, social connections, and Internet they would usually have access to at the library.

This pandemic highlights the challenges and failures of our society to address homelessness. In many cities across the United States, there are laws against camping, sitting, lying down, and being in public spaces outside of particular hours. City workers routinely "sweep" tent communities, pushing people to leave the area and sometimes throwing away their personal items. No efforts are made to provide toilets, handwashing facilities, fresh water, or any kind of protection against the elements.

Ironically, because the federal and state governments are trying to limit the spread of this potentially lethal virus, some cities have temporarily stopped these sweeps and, in addition, are providing portable toilets, handwashing stations, tents, and sleeping bags. For example:

> The city of Berkeley, California, has at this point installed 20 sanitation centers at encampments, Sacramento County has ordered batches of Purell for homeless residents and in San Francisco, Mayor London Breed released $5 million for hygiene at shelters and residential hotels. She said the city will also use RVs to isolate homeless individuals if they test positive for COVID-19. (Solomon, 2020)

It is difficult not to point out that when cities and governments want to address the needs of people experiencing homelessness, they can do so quickly.

The National Coalition for the Homeless provided a list of recommendations that directly impact and support those who are experiencing homelessness. Their list included:

- More broadly realize that everyone who may be experiencing homelessness would not be in as great a risk of poor health outcomes, or spread of COVID-19, if they had access to safe, decent, affordable, and accessible housing. We still have a lot of work to do to address the underlying income inequality and lack of low-cost housing that has perpetuated homelessness for decades.

- Ensure that national, state, and community-level public health/pandemic planning and response includes the homeless population and homeless service agencies.

- Cities should provide hygiene facilities (port-a-potties, handwashing stations) and trash pickup for residents of encampments—during and after any pandemic has passed.

- There should be a moratorium on encampment sweeps that displace already displaced households and that often cause the loss of personal property that includes medication and other life-sustaining items.

- All tests, treatment, and quarantine locations should be offered without cost for all members of the community—housed or not, with or without health insurance.

- Each community should identify space that those who do not have a permanent home can access in case of quarantine. Any costs should come out of community-level public health resources.
- Federally, we would discourage homeless dollars from being used to provide quarantine, testing, or treatment. Homeless services are already woefully underfunded, and widespread homelessness was *already* a public health emergency!
- Finally, we are concerned for the safety of unhoused folks who may be discharged from medical care to make room for COVID-19 treatment. This has happened in other emergency settings. (National Coalition for the Homeless, 2020)

This pandemic provides an opportunity for communities and governments to take much-needed action. Even though many if not most libraries are closing to the public, they are still determined to provide the services they are able to support. Keeping their wi-fi live 24 hours a day can help those who are experiencing homelessness and who have devices to be able to continue using the Internet. For those without devices, this is a time when libraries could be proactive in addressing the needs of their unhoused community members. In Chapter 6 we look at what libraries can do to address homelessness. Included in that chapter are suggestions for how libraries could address the needs of their community members who are experiencing homelessness during an emergency, such as the pandemic of 2020–2021, as well as examples of what libraries have done.

Antiracism Police Demonstrations

In 2020, added to the pandemic were demonstrations happening across the country in reaction to the police killings of people of color, in particular, African Americans. Although these protests are not about homelessness, racism and the history of government policies that have created barriers for people of color lead to housing and food insecurity and homelessness. As the National Alliance to End Homelessness states so clearly:

> Racial inequity causes homelessness. As part of its mission to prevent and end homelessness in the United States, the National Alliance to End Homelessness re-commits itself to the goals of ending racial disparities in the homelessness sector, and confronting structural racism in our nation. (NAEH, 2020b)

The topic of racism and antiracist work is a huge one, and in this book we won't cover specifically what needs to be done to address these ongoing systemic challenges. However, addressing the needs of people experiencing homelessness and creating a welcoming and respectful library environment both contribute to mitigating some of the impact of systemic racism.

Specific Community Statistics

Each year HUD offers the "CoC Homeless Populations and Subpopulations Reports" (HUD, 2021a). These reports can be filtered by year and scope and are useful for gathering statistics about your community and various populations. HUD Exchange also has a library of resources that offer extensive insight into funding, subpopulations (such as veterans), challenges to communities, and much more. The resources provide libraries with an opportunity to know more about what is being done at federal, state, and local levels; about available programs; and about numerous related reports, such as "Preventing Harassment in Housing" (HUD, 2021b). We'll talk more about using these resources in Chapter 4, when we discuss creating a plan to serve your specific community.

Students

Information about students experiencing homelessness is another category that isn't included in the tables. Students include children living with their families, as well as unaccompanied youth who are attending high school, community college, or college/university. All are impacted by homelessness. As the National Network for Youth (NN4Y) points out in their issue brief, "Education Barriers for Homeless Youth": "The absence of a stable living arrangement has a devastating impact on educational outcomes for youth" (n.d.). Their list of barriers includes:

- "Paper" barriers created by the lack of proper school records, medical records, residency documents, and parental permission slips for unaccompanied youth.
- The impact of changing schools frequently: lack of transportation and educators being able to correctly identify their needs

Other barriers include:

- Lack of school supplies.
- The stigma of being unhoused.
- Lack of a quiet safe space to study.
- Lack of privacy.

College and university students are also impacted by homelessness. In recent years, this topic has attracted more attention and schools are providing a range of services, including food pantries, support services, and information about local resources. According to Broton (2019), "Nearly seven hundred colleges and universities have on-campus food pantries, and others have meal voucher programs, free clothing closets, short-term housing accommodations, and other programs designed to respond to emergency situations." For instance, Luria Library at Santa Barbara, California City College, provides information on their website about accessing food, clothing, showers, housing, financial aid, and more (Luria Library, n.d.). An excellent source of information about student homelessness is "The Hope Center for College, Community and Justice," which was created to do research and take action on student housing instability and food insecurity. On their website you'll find projects, publications, and more. You can also sign up for their newsletter (The Hope Center, n.d.).

Statistics on student homelessness are difficult to gather, since many students don't identify as "homeless" and in fact may not even recognize themselves in that description. They may sleep on the floor of a friend's room for a few nights, then another friend, then in their car, and so on. However, to give you an idea of the extent of this challenge, Broton (2019) provides us with some sobering information, based on a study of 46,000 students in 66 institutions in 20 states and Washington, DC:

- Approximately half of undergraduates are food and/or housing insecure.
- Students from marginalized groups, including former foster youth, racial/ethnic minorities, LGBTQ students, and students from low-income families are at an increased risk.

Both academic and public library staff can help students who are unstably housed and/or food insecure. We'll be looking at what libraries can do in future chapters, so if this aspect of homelessness is important to you, collecting relevant information will be an important first action.

Persons Who Have Been Incarcerated

Another group that isn't included in this count are people who have been formerly incarcerated. As with other groups, their incarceration intersects with other characteristics, in particular being a person of color. Couloute (2018), representing the "Prison Policy Initiative," provides sobering and much-needed insights into the challenges of being housed after being incarcerated. He begins his report, "Nowhere to Go: Home-lessness Among Formerly Incarcerated People," with this statement:

> In this report, we provide the first estimate of homelessness among the 5 million formerly incarcerated people living in the United States, finding that formerly incarcerated people are **almost 10 times more likely to be homeless** than the general public.

He goes on to explain: "We find that rates of homelessness are especially high among specific demographics:

- People who have been incarcerated more than once
- People recently released from prison
- People of color and women."

He also makes this point: "Unfortunately, being homeless makes formerly incarcerated people more likely to be arrested and incarcerated again, thanks to policies that criminalize homelessness" (Couloute, 2018).

As library staff, we can be aware of the challenges for those who have been formerly incarcerated and provide local information and resources in a welcoming and respectful way. In Chapter 6, we look at specific examples of what libraries are doing to reach out and support previously incarcerated community members.

Older Adults

Another important subgroup are older adults. In "How to Prevent and End Homelessness Among Older Adults," Goldberg and colleagues (2016) offer some sobering statistics and challenges for those who are aged 50 and older. As they write:

> Older adults are at greater risk of homelessness than at any time in recent history. The population is aging, and more adults are aging into poverty. At the same time, housing is becoming more unaffordable and the costs of necessities like health care are rising, leaving older adults at risk of pov-erty and homelessness. (Introduction)

Among the challenges they list are:

- "Homelessness among people 65 and older will more than double by 2050, from more than 44,000 in 2010 to nearly 93,000 in 2050"
- "45% of those 65 & older are 'economically vulnerable'"
- "Many poor and economically vulnerable seniors are paying too large a proportion of their incomes for basic necessities like housing and health care, leaving little left for emergencies"

- "The average older adult pays \$4734 in out-of-pocket health care costs, three times more than non-Medicare households. These high healthcare costs can leave older adults on the brink of homelessness, facing difficult choices between having enough money to pay rent and paying for needed medical services and prescriptions."
- "Among homeless adults age 50 & over, 44% were never homeless before 50"
- "Frequent falls, loss of mobility, and other common conditions of aging that impact mobility are more difficult to manage on the streets and in homeless shelters"
- "Homelessness can age a person prematurely and lead to life expectancies that can be years lower than the general [housed] population."
- Crime: A legitimate fear of violent crimes deter some unhoused older adults from using shelters.
- Accessing benefits: "Physical and cognitive difficulties as well as the lack of a permanent address can be a barrier to applying for and receiving benefits that provide basic income support and health care." Some may be unaware of available benefits and/or may need help navigating applications.
- Institutionalization: "Without affordable housing options and supportive services, thousands of Americans are at risk of institutionalization and chronic homelessness at the same time."

Being aware of these challenges can help library staff provide relevant and critical information and resources, such as free legal services, connections to low-cost health care providers, expertise in navigating online forms, information about local truly affordable housing, and simply a safe space to be off the streets and in a respectful, caring, and welcoming environment. It should also be noted that many if not most libraries already provide services like these for older adults.

Rural Areas

Experiencing homelessness in rural areas doesn't look the same as suburban or urban areas, even though these areas—especially urban ones—attract most of the attention. Stigers (2019) prepared a report that looks at rural housing and gives us an idea of the challenges of finding affordable housing, one of the biggest barriers to moving out of homelessness or preventing homelessness. As Stigers writes: "Access to affordable housing is in a crisis" (2019, p. 1). Reasons for this include low incomes, high energy costs, persistent poverty, and declining support for housing subsidies.

Most of the people impacted by these are rural renters, and there is a severe shortage of truly affordable rentals. In addition, construction costs and aging properties impact the availability of housing, as does the relatively ineffective solution of building multifamily buildings in rural areas because of the geography (Stigers, 2019). In Chapter 6, we will talk more about what libraries can do to address rural homelessness. Although it is challenging, there are resources and strategies that can be used to identify and serve well those who are unstably housed in your communities.

CULTURE

Once we have an idea of who is experiencing homelessness in our communities, we need to look at culture and how it applies to libraries and the communities we serve.

We can ask: What is culture? How does it relate to addressing homelessness? Culture can be a difficult word to define precisely, and it's interesting to note that the Merriam-Webster website shows it is currently (in 2020) in the top 1% of lookups. Their simple definition of culture is: "the beliefs, customs, arts, etc. of a particular society, group, place, or time; a particular society that has its own beliefs, ways of life, art, etc.; a way of thinking, behaving, or working that exists in a place or organization (such as a business)."

Two of the cultures we are looking at in this case include homelessness and libraries. For people experiencing homelessness, their daily lives are affected by multiple factors, including who they are, their life experiences, mental and physical health, goals, needs, friends, family, and so on—just like a housed person. But one of their overarching characteristics is that they don't have a regular and safe place to sleep at night. As already mentioned, this means they come with the baggage of certain stereotypes that can serve as barriers to service for them because of attitudes and assumptions.

It's important to remind yourself that when you know someone is experiencing homelessness, that's *all* you know about them. Unless they share this information with you, you don't know anything about their education, their employment status, their physical and mental health, their substance use, or their hygiene. All you know is their housing status. It's critical to always keep this in mind.

In her *HuffPost* piece, Sarah Ruiz-Grossman describes "5 Things People Get Wrong About Homelessness" (2018). The assumptions she mentions are ones many housed people, including library staff, may have made about unhoused community members. They include: that everyone who is unhoused lives on the streets, has a mental health challenge, has a substance use disorder, "just need to get a job," and "it's their fault they're homeless" (Ruiz-Grossman, 2018). In her article, she uses quotes and statistics to refute all of these. One of the most compelling points she makes is a quote from Shahera Hyatt, director of the California Homeless Youth Project:

> When folks say that people become homeless because of a mental health issue or a substance use issue, I usually like to say, "people don't become homeless because of those issues, it's because we don't have a system in society to support people having a mental health crisis or a substance use issue. . . . Because not all people having those issues experience homelessness. . . . It's the folks living in poverty who often lack the social safety net to buoy them through the storm." (Ruiz-Grossman, 2018)

In this book, we look at how libraries can be part of this social safety net.

The other "culture" is the culture of libraries, with our common language, specific goals, funding challenges, and the other myriad ways our culture is demonstrated. Although we are all individuals, we are also encumbered with the baggage of stubborn stereotypes, and these can also act as barriers because assumptions are made about us: what it's like to be in a library, what public libraries are for, what they're interested in doing, and so on.

The stereotypes of both groups make it difficult to create relationships. In fact, members of each group may have low expectations of those from the other group. Library staff may assume those who are experiencing homelessness or those who work with them, such as service providers, aren't interested in working with libraries. In most cases, service providers and those who are experiencing homelessness assume libraries don't have any interest in partnerships or active support.

One way to address the challenge for library staff is to consider the concept of "cultural humility," first described by Tervalon and Murray-Garcia in 1998. As they define it:

> Cultural humility incorporates a lifelong commitment to self-evaluation and self-critique, to redressing the power imbalances in the patient-physician [library staff–library user] dynamic, and to developing mutually beneficial and nonpaternalistic clinical and advocacy partnerships with communities on behalf of individuals and defined populations. (brackets added)

Or as these authors describe it: "Cultural humility takes into account the fluidity and subjectivity of culture and challenges both individuals and institutions to address inequalities" (Fisher-Borne et al., 2015).

Some of the most important points about cultural humility are looking at ourselves and our culture and assumptions, and looking at our institutions. It isn't unusual to find people in an institution like a library where some are committed to looking at power and inequities and some aren't—there's no institutional commitment. We can engage in critical self-reflection by looking at the assumptions we are making, the experiences that have shaped those assumptions, our own life experiences with housing and income stability, and how these may be impacting our assumptions and expectations about our library patrons, our services, and our rules and policies.

We can remind ourselves of the power imbalances that exist between our unstably housed library users and us, and we can consider how we could mitigate them with respectful and engaged personal interactions, flexible and informed service, positive signage, partnerships, and relevant resources presented in ways that are not reliant on rigid rules and policies. In addition, homelessness creates and is created by power imbalances, and as respected institutions, we can partner and advocate for services and housing that will redress some of these power imbalances at a local and even national level. We can consider our institutions and how they are or are not supportive of these kinds of reflection and action and how we could begin to make changes if they are not.

In libraries we have certain expectations about who we are serving, what their information needs are, and how we will meet those needs. Using cultural humility as a guide, we can consider that there may be more to know about our library users. They may need us to adjust what we're doing so we can serve everyone well.

Cultural competence is a more common term used in libraries, and so a brief comparison of the two concepts may be helpful. According to the authors, some of the primary differences between these two include:

- Cultural humility emphasizes not only understanding the "other" but also understanding ourselves.
- Cultural competence implies an end point—it assumes "a lack of knowledge, awareness, and skills" that must and can be overcome, while cultural humility acknowledges this is a "lifelong and ongoing process."
- Cultural competence focuses on knowledge acquisition, while cultural humility looks at institutional accountability and challenges power imbalances. (Tervalon & Murray-Garcia, 1998)

This can be partly semantics—some who use the term "cultural competence" are talking about more than simple competence on a personal level, and these other concepts are included. But frequently cultural competence implies an end point, without considering where we are coming from or how our institutions may be addressing societal power imbalances. Consequently, for clarity, we will be using the term "cultural humility."

Trauma-Informed Approach

"When a human service program takes the step to become trauma-informed, every part of its organization, management, and service delivery system is assessed and potentially modified to include a basic understanding of how trauma affects the life of an individual seeking services. Trauma-informed organizations, programs, and services are based on an understanding of the vulnerabilities or triggers of trauma survivors that traditional service delivery approaches may exacerbate, so that these services and programs can be more supportive and avoid re-traumatization" (Community Reach Center, n.d.).

This quote sums up what it means to be a trauma-informed agency. It's challenging to be trauma informed—it means understanding and possibly setting aside your own reactions to someone's behavior based on trauma they've experienced. If someone acts in a way that feels belligerent to you because they've experienced trauma on the streets, it takes practice, awareness, and kindness to be able to get past your own feelings and realize it's not personally aimed at you. One excellent point that briefly offers insight into what a trauma-informed approach looks like is the difference between asking "What's wrong with you?" and asking "What happened?" By asking what happened, we can acknowledge the trauma but avoid blaming the person. This kind of respectful interaction can lead to more positive results for both the library user and library staff.

Some libraries offer trauma-informed trainings to their staff, frequently through an outside agency that can provide relevant information and valuable resources. These trainings can be offered in conjunction with staff trainings related to serving community members who are experiencing homelessness and poverty and those (both housed and unhoused) who have mental health life experiences that may affect their interactions with library staff and their fellow library users. As the Substance Abuse and Mental Health Services Administration (SAMHSA) points out: "A trauma-informed approach can be implemented in any type of service setting or organization and is distinct from trauma-specific interventions or treatments that are designed specifically to address the consequences of trauma and to facilitate healing" (SAMHSA, 2018).

That is to say, as library staff, there isn't an expectation that you are expected to provide treatment, such as counseling. Instead, the trauma-informed approach means "the program, organization, or system

1. *Realizes* the widespread impact of trauma . . . ;
2. *Recognizes* the signs and symptoms of trauma in clients, families, staff, and others involved with the system;

3. *Responds* by fully integrating knowledge about trauma into policies, procedures, and practices; and

4. Seeks to actively resist *re-traumatization.*"

SAMHSA also offers "Six Principles of a Trauma-Informed Approach" (SAMHSA, 2018):

1. Safety
2. Trustworthiness and transparency
3. Peer support
4. Collaboration and mutuality
5. Empowerment, voice, and choice
6. Cultural, historical, and gender issues

As you can see, the recognition of trauma and the inclusion of awareness of its impact on any of the library users can help staff serve all who have experienced trauma. As with other lived experiences related to homelessness, the reality is that housed library users also appreciate a trauma-informed approach to providing services. You may already be doing this without consciously being aware of it. Patience, a sense of humor, listening, showing respect, examining your policies and procedures, having signage that uses positive language rather than shouting "no, no, no"—all of these contribute to an environment that feels welcoming and safe. Becoming a trauma-informed library is "a transformation and no easy feat!" (Evans, 2013). But it's worth working toward, for the sake of those you serve and the library staff themselves.

One library that has implemented a trauma-informed approach is the Athens-Clarke County (GA) Library, by using IMLS funding to partner with the University of Georgia School of Social Work. The partnership is called "Trauma-Informed Library Transformation," or TILT. TILT is "designed to create a trauma-informed environment at the library" (Eades, 2020).

A trauma-informed approach includes treating each person with the recognition that their needs are unique to them. In libraries, we tend to say, "We treat everyone the same," despite the fact we actually don't do that. If a child falls asleep in a stroller, we don't wake them up, or if someone needs us to speak more loudly, we do that—because that's good customer service.

This topic is addressed well in the *Community-Led Libraries Toolkit* (2008), which provides excellent examples in its report on the "Working Together Project," which ran from November 2005 to April 2008, during which time it "explored the application of community development techniques in developing more inclusive public library services in Canada" (Working Together Project, 2008). This 4-year project offered disengaged or underserved community members a chance to relate their library experiences, impressions, and expectations. The resulting toolkit provided what they call "six key lessons":

1. Library culture, along with rules and procedures, create significant barriers to inclusion.

2. Libraries must recognize that *same* or *consistent* customer service, which does not take into account socioeconomic disparity, results in inequitable services that further disadvantage socially excluded people.

3. Planning relevant and effective library services for socially excluded community members requires a collaboration of equals between the community members and the library.

4. Relationship building is at the core of effective service planning.

5. Staff "soft skills" such as empathy, interpersonal competence, and open-mindedness are essential.

6. People want to see themselves represented in the library and have an opportunity to participate. (p. 8)

All of these key lessons relate directly to addressing homelessness in your library. We'll be expanding on some of these points later in the book.

Adverse Childhood Experiences

Closely related to a trauma-informed approach is an awareness about adverse childhood experiences (ACEs). This term first emerged from a 1995 study by Kaiser Permanente and the Centers for Disease Control (Tait, 2019). A questionnaire asked about negative childhood experiences, such as physical or emotional abuse, divorce, incarceration of a parent, and other factors. These childhood experiences had an impact on the future physical and mental well-being of adults.

Tait (2019) also describes a study about the impact of positive experiences and how they may be able to mitigate some of the harm caused by ACEs. As she states: "A new study published in the journal *Child Abuse and Neglect* has found that *positive* experiences, such as having a teacher who cares about them, can buffer against these negative outcomes."

As library staff, we can make a difference to children who are experiencing the trauma of poverty and homelessness, by offering these positive experiences, by creating respectful, encouraging, supportive, and welcoming environments.

Harm Reduction

Another term you may encounter is "harm reduction." As the National Health Care for the Homeless Council (NHCHC) describes it:

> Harm reduction is one treatment approach among many that is necessary to provide the client with choice. Understanding the realities of poverty, class, racism, social isolation, past trauma, sex-based discrimination, and other social inequalities that affect both people's vulnerability and capacity to effectively deal with substance use, the harm reduction approach provides a holistic perspective for creating change. This paradigm recognizes that the client is the change agent who through individual self-direction seeks to minimize unhealthy practices and improve her overall health. (2010)

The principal tenet of harm reduction is the emphasis on the word "choice." It can be challenging to hold back from making suggestions or creating expectations about another person's life. If, for example, you know someone who is trying to quit smoking, yet you see them smoking cigarettes regularly, it can be difficult to not say something—a suggestion, a comment. Yet we know that for ourselves we don't make changes until we're ready, and we not only need to be in charge of making those changes, we need to be able to do it our own way.

So, one person may decide to simply quit smoking one day, while another may decide to gradually cut back, while another may decide to use a nicotine patch. And any of these people may talk about it for weeks, months, even years before they are ready. A non-harm reduction approach would be to issue an edict of some kind: "You have one month to quit" or "I insist you stop" or "I'm worried about your health, so you have to stop now." A harm reduction approach would be to listen respectfully, offer examples of strategies, keep your opinions to yourself, and always be ready to engage in action or conversation that is initiated by the person. That way, each person makes the decision for themselves, and they feel supported while they are working toward that decision, whatever it is.

Needle exchange is an excellent example of a harm reduction approach. Although providing people with free needles may not seem like a good idea, the relationships and conversations that emerge from these programs, as well as the obvious health benefits to using a clean needle, provide support, connections, and options. And gradually, as trust is created, participants may ask questions about programs that will help them use fewer or no drugs. But that can't be the expectation.

Person-First/Identity-First Language

"Language not only describes our reality, but also designs it" (Hyams et al., 2018).

One way to support community members who are experiencing homelessness is to use people-first/person-centered language. People-first/person-centered language is just that: The person comes first. As Hyams et al. put it: "Using person-centered language is about respecting the dignity, worth, unique qualities and strengths of every individual. A person's identity and self-image are closely linked to the words used to describe them" (2018).

For instance, in this book, we use "people experiencing homelessness" rather than "the homeless," because no one is defined by their housing status. Other examples of person-first language are:

• A person with a mental health diagnosis or condition versus "the mentally ill."

• A person with depression versus a depressed person.

• A person with a disability versus "the disabled."

If you don't already use person-centered language, this may feel uncomfortable or awkward at first. For example, saying "people experiencing homelessness" every time you want to discuss this topic is longer than simply saying "homeless person" or "the homeless." I have found for myself that I tend to mix it up, as you'll notice as you read this book. Sometimes I say person experiencing homelessness, other times I say a person who is unhoused or unstably housed. Whatever I say, I want to show respect for a person's living situation and make it clear I don't equate who they are with their housing status.

A caveat for this is that some people prefer you don't use person-first language for them, and they don't use it for themselves. One way this is expressed is through the term "identity-first language" (IFL). In her blog post on "Think Inclusive," Emily Landau describes the conflict between these two approaches and defines IFL. As she puts it:

> IFL is a linguistic concept embraced and actually preferred by countless people within the disability community. In the ideology of identity-first, "disabled" is a perfectly acceptable way for a person to identify. Instead of going out of your way to say "person with a disability," when using IFL you would instead say "disabled person." This is how I personally choose to identify myself. **I am a disabled person.** (2015)

She goes on to explain that by separating a person from their disability, there's an implication that "disabled" and "disability" are "negative, derogatory words." She points out that for her (and many others) it is "an identity and culture unto itself."

Metaphors

Another aspect of language and disabilities are the metaphors that are "deeply engrained in everyday language, news, and literature, although many remain oblivious to their impact" (Nario-Redmond, 2020). Nario-Redmond offers several examples, including "blind to," "lame duck," and "crippled or paralyzed by fear" (p. 101). Other common words include "crazy," "insane," and "bonkers." Being aware of the metaphors we use and finding alternative ways of expressing our ideas can help change the subtle, yet powerful, stories told about people with disabilities.

Strengths-Based Language

Yet another approach to language is what is called "strengths-based language" versus "deficit-based language." As Hyams et al. write:

> When a practitioner uses deficits-based language filtered through a diagnostic label, they may become negatively biased and depersonalize the individual they are working with. Practitioners sometimes use casual labels when describing individuals, such as "junkie" for an individual with a substance use history or "cutter" for an individual that engages in self-harm. Typically, practitioners are not intending to demean individual but using this language can become an accepted part of the agency's culture. These narrow and negative labels are stigmatizing and can result in discriminatory and ineffective care. (2018)

Elissa Hardy, community resource manager at the Denver Public Library, created a table that compares these three approaches to language. Table 1.7 is an adapted version of her table (personal communication, 2020).

You may notice the last section of Table 1.7 does not mention the person's housing status. This is an important point, especially for our work in libraries. Although we may be more aware of the substance overuse of people who are living their private lives in public, their housing status isn't really relevant to whether or not they would like help working on their substance use.

Using Language

With all this information, you may be wondering what language you should use, especially when talking about a person within hearing distance or talking directly with them? The best guide is to follow the lead of the person you're interacting with, especially as it relates to people with disabilities or disabled people. When talking about a person's housing status, the most important point is to try to ascertain what they need. Do

Table 1.7   Strengths-Based Language

Deficit-Based Language	Person-Centered Language	Strengths-Based Language
Homeless person	Person experiencing homelessness	Persons who have developed ways to survive related to housing challenges
Crazy person/ mentally ill person	Person with a mental health challenge	Persons who thrive and survive while living with a mental health challenge
Disabled person	Person with a disability	Persons who thrive and survive while living with a disability
Addict	Person who uses drugs Person who injects drugs	Persons who have overcome adversities in life and found ways that work for them to cope
Alcoholic	Person who uses alcohol	See above
We are developing programming for our customers who are homeless and addicted.	We are developing programming for our customers who are experiencing homelessness and who use drugs or alcohol.	We are developing programming for our community members who have overcome adversities and trauma in their lives by finding ways to cope that work for them. We want to honor this strength and survival in this program development.

they have a predictable and safe place to sleep that night? Is it temporary? Many people who are experiencing homelessness don't think of themselves as homeless and using the term—especially calling them "homeless"—may be rejected by them. It can also affect how they feel about themselves and their housing status.

In fact, Walter et al. (2015) did a study looking at the impact on a person's personal well-being and mood based on having to self-categorize themselves as homeless. They found that people who had to self-identify as homeless so they could receive services were more likely to have lower personal well-being and more negative moods. The stigma and stereotype associated with homelessness is so strong that it impacted how they felt about themselves. On the other hand, 31% of the people who were studied rejected the label of homeless, even though it was a requirement for being able to take advantage of services.

Knowing this, library staff are encouraged to focus on the needs of their community members, rather than on a category in which to put them.

ON THE STREETS

Being unstably housed or experiencing homelessness can be a demoralizing, disorienting, and traumatic experience. When someone who is experiencing homelessness enters a library, they come from an unstable or unpredictable living situation, where they must live their private life in public. If you are housed, think about all the activities you pursue inside your home and imagine being watched and sometimes judged for pursuing them. For instance, if you have a glass of wine or a beer in the privacy of your home, that's socially acceptable. However, if you were to do that sitting on the sidewalk, you might be stared at, avoided, or even berated. Or if you raise your voice in an argument with a friend or partner, no one calls the police or veers around you or makes belittling comments. If you talk to yourself as you go about your work (and I know I certainly do), there is no one ready to pass judgment on you. You probably have a place where on the whole you can be yourself. When you live on the streets, that's much more challenging.

Experiencing homelessness also means living in a hostile environment much of the time. In general, public spaces are not welcoming or friendly toward those experiencing homelessness. As a society, Americans hope to not have to deal with homelessness. Folks are moved out of public spaces, like libraries, by the creation of public conduct policies and antihomeless environments that target people without homes. An examination of homelessness begins to reveal the ways in which public spaces can be created to either validate those who occupy them or seek to expel them. These spaces communicate with the public, whether or not they realize it, and those who do are most often those who are negatively impacted. Kerrigan (2018) calls this concept "hostile design, hostile architecture or defensive design." As she states: "This refers to design features implemented into city and town planning which were created specifically to deter homeless people from finding somewhere to sleep." Or as Jock (2019) puts it:

> When the city builds an armrest in the middle of a park bench, it says to someone who needed to sleep there, "You are not welcome here." When the city adds spikes to the cement of an already hard and uncomfortable sidewalk, it says to the person who needed to sit there, "You are not welcome here." It makes the message rather clear. It does not need words on a sign, only metal and concrete.

Examples of this kind of architecture are ever-present in the urban environment, although people who are housed may not notice. Hostile architecture includes metal prongs in window wells, benches with arms placed close together, hard metal benches that are cold in the winter and hot in the summer, awning gaps, and raised grate covers. That is, purposeful choices are being made about who should be encouraged to inhabit public spaces and who should not.

Your community members and library users who are unstably housed—who have no other place to go—are having these experiences and are carrying them with them when they enter your library.

The following photographs (Figures 1.1 to 1.3) are examples of hostile architecture in New York City.

Experiencing homelessness is also dangerous. Although housed people can be fearful around people who are unhoused, particularly those who are more visibly unhoused, the reality is that a person living on the streets is much more likely to be the victim of violence than the perpetrator. "Vulnerable to Hate" (Leomporra & Hustings, 2018) is a regular report from the National Coalition for the Homeless. One of their motivations for creating these reports is to raise awareness of crimes and violence against those who are experiencing homelessness. As they write in their most recent report:

> In order to build healthy and compassionate communities, the civil and human rights of poor people and people experiencing homelessness must be protected and enforced. At this time, there must be commitment by our lawmakers to combat bias-motivated violent acts against people who experience homelessness. (2018, Executive Summary)

Figure 1.1   Hostile architecture bench in New York City.
(Photo by Katie Winkelstein-Duveneck)

Figure 1.2 Hostile architecture subway grate in New York City. (Photo by Katie Winkelstein-Duveneck)

Figure 1.3 Hostile architecture window spikes in New York City. (Photo by Katie Winkelstein-Duveneck)

According to the report, across 2016–2017 there were 112 documented "antihomeless" attacks, 48 of which were fatal attacks. As they point out, these numbers are necessarily an undercount and only include those that are reported and that were by housed perpetrators. People experiencing homelessness do not have protected status by the FBI, so these are not considered hate crimes. This is one example of an action libraries can take. Raising awareness of the ongoing violence against unhoused community members could help change public perceptions as well as moving toward creating legal protections against this kind of violence.

The report also includes a list of what they call "How People Experiencing Homelessness Are Dehumanized" (Leomporra & Hustings, 2018). As they point out: "Structural violence . . . has created growing income inequality and homelessness in the United States. This ongoing structural violence can lead to direct violence when a community is thoroughly dehumanized (p. 16). This list includes:

- Segregation.
- Fear.
- Illegal to be poor.
- The criminal label.
- Attacked by police.
- Refused a place to sleep.
- Property stolen illegally.
- Denied food, bathrooms, and health care.
- Existence denied.
- Verbally abused.
- Attacked. (p. 16)

Other experiences on the streets are rules about what can and can't be done in a public place and the resulting citations and tickets when these rules are necessarily broken. Cities have so-called "sit/lie" laws that prohibit people from sitting or lying down in a public space, such as a sidewalk, even on the edge of the sidewalk or in a doorway. These laws, what the Western Regional Advocacy Project (WRAP) calls "the criminalization of poor and homeless people's existence" (WRAP, n.d.)., target those who have no other place to be during the day and at night.

In many cities, these laws include a prohibition against sleeping in a legally parked vehicle, sleeping in parks, and creating communities on the streets, using tents, tarps, or other protections from the weather, and for privacy. These laws are sometimes referred to as quality-of-life laws, and cities across the United States are increasingly adopting them. In their "National Civil Rights Fact Sheet," WRAP lists the preliminary findings of their street outreach to almost 1,600 people in 15 communities. Their statistics include:

Eighty-two percent of survey respondents reported being harassed, cited, or arrested for sleeping.

Seventy-seven percent of survey respondents reported being harassed, cited, or arrested for sitting or lying on the sidewalk.

Seventy-five percent of survey respondents reported being harassed, cited, or arrested for loitering or hanging out.

Only 25% of the respondents said they knew of a safe place to sleep at night. (WRAP, 2016)

These are excellent examples of the challenges people who don't have a safe and habitable place to call home are encountering.

Chelsea's Story

Example: A young woman, we'll call her Chelsea, received multiple citations and tickets for sleeping in her car, loitering, and asking for money. She couldn't afford to pay the fees that accrued, and so the local police confiscated her car and sold it at auction, using the money to pay off her tickets and citations. Now she no longer has a private space to sleep at night.

It should be noted that in cities that have sit/lie laws, like San Francisco, there have been some efforts to examine the effects of these laws and try to mitigate their effects. As San Francisco Police Department sergeant Michael Andraychak said in a 2018 interview: "[T]he Department and City realized many years ago that we cannot arrest our way out of the homeless crisis" (Andersen, 2018). However, cities continue to respond to concerns by shopkeepers and housed community members by moving and citing people, using a range of approaches.

Housed Privilege

As we've mentioned, there are differences between how we are allowed to act in public and in private. There are also other privileges of those who are housed. The following are examples of housed privileges, although it's important to point out that not all of these are true for people who are housed:

- Having control over where you live
- Knowing where you're going to sleep that night
- Being able to have a daily routine

- Having access to electricity for charging devices/electronics
- Having a safe space, without fear of being verbally or physically attacked
- Having a place to store your personal items
- Being able to put down roots
- Having the ability to preserve and store family artifacts, heirlooms, photos, and other ways of keeping family memories
- Having a previous address when applying for housing
- Having an address when applying for employment, school, and at other times you need one
- Being able to engage in intimate activity in a private, safe, and comfortable setting
- Being able to have a disagreement with a partner without being judged or having an audience
- Having control over the climate where you live
- Not having to worry about bodily functions
- Being able to easily register to vote and to cast a ballot
- Having the ability to entertain yourself with movies, television, and video games
- Having your own place to garden
- Having an address for receiving mail
- Being able to host guests
- Being able to provide shelter to someone else
- Knowing where your personal belongings are at any given moment
- Being able to safely and privately take a shower or bath
- Being able to talk aloud to yourself without being judged, ridiculed, or abused
- Being able to drink a glass of wine, beer, or other alcoholic beverages without being chastised, avoided, verbally accosted, or denigrated
- Being able to simply sit and think or do nothing at all
- Having access to a kitchen where you can safely store and prepare food
- Having control over the air you breathe
- Being able to stay healthy by getting enough sleep and healthy food, and avoiding contaminants, insects, and rodents

As you read this list, ask yourself: Is there a way the library could help with any of these? Some are probably out of the reach of the library, but others may be possible. For example, a library could work with unhoused community members to make sure they are able to vote no matter their housing status. The National Coalition for the Homeless (2018) has created a downloadable manual, "You Don't Need a Home to Vote," which provides relevant and useful information about this topic. One of the challenges of voting while unhoused is not only registering to vote, but also receiving any related mailings, such as a vote-by-mail ballot. During the 2020 pandemic previously described, there was a nationwide effort to increase mail-in balloting, to protect the health of voters and poll workers. However, to receive one of these ballots, a person has to have a mailing address. Some shelters and other service agencies provide these for unhoused community members. Libraries, too, could offer their addresses so everyone is able to vote, housed or not.

Another action a library could take is to partner with an agency or even the city to provide lockers for people experiencing homelessness. A good example of a program like this is San Diego's "Think Dignity Transitional Storage Center (TSC)" (Think Dignity, n.d.). TSC provides 104 lockers and about 130 bins for people experiencing homelessness. As they describe on their website:

> The TSC is a place for homeless individuals to safely store their personal belongings, allowing them to use public transportation, job hunt, work, attend classes, meet with health professionals and other service providers, and begin to transition off the streets, while freeing the streets of over 30,000 pounds of personal belongings. It is a win-win solution for all. (Think Dignity, n.d.)

On their website, they also ask for donations to support this program—a dollar a day will pay for someone's locker for a year. This would make a good campaign at your library and would also help mitigate policies you may have around baggage and other belongings in the library. In their survey on addressing homelessness in public and academic libraries, Bales and Winkelstein found that 15 out of the 812 respondents provided lockers (2019).

IN THE LIBRARY

As you can see, it is challenging to feel safe and included while experiencing homelessness. Creating a supportive and welcoming environment in your library for all your library users, including those who are unhoused, can make a huge difference in their lives. The lack of truly affordable housing, income inequalities, political decisions, local measures, and more all contribute to homelessness, and it's unlikely your library will be able to address all or any of these. But you can make a difference by simply letting your unhoused community members know that they are welcome at your library and that you look forward to meeting their library needs.

CONCLUSION

In this chapter we've looked at what it means to be experiencing homelessness, the importance of tone and support, various populations who are unhoused, daily realities, and some related vocabulary. It is hoped this information will help you as you find out more about your community and focus on some actions your library can take to address the needs of those who are unstably housed.

In Chapter 2, we look at the library's past and current role and actions in addressing homelessness and how attitudes are changing—as we learn more about this social issue.

REFERENCES

Andersen, T. (2018, October 18). What happened to SF's controversial "sit-lie" ordinance? *SFGate.* https://www.sfgate.com/bayarea/article/What-happened-to-SF-s-controversial-sit-lie-13303216.php

Bales, S., & Winkelstein, J. A. (2019). [Libraries and homelessness]. Unpublished raw data.

Beck, E., & Twiss, P. (2018). *The homelessness industry: A critique of US social policy.* Lynne Rienner.

Broton, K. M. (2019). The reality of today's college students: Addressing students' economic and material well-being. *Bringing theory to practice.* https://bttop.org/news-events/feature-reality-today%E2%80%99s-college-students-addressing-students%E2%80%99-economic-and-material-well

Centers for Disease Control and Prevention (CDC). (2020, August 16). *Coronavirus 2019 (COVID-19): Older adults.* https://www.cdc.gov/coronavirus/2019-ncov/need-extra-precautions/older-adults.html

Coalition on Homelessness. (2015). *Punishing the poorest: How the criminalization of homelessness perpetuates poverty in San Francisco.* http://www.cohsf.org/what-we-do/reports

Community Reach Center. (n.d.). *Trauma-informed care (TIC).* https://www.communityreachcenter.org/services/adult-and-senior-services/trauma-informed-care-tic

Couloute, L. (2018, August). *Nowhere to go: Homelessness among formerly incarcerated people.* Prison Policy Initiative. https://www.prisonpolicy.org/reports/housing.html

Eades, R. B. (2020, April 17). Implementing a trauma-informed approach. *Public Libraries Online.* http://publiclibrariesonline.org/2020/04/implementing-a-trauma-informed-approach

Evans, J. K. (2013, May 1). What does trauma-informed care really mean? *The Up Center.* https://www.theupcenter.org/wp-content/uploads/2014/05/TIC -05.14.14.pdf

Evans, J. K. (2015). What every child welfare professional needs to know. *The Up Center.* https://www.theupcenter.org/tic

Fisher-Borne, M., Cain, J. M., & Martin, S. L. (2015). From mastery to account-ability: Cultural humility as an alternative to cultural competence. *Social Work Education: The International Journal, 34*(23), 165–181.

GAO (U.S. Government Accountability Office). (2019, January 9). *Better infor-mation could help eligible college students access federal food assis-tance benefits.* https://www.gao.gov/products/GAO-19-95#summary

Goldberg, J., Lang, K., & Barrington, V. (2016, April). How to prevent and end homelessness among older adults. *Justice in Aging.* https://www .justiceinaging.org/wp-content/uploads/2016/04/Homelessness-Older -Adults.pdf

Griswold, E. (2020, March 26). How do you shelter in place when you don't have a home? *The New Yorker.* https://www.newyorker.com/news/dispatch /how-do-you-shelter-in-place-when-you-dont-have-a-home

Harris, M. D. (2006). *Colored pictures: Race and visual representation.* Univer-sity of North Carolina Press.

Henry, M., de Sousa, T., Roddey, C., Gayen, S., & Bednar, T.J., Abt Associates. (2021, January). Part 1: Estimates of homelessness in the United States: The 2020 annual homeless assessment report (AHAR) to Congress. *U.S. Department of Housing and Urban Development.* https://www.huduser .gov/portal/datasets/ahar/2020-ahar-part-1-pit-estimates-of-homeless-ness-in-the-us.html

Henry, M., Watt, R., Rosenthal, L., Shivki, A., & Abt Associates. (2018, October). Part 2: Estimates of homelessness in the United States: The 2017 annual homeless assessment report (AHAR) to Congress. *U.S. Department of Housing and Urban Development.* https://www.hudexchange.info/resource /5769/2017-ahar-part-2-estimates-of-homelessness-in-the-us

The Hope Center for College, Community and Justice. (n.d.). *About the Hope Center.* https://hope4college.com

HostileDesign.org. (n.d.). *Designs against humanity.* https://hostiledesign.org

Hyams, K., Prater, N., Rohovit, J., & Meyer-Kalos, P. S. (2018, April). Person-centered language. *Clinical Tip No. 8.* Center for Practice Transformation, University of Minnesota.

Jock, K. (2019, June 7). *You are not welcome here: Anti-homeless architecture crops up nationwide.* https://www.streetroots.org/news/2019/06/07/you -are-not-welcome-here-anti-homeless-architecture-crops-nationwide

Kerrigan, S. (2018, May 22). 15 Examples of "anti-homeless" hostile architecture that you probably never noticed before. *Interesting engineering: Archi-tecture.* https://interestingengineering.com/15-examples-anti-homeless -hostile-architecture-that-you-probably-never-noticed-before

Landau, E. (2015, July 20). Why person-first language doesn't always put the person first. *Think inclusive.* https://www.thinkinclusive.us/why-person -first-language-doesnt-always-put-the-person-first

Leomporra, A., & Hustings, M. (Eds.). (2018). Vulnerable to hate: A survey of bias-motivated violence against people experiencing homelessness in 2016–2017. *National Coalition for the Homeless.* http://nationalhomeless .org/vulnerable-to-hate-2016-2017

Luria Library. (n.d.). Hunger or homelessness—resources for and about: Home. *Santa Barbara City College.* https://sbcc.libguides.com/hungerorhome lessness

Merriam-Webster. (n.d.). *The definition of culture.* https://www.merriam-webster .com/dictionary/culture

NAHRO. (2015). *HUD publishes final definition of "chronically homeless."* http:// www.nahro.org/hud-publishes-final-definition-%E2%80%9Cchronically -homeless%E2%80%9D

Nario-Redmond, M. R. (2020). *Ableism: The causes and consequences of disability prejudice.* Wiley.

National Alliance to End Homelessness (NAEH). (2020a). *Events: Upcoming events. COVID-19 Webinar Series.* https://endhomelessness.org/events /upcoming-events

National Alliance to End Homelessness (NAEH). (2020b). *National Alliance to End Homelessness statement on structural racism and racial inequity.* https://endhomelessness.org/national-alliance-to-end-homelessness -statement-on-structural-racism-and-racial-inequity

National Center for Homeless Education (NCHE). (n.d.a). *National Center for Homeless Education.* https://nche.ed.gov

National Center for Homeless Education (NCHE). (n.d.b). *The McKinney-Vento definition of homeless.* https://nche.ed.gov/mckinney-vento-definition

National Coalition for the Homeless. (2018). *You don't need a home to vote.* https://www.nationalhomeless.org/wp-content/uploads/2018/08/2018 -Manual_for-web.pdf

National Coalition for the Homeless. (2020, March 10). *What homeless folks should know about coronavirus (COVID-1).* http://nationalhomeless.org /coronavirus-covid-19

National Health Care for the Homeless Council (NHCHC). (2010, April). *Harm reduction: Preparing people for change.* http://homelesshub.ca/resource /harm-reduction-preparing-people-change

National Health Care for the Homeless Council (NHCHC). (2012). *Disability, employment and homelessness: 2012 policy statement.* https://www.nhchc .org/policy-advocacy/issue/disability

National Network for Youth (NN4Y). (n.d.). Education barriers for homeless youth. *NN4Y Issue Brief.* https://www.nn4youth.org/policy-advocacy/fact -sheets-and-issue-briefs

Olivet, J., & Dones, M. (2017). *Racial equity: An essential component in our nation's homelessness response.* United States Interagency Council on Homelessness. https://www.usich.gov/news/racial-equity-an-essential-component-of -our-nations-homelessness-response

Ruiz-Grossman, S. (2018, December 15). 5 things people get wrong about homelessness. *HuffPost.* https://www.huffpost.com/entry/homeless-stereotypes -myths-housing-crisis_n_5c05a9a7e4b0cd916faefb18

Sabatini, J. (2016, June 1). SF's sit/lie law may be told to take a hike. *San Francisco Examiner.* http://www.sfexaminer.com/sfs-sit-lie-law-may-told-take-hike/#

Said, E. (1993). *Culture and imperialism.* Chatto & Windus.

SAMHSA. (2018). *Trauma-informed approach and trauma-specific interventions.* https://www.samhsa.gov/nctic/trauma-interventions

Saoirse, K. (2018, May 22). 15 examples of "anti-homeless" hostile architecture that you probably never noticed before. *Interesting engineering.* https://interestingengineering.com/15-examples-anti-homeless-hostile-architecture-that-you-probably-never-noticed-before

Scarlett, E. (2020, March 18). Homeless during a pandemic: The challenge to self-isolate and be protected from COVID-19. *WIS News10.* https://www.msn.com/en-us/health/medical/homeless-during-a-pandemic-the-challenge-to-self-isolate-and-stay-protected-from-covid-19/ar-BB11lVHX

Solomon, M. (2020, March 13). California races to defend homeless population from COVID-19. *Marketplace.* https://www.marketplace.org/2020/03/13/california-races-to-defend-homeless-population-from-covid-19

Stigers, K. (2019, May). Summary of issues facing rural housing. *FAHE.* https://fahe.org/rural-housing-memo

StigmaWatch. (n.d.). What is StigmaWatch? *SANE.* https://www.sane.org/services/stigmawatch

Tait, V. (2019). Ways to counter the effects of adverse childhood experiences. *Psychology Today.* https://www.psychologytoday.com/us/blog/pulling-through/201910/ways-counter-the-effects-adverse-childhood-experiences

Technical Assistance Collaborative (TAC). (2016). *Priced out in the United States.* http://www.tacinc.org/knowledge-resources/priced-out-v2

Tervalon, M., & Murray-Garcia, J. (1998). Cultural humility versus cultural competence: A critical distinction in defining physician training outcomes in multicultural education. *Journal of Health Care for the Poor and Underserved, 9*(2), 117–125.

Think Dignity. (n.d.). *Transitional storage center (TSC).* https://www.thinkdignity.org/transitional-storage-center-tsc

Ting-Toomey, S. (1999). *Communicating across cultures.* Guilford Press.

Tufts. (2020, July 10). *Why people of color are suffering more from COVID-19.* Tufts University School of Medicine. https://medicine.tufts.edu/news/2020/07/why-people-color-are-suffering-more-covid-19

United States Census Bureau. (2019). *Quick facts United States.* https://www.census.gov/quickfacts/fact/table/US#

United States Interagency Council on Homelessness (USICH). (2018, August). *Homelessness in America: Focus on chronic homelessness among people with disabilities.* https://www.usich.gov/tools-for-action/homelessness-in-america-focus-on-people-with-disabilities-experiencing-chronic-homelessness

U.S. Department of Housing and Urban Development (HUD). (n.d.). *Homeless management information system.* https://www.hudexchange.info/programs/hmis

U.S. Department of Housing and Urban Development (HUD). (2021a). CoC homeless populations and subpopulations reports. *HUD Exchange.*

https://www.hudexchange.info/programs/coc/coc-homeless-populations-and-subpopulations-reports

U.S. Department of Housing and Urban Development (HUD). (2021b). *Resource library.* https://www.hudexchange.info/resources/

Vaughan, A. (2018, February 22). Closing session. *Coming Up Together* conference. Ottawa, Canada. http://www.coming-up-together.ca

Walter, Z., Jetten, J., Parsell, C., & Dingle, G. A. (2015). The impact of self-categorizing as "homeless" on well-being and service use. *Analyses of Social Issues and Public Policy, 15*(1), 333–356.

Western Regional Advocacy Project (WRAP). (n.d.). *Homeless bill of rights.* https://wraphome.org/what/homeless-bill-of-rights

Western Regional Advocacy Project (WRAP). (2016, October 4). *National civil rights fact sheet.* https://wraphome.org/what/homeless-bill-of-rights

Working Together Project. (2008). *Community-led libraries toolkit: Starting us all down the path toward developing inclusive public libraries.* http://www.librariesincommunities.ca/resources/Community-Led_Libraries_Toolkit.pdf

World Population Review. (2021). *Native American population 2020.* https://worldpopulationreview.com/state-rankings/native-american-population

Worldometer. (2021, March 26). *COVID-19 coronavirus pandemic.* https://www.worldometers.info/coronavirus

2

The Library's Role: Then and Now

INTRODUCTION

In Chapter 2, we look at reasons why libraries are and should be involved in addressing homelessness in their communities. We also look at how libraries have interfaced with their unhoused community members in the past and how that is changing. We conclude with a discussion of compassion fatigue and related concepts and some tips on coping with the demands of a library job that places library staff in the middle of social issues that aren't being solved in society at large.

WHY LIBRARIES?

We'll start with the Universal Declaration of Human Rights. This is included because everyone has the same rights, and we need to remember that when working with people who may be culturally or economically different from ourselves, such as people experiencing homelessness when we are housed. Article 25 is particularly relevant.

Articles 1, 2, and 25 tell us:

Article 1.
- All human beings are born free and equal in dignity and rights. They are endowed with reason and conscience and should act towards one another in a spirit of brotherhood.

Article 2.
- Everyone is entitled to all the rights and freedoms set forth in this Declaration, without distinction of any kind, such as race, colour, sex, language, religion, political or other opinion, national or social origin, property, birth or other status.

Article 25.
  * Everyone has the right to a standard of living adequate for the health and well-being of himself and of his family, including food, clothing, housing and medical care and necessary social services, and the right to security in the event of unemployment, sickness, disability, widowhood, old age or other lack of livelihood in circumstances beyond his control. (United Nations, n.d.)

Addressing homelessness and the precursors and outcomes of homelessness are human rights issues for libraries and their communities.

Second, the American Library Association has the updated Policy B.8.10 (the old policy 61, previously called "The Poor People's Policy"): "Addressing Poverty, Inequality and the Responsibilities of Libraries" (ALA, 2019). This policy provides guidance, resources, and support to libraries and library staff related to the role of libraries in addressing homelessness and poverty. The full text of this is in Appendix K.

The reality, though, is this policy hasn't received much attention in the library world. In his 2005 Jean E. Coleman Outreach Lecture, "Classism in the Stacks: Libraries and Poverty," Sandford Berman provided an excellent critique of library attitudes toward homelessness and poverty. As he points out, although the Library Bill of Rights has been adopted by "hundreds of institutions," he could find "no library that has similarly adopted and publicized the Poor People's Policy (PPP)" (Berman, 2005). He offers examples of library policies and programs and suggestions for ways in which libraries can be more supportive and less punitive. It's a lecture well worth reading and as applicable to many of today's libraries as it was in 2005.

Another reason for libraries to be actively addressing homelessness and poverty is directly related to the health of a community. Sir Michael Marmot, who is chair of the Commission on Social Determinants of Health, part of the World Health Organization (WHO), has spent his professional life looking at the social determinants of health. His research focuses on social gradients and the impact they have on the health of individuals and communities. As he says in an interview on Australian radio, "There's good evidence that if people are disempowered—if they have little control over their lives, if they're socially isolated or unable to participate fully in society—then there are biological effects" (Marmot, 2011). Our libraries are part of these communities, and when we are able to strengthen the health of some of our community members, such as people experiencing homelessness, we make our entire community stronger. Conversely, poor health in some of our community members weakens our communities. It may not be obvious that investing in, supporting, and educating all our community members can affect health, but Marmot makes an excellent case for this.

As Mỹ Dzung Chu writes in her piece, "Why Housing Security Is Key to Environmental Justice": "I am passionate about housing security because it determines where we can afford to live and the quality of housing we can live in—all of which affects our health, the health of our communities, and of future generations" (Chu, 2020).

As mentioned in Chapter 1, this book is being written during the COVID-19 worldwide pandemic. At this writing, the United States has the greatest number of virus-related deaths of any country in the world, topping 561,142 as of March 26, 2021, with more than 30,863,052 people diagnosed with it in the United States (Worldometer, 2021). This virus is an excellent example of the importance of supporting all of our community members in their efforts to stay healthy, because everyone's health impacts the community—in this case, by either speeding up or slowing down the transmission of a fatal virus.

In addition, libraries—especially public libraries—are in theory there for everyone. By looking at how we can address homelessness and poverty, we help make that statement a reality.

Finally, the reality is that there are thousands of people experiencing homelessness every day in the United States. Those who are living on the streets or in cars, under bridges or overpasses, in alleys or in doorways, as well as those who stay in emergency shelters, motels, hotels, and doubled up in small apartments, need a place to go during the day. A public library, as a free and safe public space out of the elements, is an obvious choice. In Chapter 3 we'll be looking at how people experiencing homelessness are using the library and the barriers they encounter, but as many of you know, both housed and unhoused folks are using our libraries. We can choose to create more and more rules to control who is acceptable in our libraries and who isn't, or we can take positive action that means we have provided the resources and personal connections that will help people who need it find permanent and stable housing, while also becoming library users who contribute to our libraries and to our communities. Ultimately, in this second scenario, we all benefit.

BARRIERS TO LIBRARY USE: PAST AND PRESENT

For all library users, there can be many barriers to using the library. For those who are housed, these barriers can be frustrating and can prevent library users from accessing the resources, programs, and materials they need. For those who are experiencing homelessness, the same applies, but there is also the use of the space itself. Experiencing homelessness means not being able to have a safe (and private) space out of the general public eye. It also means not necessarily having access to safe, free showers, safe places to sleep, facilities to wash clothes or bedding, access to toilets, and places to store personal items. In addition, it can include not having personal connections that create social capital. Because of these challenges, using a library can mean more than the critical resources provided.

Public Conduct Policies

Public conduct policies are frequently the largest barrier. These policies include no sleeping, no strong odors, the requirement to be actively engaged with library materials at all times, no washing of clothes or person in restrooms, and a limit on the amount of baggage allowed. For those who stay awake all night because they feel unsafe, dozing off in a safe and comfortable place can and does happen. Libraries with no-sleeping policies can make it difficult for these library users to take advantage of the space as well as the resources.

Of the libraries surveyed for the IFLA "Guidelines for Library Services to People Experiencing Homelessness," more than half of them had policies specifically related to sleeping in the library (IFLA, 2017). Although this was an international survey, many of the libraries were U.S. libraries. One example of a library that is flexible is the Forbes Library in Northampton (Massachusetts), where "sleeping is allowed but no lying down" (IFLA, 2017).

Baggage limits can mean those who need to carry all of their possessions with them can't use the library, unless there are secure lockers or other storage facilities made available. Odor policies can prevent some library users from staying in the library, and for those who don't have access to bathing facilities, they probably can't return. Odor policies were much less common than no-sleeping policies among the libraries that replied to the survey—of the 50 responses to the survey, only 10 had odor policies (IFLA, 2017).

No washing in the restrooms means that those who have been ejected due to strong odors can't address their lack of basic hygiene options and therefore can't use the library.

Most public conduct policies have been designed to create an atmosphere that is acceptable to housed, well-rested, and well-bathed library users. It makes sense for libraries to do this, because these library users tend to be the most outspoken about what is acceptable and what is not acceptable to them, they probably pay taxes that contribute to the funding for libraries (although it should be noted that many people experiencing homelessness are employed and also pay taxes), and it is the unspoken assumption that they are the default library users.

Other Policies and Procedures

This is also true for other policies and procedures, such as the requirements for getting a library card, for using a meeting room, for using a library computer, and for paying fines and fees. Requiring a permanent address for a library card automatically excludes those who are experiencing homelessness, although some libraries offer the option of using a shelter address. However, these cards are usually limited, and they also "out" the person as unstably housed and, especially for unaccompanied youth and for families, this may be a secret they're trying to keep.

Thomas's Story

Thomas spent most days at the main branch of an urban library system. He loved to read and really wanted to be able to check out some books. The library he used will accept a shelter address, so he could get a limited card—one that allowed him to check out one print item at a time and also use the Internet computers for an hour. When I spoke to him, his dilemma was that he didn't want to reveal his housing status. He had been careful to wear clean clothes, he'd found a place to safely shower, and he only carried with him a small student backpack, since all of his other belongings had been stolen at the bus station when he arrived in the city. He was fully aware of the stigma attached to housing status, and he resisted having that stereotype applied to him. On the other hand, he wanted a library card—he'd always had a library card in the small town where he grew up, and he loved libraries.

Thomas is an excellent example of the impact of library policies on the lives of those experiencing homelessness and the need for a different approach to serving all library users. The one-size-fits-all theme that is reiterated over and over doesn't work for everyone, and libraries need to be ready to serve all their community members equally well. As mentioned in Chapter 1, the Working Together Project (2008) points out in their "Six Key Lessons": "Libraries must recognize that *same* or *consistent* customer service, which does not take into account socio-economic disparity, results in inequitable services that further disadvantage socially excluded people" (p. 10).

This can be challenging for library staff, because it may seem easier to have specific clear rules that can be pointed to when a library user doesn't fit in with expectations. And since there are no rules that work for everyone, exceptions are made. But we must note that if exceptions are going to be made, then library staff must be transparent about what is possible and what isn't possible. For example, if a housed middle school student comes to the library with their tuba, most libraries would overlook its size or even offer to store it temporarily, because the student is seen as somehow "acceptable."

On the other hand, if a person experiencing homelessness arrived with a suitcase of the same size, and if there is a rule against large items, chances are good that the library user would be asked to either leave their belongings outside or leave the library. If there is a no-sleeping policy, is it enforced for babies sleeping in strollers? If there's a strong odor policy, is it enforced for that sleeping baby who also needs a diaper change?

Library staff may be willing to make exceptions in some cases, but because experiencing homelessness is both traumatic and a challenge to one's self-esteem, if it's not obvious that exceptions are made, the person with the suitcase probably won't ask.

Lowering or Removing Barriers

Some libraries are reconsidering their policies and procedures, taking into account the barriers they may pose. For instance, according to an article in the *South Seattle Emerald* about the impact of the public conduct policies of the Seattle Public Library, the King County Library System (KCLS) did away with their no-sleeping policy. The article quotes KCLS librarian Maggie Block, who states:

> I, and also the people who are making patron behavior policy, want patrons experiencing homelessness to be able to use our libraries and feel safe doing so. . . . We see how having punitive responses for folks who are sleeping affects folks in unstable housing more than other populations. And I really don't like that. (Graham, 2017)

The KCLS "Code of Conduct" provides a general statement about their policy, which gently and clearly sets expectations without using negative or punitive language. It's a good example of how a policy can be in place that highlights a commitment to welcoming "every member of the community" (King County Library System, 2017).

If you have library policies that are acting as barriers to services and resources for your unhoused library community, ask yourself: Why do you have the policies? What changes could you make? What would be the reaction of the housed community members and the library staff? How could you work with them to find ways to create rules that work for all of your library users?

In a 2019 online survey of public and academic library staff, one of the questions asked staff what actions their libraries are taking to address homelessness. The answers included some changes to their policies and procedures, including:

- Allowing food in the library, and allowing people to heat up food or drink.
- Creating a card that doesn't require a permanent address.
- Providing computer day/guest passes (493 out of the 812 respondents).
- An academic library honoring public library cards that are providing for unhoused community members.
- Allowing anyone without an address to use computers.
- Allowing people to sleep on city property.
- Allowing the use of library telephone.

These changes were based on getting to know their community members and helping meet their ongoing and daily needs. Several of the respondents also expressed frustration with the rules and policies of their libraries—for example, the no-sleeping policies, library card rules, and the limit on personal items (Bales & Winkelstein, 2019).

The Good News

The good news is that public libraries are taking a harder look at homelessness and their role in addressing this community challenge. In Chapter 6, there are specific examples of library programs related to homelessness. But for now, it's important to stress that across the United States, there are more discussions, programs, presentations, trainings, and partnerships that help libraries in their efforts to serve all of their community members well. While in the past, an Internet search for "libraries and homelessness" resulted in only complaints and suggestions on how to "deal" with these "problem patrons," current searches reveal news articles, webinars, classes, and other sources of shared information that will benefit all community members. There are still articles, especially related to concerns expressed by housed library users and the challenge for library staff in addressing these concerns while still supporting all library users. But the addition of social workers and public health interns to library services has created new relationships and a more positive and supportive attitude toward those experiencing homelessness.

On September 4, 2018, *American Libraries* magazine published a letter from public library directors and social workers (American Libraries, 2018). As they state in their letter:

> We represent libraries that have hired and collaborated with social workers, and we are at the forefront of serving these customers in new and innovative ways. We've seen firsthand the power of providing thoughtful,

trauma-informed care and the positive impact it has on our libraries, customers, staffs, and communities. . . . We pay close attention to language and labels when working with customers experiencing life challenges. Specifically, we use terms such as "people experiencing homelessness" or "having an experience of being homeless" rather than a blanket statement of "homeless." The same applies with other conditions such as substance use. These experiences do not define people; people define their experiences. . . . We train and educate library staffers on being part of the solution to homelessness. We explain how policy work, advocacy, and compassion must be used together to systematically address homelessness and the effects it has on individuals, families, and communities.

As you can see, these library directors and social workers are taking a comprehensive and active approach to providing library services and spaces for all of their library users. This new attitude has made a difference in libraries and communities, and it is heartening to see the progress that has been made.

We could call this a new approach, but in reality public libraries have always reached out to their communities in an effort to understand and serve them. Unfortunately, increasing economic inequities, inadequate health care, and a lack of affordable housing has created challenges for larger and larger numbers of Americans. Combined with the increasingly hostile and stigmatized views of homelessness, library staff have been left to grapple with social issues that are difficult at best. As with the awareness of the impact of racism, homophobia, transphobia, ableism, and classism on our communities, libraries are now tasked with learning more about a systemic challenge that is only getting worse, especially with the pending impact of the pandemic 2020–2021. Learning more, taking action that works for your library and your community, and becoming part of the caring community that is much needed as we address homelessness and poverty—all of these are possible and necessary.

In Chapter 6, there are specific examples of both small and large steps libraries are taking to address homelessness in their communities. These libraries are responding to the needs of those experiencing homelessness by listening, reaching out, partnering with local organizations, and using their positions as respected institutions to make a difference, so all community members have the opportunity to thrive.

KNOWING YOUR LIMITS OR WHEN TO ASK FOR HELP

As you read this book, you'll see that most of all it provides information about how to meet the information and resource needs of community members who are experiencing homelessness. It is necessary for libraries to play a role in addressing homelessness for the reasons outlined earlier. But this doesn't mean it will necessarily be easy to decide which role your library will play or how this decision will impact library staff.

The key point that can be made about this role is it's not your responsibility to make sure unhoused folks find housing or resources that lead to fulfilling lives. That is, it's not your responsibility to solve anyone's challenges, including those who are experiencing homelessness. As shelter and housing specialist John Petroskas put it:

> You don't have to solve a person's problems. I work with homeless people every day and I don't solve anybody's problems. Homeless people don't ask me to. . . . They have to do the work. I can connect them to a resource, but I can't do the work. And librarians can't do the work for people either. But you can connect them to resources, and that's what your jobs are. (Gehner & Freeman, 2005)

A library may provide employment resources or lists of local senior services or information about local preschools, but there is no library responsibility to make sure someone finds a job or senior community or a place for their young child to go to school. Our strength as libraries is to listen to our community members so we know what they are looking for and then try to connect them to the resources that will make a difference in their lives.

This is not to say there aren't challenges. The stigma, anxiety, trauma, and uncertainty in the lives of those experiencing homelessness indirectly or directly impacts library staff. We are used to being able to help, and even though we may know we don't have to solve people's problems, we naturally want to do just that. And when we're not able to, we're frustrated or anxious or sad or disillusioned. If the interactions are intense, frequent, and prolonged, we may experience secondary trauma/compassion fatigue.

Secondary Trauma/Compassion Fatigue

Naomi Rachel Remen writes about secondary trauma or burnout in her book *Kitchen Table Wisdom* (1996). A popular quote from her is: "The expectation that we can be immersed in suffering and loss daily and not be touched by it is as unrealistic as expecting to be able to walk through water without getting wet" (p. 52).

So, a recognition of how we are reacting is a first step. Looking at the symptoms of burnout, we can acknowledge how our own feelings may be affecting us as well as our library users. Alessandra Pigni (n.d.) writes about "the exhaustion funnel," developed by Professor Marie Asberg at the Karolinska Institute in Stockholm, Sweden. Some of the symptoms of burnout include insomnia, low energy, aches and pains, joylessness, and depressed mood and exhaustion. For library staff, there may also be anger, resentment, or resignation, depending on the library, the community, and the amount of institutional support.

Compassion fatigue is related to secondary trauma. The "Compassion Fatigue Awareness Project" (n.d.) offers Dr. Charles Figley's definition of compassion fatigue:

> Compassion Fatigue is a state experienced by those helping people or animals in distress; it is an extreme state of tension and preoccupation with the suffering of those being helped to the degree that it can create a secondary traumatic stress for the helper. ("Did you know?," n.d.)

Whether or not we are aware of it, the daily work of serving the public, whether they are housed or unhoused, can take its toll and create compassion fatigue, burnout, and secondary trauma—however you describe the daily feelings you may have in doing your job. These are feelings you experience not only at work, but that you carry away with you when you leave each day. There are numerous websites, readings, webinars, and online talks about these topics, and it's worth taking the time (a first step in self-care) to find one that is helpful. WebJunction addresses library compassion fatigue in their webinar given by Linda Bruno (Bruno, 2012). Included on that page are also some relevant resources.

Another presentation is offered on Floridawebinars.org (Dubiel, 2016). This one includes two useful handouts that can be downloaded. One final recommendation of the many resources available is a TEDxFargo talk by Juliette Watt (2018). Although she's not directly addressing library staff, her insights, personal story, and suggestions are for a wide audience. She offers this quick definition of compassion fatigue, again from Dr. Figley: "The emotional and physical burden created by caring for others in distress" (Watt, 2018).

Emotional Labor

"Emotional labor" is a related term. There are numerous definitions for emotional labor, but here's a simple one: "In a work context, emotional labor refers to the expectation that a worker should *manipulate* either her actual feelings or the appearance of her feelings in order to satisfy the perceived requirements of her job" (Hackman, 2015).

Like most public service jobs, working in a library means being nice to the customers. As library staff, we may have particular expectations about what this looks like and who we are expected to serve. When it appears our workload has expanded—there are fewer staff, more responsibilities, increased job duties, and new services—this can be not only stressful but also emotionally draining. When this includes working with library users who are new to us, whose needs we don't understand, who have challenges we can't solve, and who are experiencing daily trauma, that adds to our emotional labor.

Addressing These Challenges

So how do we address all of this and still do our jobs? Again, there are numerous lists of self-care suggestions, some specifically tailored to those who work in libraries. They include:

- Leaving the building during the work day, even if it's briefly.
- Meditation or practicing conscious awareness.
- Saying no/defining your boundaries.
- Setting small goals.
- Eating well.
- Exercising.
- Doing something you enjoy.

Although all of these (and others) are useful, they can feel beside the point. Yes, you can take better care of yourself, but what if you still feel overwhelmed at work? What if you are resentful that you have to put aside your fears, your anxiety, and your hopelessness so you can still help unhoused library users find the connections they need to move on with their lives?

Himmelstein (2020) offers examples of actions some school and public libraries are taking to address compassion fatigue. One major point in his article relates to administrative support. In one example, one school librarian has a library technician who "helps with administrative tasks," while another, who is retiring because of the stress of the job responsibilities, does not have this kind of support. Other kinds of support include providing "training in compassion fatigue, mental health first aid, and self-care strategies . . . regularly checking in on staff well-being; and staff mental health support after traumatic events."

Twinsburg (Ohio) Public Library (TPL) supports staff by offering training opportunities on such topics as mental health and working with patrons in distress. Like the Denver Public Library, TPL also provides access to free counseling services (Himmelstein, 2020).

Himmelstein also highlights an article by Fobazi Ettarh, who writes about "vocational awe" and library staff. Ettarh discusses the dangers of "vocational awe," which is defined as "the set of ideas, values, and assumptions librarians have about themselves and the profession that result in beliefs that libraries as institutions are inherently good and sacred, and therefore beyond critique" (Ettarh, 2018). As Himmelstein and Ettarh point out, seeing librarianship as a "sacred profession" can interfere with the need to be honest about the daily challenges of your job. It's difficult to set boundaries or limits and be clear about what you can and cannot do when there's an expectation that you'll do anything for your job because that's the definition of librarianship.

As a follow-up to the Himmelstein article, *School Library Journal* (SLJ) used Twitter to ask librarians: "How should your employers/institutions/schools support you in the face of burnout and compassion fatigue?" Answers included:

- Check in with staff regularly. Create an environment where they can express frustration and burnout. Validate their feelings. Give them "mental health" time off when/if needed.

- Generous leave helps tremendously. My college even gives a good amount of free counseling per year at the local hospital/clinic. Shared governance and a sense of belonging does wonders.

- Support us by promoting a healthy environment, that is, don't allow/promote/ignore/look past toxic behaviors by others. Address them, because it affects everyone.

- Success story: My principal regularly checks in to see if I am taking care of myself. She acknowledges how many of our kiddos come to me for a place of support/safety, and she understands the emotional toll. She pops in to visit, and she offers to cover if needed. I'm VERY lucky! (Himmelstein, 2020)

In future chapters, we'll be looking specifically at what libraries can do, and my hope is that by having a plan—and by tailoring that plan to your community, your library, and your library staff—this will help lessen compassion fatigue and burnout related to addressing homelessness. Creating partnerships in particular will provide opportunities to not feel alone in doing this work. Partnerships not only lessen the burden, share the work, and provide insights and information, but they can also let you know you're not doing the work on your own.

Because you aren't alone, even though it may sometimes (or always) feel like that. Across the United States libraries are engaged in this work, and so support is there. Engaging with a highly stigmatized population can challenge us, so we also need to help lessen the stigma and the misconceptions that color their lives so we can be free to do our work while feeling supported and with a strong sense of how crucial it can be.

CONCLUSION

In this chapter we've looked at why libraries are addressing homelessness and the challenges experienced by our unhoused community members, as well as the necessity for supporting library staff in doing this work. In Chapter 3, we'll look at the practical and emotional needs of those who are experiencing homelessness, so we can understand how our libraries fit into their lives.

REFERENCES

American Libraries. (2018, September 4). *Letter from public library directors and social workers.* https://americanlibrariesmagazine.org/blogs/the-scoop/letter-from-public-library-directors-and-social-workers

American Library Association. (2019). B.8 services and responsibilities of libraries (old number 52). *Policy manual: American Library Association.* http://www.ala.org/aboutala/governance/policymanual/updatedpolicymanual/section2/52libsvcsandrespon

Bales, S., & Winkelstein, J. A. (2019). [Libraries and homelessness]. Unpublished raw data.

Berman, S. (2005). Classism in the stacks: Libraries and poverty. 2005 Jean E. Coleman Outreach Lecture. *American Library Association.* http://www.ala.org/aboutala/offices/olos/olosprograms/jeanecoleman/05berman

Bruno, L. (2012). Understanding compassion fatigue in your library. *WebJunction.* https://www.webjunction.org/events/webjunction/Understanding_Compassion_Fatigue_in_Your_Library.html

Chu, M. D. (2020, April 16). Why housing security is key to environmental justice. *Environmental Health News.* https://www.ehn.org/affordable-housing-environmental-justice-2645687591.html

Dubiel, C. (2016). Do you have compassion fatigue? *FloridaLibraryWebinars.org.* https://floridalibrarywebinars.org/do-you-have-compassion-fatigue-ondemand

Ettarh, F. (2018, January 10). Vocational awe and librarianship: The lies we tell ourselves. *In the library with the lead pipe.* http://www.inthelibrarywiththeleadpipe.org/2018/vocational-awe

Gehner, J., & Freeman, K. (2005). Just a little understanding: A social-service provider's perspective on homeless library users. *Hunger, Homelessness & Poverty Task Force of the Social Responsibilities Round Table of the American Library Association.* http://hhptf.org/article/5

Graham, N. (2017, February 16). Seattle Public Library rules a bane to the homeless. *South Seattle Emerald.* https://southseattleemerald.com/2017/02/16/seattle-public-library-rules-a-bane-to-the-homeless

Hackman, R. (2015, November 8). "Women are just better at this stuff": Is emotional labor feminism's next frontier? *The Guardian.* https://www.theguardian.com/world/2015/nov/08/women-gender-roles-sexism-emotional-labor-feminism

Himmelstein, D. (2020, February 17). As compassion fatigue takes its toll, schools and public libraries take steps to support librarians. *School Library Journal.* https://www.slj.com/?detailStory=as-compassion-fatigue-takes-its-toll -schools-public-libraries-take-steps-to-support-librarians&utm_source =Marketing&utm_medium=email&utm_campaign=top5

IFLA. (2017). *IFLA guidelines for library services to people experiencing homelessness.* IFLA Library Services to People with Special Needs. https:// www.ifla.org/publications/node/12642

King County Library System. (2017, April 1). *Patron code of conduct.* https:// kcls.org/news/conduct

Marmot, M. (2011). Highlights from an Australian interview with Sir Michael Marmot and his recent Canadian presentation to health economists. *Epimonitor.* http://epimonitor.net/Michael_Marmot_Interview.htm

Pigni, A. (n.d.). Burnout: The exhaustion funnel. *MINDFULNEXT.* http://www .mindfulnext.org/burnout-the-exhaustion-funnel

Renen, R. N. (1996). *Kitchen table wisdom.* Berkeley Publishing Group.

United Nations. (n.d.). *The Universal Declaration of Human Rights.* http://www .un.org/en/universal-declaration-human-rights

Watt, J. (2018). Compassion fatigue: What is it and do you have it? *TEDxFargo.* https://www.youtube.com/watch?v=v-4m35Gixno

Working Together Project. (2008). *Community-led libraries toolkit: Starting us all down the path toward developing inclusive public libraries.* http:// www.librariesincommunities.ca/resources/Community-Led_Libraries _Toolkit.pdf

Worldometer. (2021, March 26). *COVID-19 coronavirus pandemic.* https://www .worldometers.info/coronavirus

3

Needs of Community Members Experiencing Homelessness

INTRODUCTION

In Chapter 3, we look at the varied needs of community members who are experiencing homelessness and how libraries can help meet those needs. These needs range from information to physical and emotional needs. We also look at the specific needs of unaccompanied LGBTGQ+ (lesbian, gay, bisexual, transgender, gender-expansive, and queer/questioning) youth who are experiencing homelessness and whose needs are tied not only to their housing status, but also to the stigma and attitudes attached to being LGBTGQ+ in our society.

WHAT ARE THE NEEDS?

The McKinney Act (more about this act in Appendix A, Glossary) defined the types of services it anticipated being offered through the program as

> food, child care, assistance in obtaining permanent housing, outpatient health services, employment counseling, nutritional counseling security, security arrangements necessary for the protection of residents of facilities to assist the homeless, and such other services essential for maintaining independent living . . . (PL 100-77, Sec. 431, 42 USC 11391) (Beck & Twiss, 2018, p. 155)

This quote about the history of the McKinney Act can provide insight into the range of needs for those experiencing homelessness. A critical need, related to all of the following topics, is reliable access to the Internet, with enough time allowed for meaningful access. Besides the practical needs described here, the Internet helps unhoused community members maintain social connections to families and friends, as well as staying connected to social media and simply what is happening in the world. For community members who have Internet-ready devices, the library can provide electricity, a wireless connection or even a hotspot. For those without the devices, libraries can offer access to computers or the ability to check out a laptop. In this modern connected world, access is critical—socially, emotionally, and physically.

We begin with informational needs.

Informational Needs

Like any library users, people who are experiencing homelessness have myriad needs. Most of them will sound familiar to you, since their needs are not that different from those of your housed library users. As you read these lists, keep in mind the point made in Chapter 1 related to partnering or become part of your local Continuum of Care (CoC). Libraries can meet many of these informational needs or partner with agencies that already do that.

Housing

In keeping with the social services "Housing First" model (National Alliance to End Homelessness, 2016), we'll start with housing.

What are the informational needs related to housing? As with any of your community members who are looking for housing, these needs include searching for, applying for, affording, and maintaining housing that is safe, healthy, and financially feasible.

- Resources for housing searches
  - How to find and access listings for truly affordable housing
  - Connecting with local social services agencies
  - Connecting with local housing authority
  - Includes transportation and methods of communication (e-mail, telephone)
- Filling out applications
  - Internet access: Access to Internet computers and enough time to fill out housing applications and apply for benefits
  - References: Finding and contacting references and what to do without adequate references
  - Addressing challenges with credit ratings/credit history
  - Answering questions on forms

- Transportation
  - To agencies
  - To potential homes
  - Ease of transportation to and from prospective housing
- Financial
  - Understanding and obtaining necessary payments
  - Housing vouchers: Obtaining, using

Employment Needs

What are the informational and resource needs related to employment? As with any job seekers, looking for employment entails finding, applying for, and keeping a job. Like housed job seekers, people experiencing homelessness are looking for meaningful work—work that does more than help them pay for housing and food. Having meaningful work makes a huge difference to those who are employed and, as Sir Michael Marmot (2011) points out, it has an impact on health. This doesn't mean that people—both housed and unhoused—won't accept work that doesn't feel meaningful, but it's important to keep in mind that those who are unhoused want job satisfaction like housed folks. It can be easy to assume that someone who is living on the streets will take anything—be it housing, employment, health care, child care, even food. This attitude creates misunderstandings and assumptions and can serve as another barrier to providing library services to those experiencing homelessness.

> **Theresa's Story**: Theresa has been living in her car for the last 2 years. The city where she lives is paying an organization to help community members find housing. They've offered Theresa housing in another city, in an area where she feels unsafe. Like anyone who wants to stay in their own city, where they have friends and connections, and like anyone who wants to feel safe in their own home, Theresa has made the choice not to accept that housing. The attitude of the organization is that she should accept it and not be so picky. This isn't an attitude they would have if the person were housed. They have now labeled her "resistant" and are less enthusiastic about helping her to find appropriate housing.

Housed people are allowed to be selective—it's assumed unhoused folks shouldn't be. In fact, agencies like the one helping Theresa call her response "resistant" and describe her reluctance as "refusal"—treating her as if she were a recalcitrant child who doesn't know what's best for herself. It's important—critical, really—that all of our library users are treated with respect and acknowledgment of their autonomy. It can be easy to slip into a patronizing attitude, and this serves no one well.

- Looking for jobs—informational needs:
    ◦ Where to look: Guidance on local and national sources for jobs.
    ◦ How to look: How to search for jobs, including key words, descriptions, relevant listings, job qualifications.
    ◦ Access to Internet: Since most, if not all, job opportunities are online, it's critical for library users to be able to use the Internet. If the lack of a permanent address, lack of bathing facilities, or fatigue are going to be barriers to this access, look for ways to change these.
    ◦ Access to other sources: Does the library provide access to job listings that aren't available elsewhere?
    ◦ Transportation: Since transportation can be a major challenge for those experiencing homelessness, job seekers need to know they can reliably get to the place of employment once they're hired. They need information about public transportation and other forms of reliable and inexpensive transportation. Are there local discounted fares? Are there local buses or other transit? Does the library provide public transportation schedules or information about how to easily find these schedules? Could the library provide free bus passes, maybe donated by housed community members or in partnership with a local agency?
- Applying for jobs
    ◦ Résumé writing: Many libraries offer résumé writing workshops, guides to writing résumés, and computers for composing them. Be sure to advertise these through flyers at local shelters, churches, community centers, low-cost food providers, and any other places library users may frequent. Or consider offering the workshops at a location convenient for those who are experiencing homelessness—at a shelter or social services agency, for example. This is another example of the advantage of partnerships.
    ◦ Interview skills: Like résumé writing, some libraries provide workshops and resources on interview skills. If there are local agencies/ organizations that provide these kinds of services without charging fees, let your library users know so they can take advantage of these.
    ◦ Dressing for interviews: As with any job seekers, there can be concern about how to dress appropriately for the interview. Tips on what to wear and information about local places to find free or

low-cost professional attire are both needed and appreciated. In addition, job seekers need access to safe and free/low-cost shower and laundry facilities, as well as hygiene products.

An organization in the San Francisco Bay Area uses donated clothing to provide professional attire for those who are experiencing homelessness and poverty. They have created convenient drop-off locations throughout the area by forging relationships with local bank branches. Libraries in the area could connect with the organization to help provide clothing and also to let housed community members know about this opportunity to donate professional clothing in excellent condition. There's more information about this partnership in Chapter 5.

- Job skills
  - Training: For some employment there may be required job skills, such as familiarity with specific software, the ability to type quickly, organizing skills, people skills, and general and specific knowledge related to the job itself. The skills required to survive on the streets aren't necessarily transferable to employment, although some are. Libraries can provide information about local free access to classes or provide classes themselves.

Poudre River Public Library District in Fort Collins, Colorado, provides free computer classes and free e-media classes that cover a wide range of computer software (Poudre River Public Library District, n.d.). Although not specifically for community members who are experiencing homelessness, these kinds of classes provide the expertise needed for finding employment. Libraries that offer these kinds of classes can reach out to shelters, social service agencies, churches, and other locations with flyers and links to information.

- Job expectations: Community members may need information about specific information about job expectations and how to meet them.

Veronica has been living unstably for the last 12 years. Three years ago, she and her boyfriend were given an RV, and Veronica got a driver's license so she could drive it. They now live in the RV and have created a community with other folks who live in RVs in the area. Through her writing, speaking, and organizing, Veronica has become an experienced and effective activist for their community. She has also become an expert auto mechanic out of necessity and interest. All of these skills could be added to her résumé.

- Required education: Many jobs have specific educational requirements, for instance, a high school diploma or equivalent, an AA degree or a BA, and a master's degree or a PhD. Libraries can help community members understand these requirements and provide resources for obtaining the necessary education to meet them. Libraries across the United States are offering GED-related classes in the library itself, as well as both online and print job resources. This is a good example of how resources already available in a library are appropriate for both housed and unhoused community members.

Los Angeles County in California offers "an accredited high school diploma for free online in just 5–18 months through LA County Library and the Career Online High School program." This program is offered through the California State Library. They also offer a "career certificate in your desired field of study, in 1 of 8 high-demand fields," including child care, protection services, office management, commercial driving, food and hospitality, and more. More information is available on their website (LA County Library, n.d.).

- Internet

Free library access to the Internet is critical for community members who don't have regular and meaningful access, including those who are experiencing homelessness. Library users may need support and information related to:

  ○ Creating an e-mail account: Which one to select, how to sign up, how to create a good password, how to protect privacy.

  ○ Applying online: Most jobs and benefits require the ability to apply online. This can be a barrier for those who don't have the expertise or access. Besides access to the Internet, libraries can help with this through instruction, frequent and extended time on the Internet computers, workshops or presentations, and setting up a volunteer technology network. Including those who are experiencing homelessness and who have expertise in using technology would benefit both the library and your housed and unhoused library users.

During the COVID-19 pandemic, most public libraries were initially closed. Although a majority continued to offer free wi-fi access outside the building, those without their own devices or the electricity to charge their devices couldn't take advantage of this access. This is a good example of how libraries can provide a much-needed service that is discontinued during an emergency like this. It can be challenging to meet the needs of all community members under these stressful situations, but it's essential.

- Identification/legal documents
  - One barrier to applying for a job can be the lack of formal IDs. It can be challenging to keep track of legal documents, such as birth and marriage certificates, school records, Social Security cards, and driver's licenses, while living unstably and unpredictably. Library staff can help by connecting people to the resources they need to obtain documents or IDs and by providing opportunities for scanning any documents and attaching them to e-mails so they can always be accessed. Information about free or low-cost copies of legal documents can also make a difference. Chapter 6 includes an example of a program that helps people obtain paperwork and IDs.

- Mailing address
  - When applying for employment, a permanent mailing address is usually required. Community members who are experiencing homelessness need to have access to a reliable and free/low-cost mailing address that can be used for correspondence. Some shelters allow the use of their address, but there are many folks who don't stay at shelters or who, like Thomas (the young person mentioned in Chapter 2), don't want to reveal their housing status. Libraries can reach out to organizations or initiate conversations with local agencies about how to create and maintain a reliable permanent mailing address.

- Phone number
  - As with the mailing address, a phone number is usually required when applying for employment. Community members experiencing homelessness need information about how to access free/low-cost phones. In many areas, there are programs that provide access to phones. Libraries can provide information about these or maybe start a program that helps unhoused community members access free phones.

- Pending citations/tickets and clearing records
  - Another barrier to employment can be tickets, citations, and criminal records, usually related to quality-of-life infractions, such as sitting or sleeping in public spaces. Some cities or counties offer programs that provide a dismissal of these fines, which can follow people for years and lead to incarceration and a criminal record. Providing information about local programs or relevant resources can make a huge difference in the lives of those who have these financial and legal barriers in their lives.

The Homeless Court in San Diego was first introduced in 1989, and since 1999 has been funded by grants from the Department of Justice's Bureau of Justice Assistance and has received pro bono legal assistance from a local law firm. According to Steve Binder, one of the original founders of Homeless Court, over the years tens of thousands of charges have been dismissed (Warth, 2015).

Health

The lack of stable, affordable, and adequate housing has a negative impact on a person's health (Diaz, 2018). So besides providing resources to help community members find housing, libraries can provide information and connections to local free or low-cost medical providers. This can include medical facilities, such as doctor's offices, as well as clinics. As described in Chapter 1, experiencing homelessness can (and usually does) have a negative impact on a person's physical and mental health. Resources libraries can provide include:

- Connections to low-cost/free clinics and/or doctors.
- Mental health training for library staff.
- Transportation.

San Francisco Public Library (SFPL) offers staff trainings on "Understanding Mental Health Challenges" through a partnership with the Mental Health Association of San Francisco (MHASF). Leah Esguerra, the social worker at SFPL, provides the trainings with MHASF (personal communication, 2018).

Legal Information

As mentioned in Chapter 1, the challenges of experiencing homelessness can (and frequently do) include citations and tickets from quality-of-life infractions. Examples of these include:

- Being in a park after dark.
- Urinating in a public space.
- Drinking alcohol in a public space.
- Walking a dog without a leash.
- Sitting or lying on a sidewalk.
- Asking for money.
- Trespassing.
- Loitering.

These infractions can go from a summons and a fine to incarceration if the fine isn't paid and/or there's a failure to show up in court. The main reason for not paying the fines is lack of money, which makes sense, since the folks who received the tickets are experiencing homelessness. As Thomas, one young person living on the streets, says: "If I had the money to pay the fine, I wouldn't be sleeping in a doorway" (personal communication, 2012).

These legal issues can act as barriers. As Brooklyn District Attorney Kenneth Thompson put it:

> Warrants never go away. So, when people apply for jobs, they come up in background checks. It could affect someone's application for citizenship. It could affect someone's ability to get housing. So, there are real consequences to outstanding warrants. (PBS, 2016)

Libraries can provide much-needed legal resources and connections to people who are trying to deal with these barriers. These include:

- "Know Your Rights" information.
- Connections to free/low-cost legal clinics.
- Free "Lawyer in the Library."
- "Community Courts."

The Brooklyn District Attorney's Office has created a program called "Begin Again," which is a periodic event that offers attendees a chance to clear outstanding summons warrants related to low-level offenses, such as unlawful consumption of alcohol in public, littering, loitering, disorderly conduct, trespassing, and many more. Libraries can provide their users with information about events like these or even offer to sponsor one themselves, by partnering with a local district attorney's office (Brooklyn District Attorney's Office, 2018).

Several libraries and cities have hosted "Community Courts." More information about Community Courts can be found in Chapter 6.

Education

People who are experiencing homelessness may encounter numerous barriers to furthering their formal education. These include:

- Interruptions to and incomplete former education.
- Missing or incomplete documents.
- No safe, quiet place to study, which is out of the elements.
- Hunger.

- Health challenges.
- Low print literacy.
- Little or no access to books or other materials and no money to buy them.
- No access to the Internet.
- No money for tuition.
- Having a criminal record due to violations from living on the streets (asking for money, sit/lie laws, loitering laws).

Libraries can help with these by providing Internet access, a quiet private place to study, access to required textbooks, information and resources for obtaining needed documents, tutoring, connections to scholarships, financial aid, and organizations that provide financial and practical support for education. In addition, addressing some of their other needs, including health challenges, literacy, and clearing legal records—as described already—will contribute to their ability to pursue and attain their educational goals. These are examples of services and resources libraries provide to their housed library users as well, and this is a point that needs to be emphasized, because it can feel overwhelming to think of adding yet more resources to the long list of needs libraries strive to meet.

Hygiene

One of the biggest challenges in living on the streets is access to free and safe places to take showers and wash clothes. We stress the "safe" aspect of this, because a shower facility that feels unsafe—for example, it's crowded, there's no privacy, and there are threats of physical violence—can't be used. Libraries can provide information about local resources, as well as becoming active partners in addressing this need. Partnerships are critical in addressing homelessness, and this is an excellent example of the potential for a library to be involved. For libraries that have odor policies, this can also be a way to ameliorate some of the impact of these policies.

San Francisco Public Library (SFPL) is one of the regular stops for lavamae[x], a mobile shower unit (lavamae[x] San Francisco, n.d.). Being able to keep clean not only creates more opportunities for unstably housed community members, but it also boosts self-esteem and helps to reduce stigma.

During the COVID-19 pandemic of 2020–2021, lavamae[x] was forced to cease operations to protect the health of the clients as well as the staff (lavamae[x], 2020a). In lieu of providing free showers, they handed out hygiene kits and encouraged housed community members to create and donate them. See Appendix J for an example of what was included in the kits (lavamae[x], 2020b). Kits like these can be created at libraries, or libraries can start a campaign to gather the various items included in them, so they can be distributed to unhoused community members even during times when there isn't a pandemic.

> The small city of Albany, California, offers free weekly showers and clean clothes through volunteers and a partnership among local community members, churches, and the high school pool facility. The city library, community center, city hall, and local YMCA post fliers providing information about this resource.

Physical and Emotional Needs

Besides the connections to resources that libraries can offer, community members experiencing homelessness have both physical and emotional needs libraries can play a part in providing.

As described in Chapter 1, life on the streets can be physically exhausting. A lack of transportation makes it difficult to go from food sources to clinics to places to sleep. Sleeping in a shelter that is noisy and/or crowded or that feels unsafe or sleeping outside leads to interrupted sleep that isn't restful. The physical challenges of poor and inadequate nutrition, accompanied by exposure to an unhealthy environment, make it difficult to focus and are a drain on energy.

Emotionally, it's challenging to be living lives that are stigmatized, misunderstood, and stereotyped. Social capital can be low, and connections made on the streets are unlikely to lead to connections needed for finding housing, employment, and education.

What Can Libraries Do to Address These Challenges

Creating a *welcoming, anticipatory,* and *supportive* environment in the library can make a huge difference to folks whose very existence is being constantly challenged, denigrated, and misrepresented.

Welcoming: A welcoming environment in a library means that all who enter the doors of the library feel as if their presence is welcomed—library staff want them to be there. Decisions about collections, displays, interior design, seating, signage, art, programs, posters, announcements, and any other ways library users experience the library all affect the environment.

For example, if displays include books and other materials that represent the lives of people experiencing homelessness, they will feel as if the library is interested in their lives. A welcoming environment also means posted signs use positive language—indicating what the library would like their users to do rather than what shouldn't be done. For instance: "Please walk" rather than "Don't run." Limiting the number of signs that are about conduct and using positive language create an atmosphere of acceptance and safety and can feel safer for those who have experienced trauma.

As part of creating a welcoming environment, it's essential we look at the stereotypes of unhoused community members. As Eberhardt writes in her excellent book *Biased: Uncovering the Hidden Prejudice That Shapes What We See, Think and Do* (2019): "Walter Lippmann, who coined the term 'stereotypes,' said it best: without individual contact that breaks through our categorization, 'we notice a trait which marks a well known type, and fill in the rest of the picture by means of the stereotypes we carry about in our heads'" (p. 219). As library staff, we need to be cognizant of this tendency and constantly question our assumptions, and we need to make sure we are using a person-centered and trauma-informed approach with all of our community members.

Anticipatory: An anticipatory environment means the library has anticipated that there will be people in the library who are unstably housed or experiencing homelessness. Similar to an approach taken for other groups served by the library, anticipating the needs of your unhoused library users means you not only want them at your library, but you've also educated library staff about their information and resource needs.

For instance, you've included children's interests in your collection, you may provide story times, games, toys, and so on. Children's librarians take classes in library school about children's librarianship and developmental stages of childhood. It's appropriate and necessary to do this, so the library can anticipate and understand the needs of children and their caregivers. Anticipating a person's presence is not the same as reacting once they're there. Anticipating means you've thought and planned in advance. Knowledge about relevant vocabulary, and approaches to personal interactions and insights into their lived experiences all contribute to an anticipatory environment.

Supportive: A supportive library environment means the library provides needed resources or connections to resources, as well a friendly attitude, all-inclusive language, and an informed approach to interactions.

A supportive library environment contributes to a general feeling of knowing one's needs and concerns are considered valid and worth addressing. A supportive environment can act as an antidote to the stigma and stereotyping that are a constant presence in the lives of those who are experiencing homelessness.

Critical to this supportive library environment is a move away from othering and excluding those who are experiencing homelessness and poverty and instead creating an all-inclusive approach. As powell and Brooks (2017) state:

> Our primary policy focus must not merely be *helping* the poor or the marginalized "other," but rather restoring them to a position in which they are *needed*—in which they are necessary, integral participants in in our economy, our communities, and our collective imagination.

In later chapters, we will be looking at ways libraries can create this all-inclusive approach.

Needs of Unhoused and Unaccompanied Youth, Including LGBTGQ+ Youth

"Inequality is a human-generated problem and can therefore be changed."

(Fisher-Borne et al., 2015, p. 15)

In this next section, we look at the needs of unaccompanied youth who are experiencing homelessness. We'll start with their general needs and then go on to the specific needs of unaccompanied lesbian, gay, bisexual, transgender, gender expansive, and queer/questioning (LGBTGQ+) youth.

Who Are the Youth?

A young person experiencing homelessness:

- Has no consistent, reliable, and safe place to sleep.
- Is unaccompanied.
- Is between the ages of 12 and 24.
- Can be both sheltered (staying in a shelter or couch surfing) or unsheltered (living on the streets, in abandoned buildings, in a car).

This is a good time to stress that, as mentioned in Chapter 1, unstably housed young people are not defined by their housing status. A good rule of thumb for working with youth experiencing homelessness is to make no assumptions.

For some youth their periods of homelessness may be short—a night or two or a few weeks. For others the time is longer—months or even years. Their homelessness can be fluid, and most don't describe themselves as experiencing homelessness; they are "couch surfing" or "traveling" or "staying with friends." They may alternate staying in emergency shelters with sleeping on the streets, in cars, or on floors.

The young people are frequently part of the population of people experiencing homelessness who are sometimes called "the invisible homeless" because they don't have the stereotypical look of what society considers someone who is without a permanent place to live. This stereotype not only stigmatizes people experiencing homelessness; it can also contribute to a lack of understanding about the range of ways a person can be unstably housed. The young people can blend in with youth who are stably housed, and this can make it challenging to identify them. However their lives are described, the youth don't have a safe and reliable place to sleep every night, and whether they are travelers, couch surfers, or alternating emergency housing with sleeping on the streets, they are at risk in the myriad ways we've already discussed.

The young people we're talking about are "unaccompanied," meaning they're not the young people who are experiencing homelessness with their families or guardians but instead are on their own. Although statistics are offered, the reality is these youth are difficult to count. They are often not connected to services or shelters.

Some of the youth may be survivors of human trafficking, which can happen anywhere, in rural, suburban, and urban areas. More about this topic can be found in Chapter 6. They may be or may have been part of the juvenile legal system. They may be coming from the foster system—either because they age out or because of the abuse they've experienced based on their gender identity or sexual orientation. Many have left school, either because they are experiencing homelessness or because of the unsafe environment—again based on their sexual orientation or gender identity. The youth are likely to come from high-conflict home environments, and for many, life on the streets may feel preferable to staying in these unsafe homes.

According to Covenant House (n.d.), which has numerous locations in both the United States and Canada: "Every year, more than 2 million kids in America will face a period of homelessness." Other statistics they provide include:

- Fifty-seven percent of homeless kids spend at least 1 day every month without food.

- In the United States, as many as 20,000 kids are forced into prostitution by human-trafficking networks every year.

- According to a study of youth in shelters, nearly 50% reported intense conflict or physical harm by a family member as a major contributing factor to their homelessness.

- More than 25% of former foster children become homeless within 2 to 4 years of leaving the system.

- Fifty percent of adolescents aging out of foster care and juvenile legal systems will be homeless within 6 months because they are unprepared to live independently and have limited education and no social support.

- Almost 40% of the homeless in the United States are under 18.

"Missed Opportunities," the report from a national survey on unaccompanied youth homelessness ("Voices of Youth Count," 2017), provides in-depth information about youth experiencing homelessness in the United States. As they note:

> While the deprivation of housing stability was the common thread in Voices of Youth Count research, the stories of youth homelessness—and the opportunities for intervention—rarely centered on housing alone. Every experience, every youth, was unique. Yet, with the data gained through Voices of Youth Count, we can begin to better understand the scale and scope of the challenge and the patterns that can guide smarter policy and practice. (Executive Summary)

This report offers some sobering statistics, including:

- One in ten young adults ages 18–25 experienced a form of homelessness over a 12-month period. *That's 3.5 million young adults. About half of them involved explicitly report homelessness, while the other half involved indicated couch surfing only.*

- One in thirty youth ages 13–17 experienced a form of homelessness over a 12-month period. *That's about 700,000 youth. About three quarters of them involved explicitly reported homelessness (including running away or being kicked out) and one quarter involved couch surfing only.*

- Particular subpopulations are at higher risk for homelessness, including Black and Latinx youth, LGBTQ+ youth, youth who did not complete high school, and youth who are parents (Voices of Youth Count, 2017, Executive Summary).

In their report, "Why They Run: An In-Depth Look at America's Runaway Youth," the National Runaway Safeline (NRS) offers some alarming statistics. As they state:

> Although youth are leaving home at all ages of adolescence, the number has accelerated more quickly in the very young (under 12) and those age 18 and over. The younger group increased 89% from 2000 to 2009, and the older group (ages 18–21) has increased by 470%. (NRS, 2010)

The NRS compiles annual data from crisis connections to its hotline and online services, and their data can provide some excellent insights into the lives of unstably housed youth. According to their report, there are multiple reasons the youth say they are on the streets, including:

- A significant family conflict.
- A parent insisted the youth leave.
- The youth feels like they should leave, even though the parent may not have insisted.
- Periods of being thrown out have alternated with periods of running away.
- Youth are kicked out because they identify as LGBTQ+, or life at home is so uncomfortable because of this that they leave (p.9).
- The research for this report also asked these young people how they feel about the term "runaway," and only one third of them considered it an accurate description.

Even more noteworthy, when asked to describe themselves, they offered 30 different descriptions, including the following list:

- A runaway with permission
- A lost child in need of help
- Looking for a better chance
- An independent person
- A person who needs space
- Living on my own
- I feel like I wasn't accepted
- I was disowned
- Neglected
- Locked out
- Traveler
- Street kid

In this author's research on LGBTGQ+ youth experiencing homelessness, the most common answer was "I just want to be me." The young people rejected the idea of having any description applied to them, which certainly seems reasonable. None of us like to be summed up by a term, as if that could take the place of actually getting to know us.

Many of the youth fall into the 18- to 24-year-old range. For this group, also known as transitional age youth, or TAY, age matters. Depending on the state, they may age out of the foster system, leaving them without physical and emotional support. There are fewer resources allocated for this age group, and so it's more difficult to find housing, social services, shelters, and programs that are specifically aimed at TAY. They are old enough to use the adult shelters, but these can be intimidating and uncomfortable spaces for them, especially for the transgender youth.

Getting Help

Figure 3.1 illustrates where youth said they would ask for help.

As you can see, the most common answer was to ask a friend. This fits well with the author's research in which word-of-mouth was the most frequent answer to how unstably housed youth received information. The second, third, and fourth choices in Table 3.1 can all relate to libraries. Library staff can be the trusted and concerned adult a young person may turn to for help. The Internet, provided at a library, is obviously a central resource.

Another finding from this research emerged from their question asking the youth if they knew where to find a range of helpful resources. Table 3.1 shows the disheartening results.

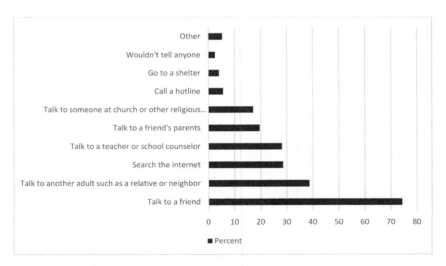

Figure 3.1 National Runaway Safeline: *Why They Run.*

Table 3.1 From *Why They Run*

	Free Meal	Medical Care	Shelter	Hotline	At Least One Service
Yes	13.5%	8.7%	8.5%	3.7%	12.8%

When asked why they didn't use available services, the three primary reasons given were:

- They do not feel they need it.
- They do not know where to find it.
- They did not know such services existed. (NRS, 2010)

Again, we can see a role for public libraries in addressing these low numbers, particularly the second and third reasons. Providing connections to resources and informing youth about the available resources easily falls into the purview of libraries. This is also where partnerships, which will be described in Chapter 5, play a critical role.

LGBTGQ+ Youth Homelessness

Vocabulary

The glossary of terms from the Human Rights Campaign (HRC, n.d.) is a great place to start if you are looking for relevant vocabulary when learning about LGBTGQ+ youth experiencing homelessness. As with any population you serve, an understanding of the vocabulary that relates to their lives is essential for communication and support. This can be challenging, since language is fluid, so the best approach is to pay attention, listen, and keep in touch with organizations who are working with the LGBTGQ+ community. Being willing to make a mistake and learn from that mistake will serve you well.

Although in this book we're using the acronym LGBTGQ+, there are many others that are commonly used. One of these is LGBTQIAA, which stands for lesbian, gay, bisexual, transgender, queer/questioning, intersex, asexual, and ally. Ally is particularly relevant because that's what we're talking about—library staff as allies. In their "Definition of Terms," the University of California, Berkeley, Centers for Educational Justice & Community Engagement (n.d.), define an ally as "someone who advocates for and supports members of a community other than their own. Reaching across differences to achieve mutual goals." Another term that is gaining in popularity is "accomplice" rather than ally. Whichever term you use, the library's role in advocating and supporting these young people is an important one.

Pronouns are another topic worth mentioning, because using a person's correct pronoun is a way of showing support and respect. We all have a pronoun, most commonly she/her/hers or he/him/his, but there are many people who use pronouns that are gender neutral. It's interesting that in

Table 3.2   Pronouns: A How-To Guide

e/ey	em	Eir	Eirs	eirself
he	him	his	his	himself
per	per	pers	pers	perself
she	her	hers	hers	herself
they	them	their	theirs	themself
ze/zie	hir	hir	hirs	hirself

English we use such gendered language, such as Mr., Miss, Mrs., or Ms., and we use the common pronouns that emphasize whether a person identifies as male or female. In fact, there are few instances in which we can't tell the gender of a person by their title, although there are some exceptions, such as doctor or professor.

For pronouns, gender-neutral pronouns can be used instead, so a person who doesn't identify on the binary of male/female has a personal pronoun that reflects who they are. The Lesbian, Gay, Bisexual, Transgender, Queer Plus (LGBTQ+) Resource Center at the University of Wisconsin, Milwaukee (n.d.), has an excellent example of gender-neutral pronouns and how to use them. Table 3.2 is a simple version of their more exhaustive list and examples.

They thought *they* looked good today in *their* new clothes.

They asked the waiter to bring *them* a glass of water.

They are proud of *themself* for *their* latest drawing.

Remember, personal pronouns are about our identities—who we are in the world. We all need to be recognized and supported in being ourselves.

Another point worth making is that gender and sex are not the same thing. As explained on the HRC website:

Sex refers to the designation of a person at birth as either 'male' or 'female' based on their anatomy (e.g., reproductive organs) and/or their biology (e.g., hormones). Gender refers to the traditional or stereotypical roles, behaviors, activities and attributes that a given society consider appropriate for men and women. (HRC, n.d.)

"Gender identity" and "gender expression" can also be confusing terms, and so the HRC definition of those is included here, too:

Gender identity refers to a person's innate, deeply-felt psychological identification as a man, woman or some other gender. Gender expression refers to the external manifestation of a person's gender identity, which may or may not conform to socially-defined behaviors and characteristics typically associated with being either masculine or feminine. (HRC, n.d.)

And finally, two more terms: cisgender and transgender. Again, the HRC definition:

Transgender—or trans—is an umbrella term for people whose gender identity or expression is different from those typically associated with the sex assigned to them at birth (e.g., the sex listed on their birth certificate). Conversely, cisgender—or cis—is the term used to describe people whose gender identity or expression aligns with those typically associated with the sex assigned to them at birth. (HRC, n.d.)

It's imperative to mention that a person's gender identity—who they are—doesn't tell you anything about who they are attracted to sexually, physically, or romantically. This is true for a person who is cisgender or transgender. For example, a person who is transgender may be gay, lesbian, pansexual, asexual, bisexual, heterosexual, or however they describe themselves. If they are transgender, all you know is that they fall under the umbrella of that term.

One final word about vocabulary. As you know, language is constantly evolving, so terms you learn now may change or become less popular. Staying informed and being willing to listen to and respect the young people's own vocabulary will make a big difference in the relationships you're able to create.

About the Youth

Statistics show that up to 40% of youth experiencing homelessness identify as LGBTQ+ (True Colors United, n.d.). When you consider that LGBTGQ+ youth represent an estimated 7% of the total youth population, you can see this statistic is disproportionately high. The young people may leave home so they can be themselves, or they are kicked out once their gender identity or sexual orientation is revealed. In addition, their home environment may be so uncomfortable or even abusive that they choose to leave as a way of taking care of themselves. When they choose to leave, it's a matter of practicing personal agency—taking control of their lives—even though the alternative is being unstably housed. Sometimes they have time to gather some belongings—or at least their cell phone if they have one; other times they are simply out on the streets.

Thomas was thrown out of his family home on his 19th birthday because his sister saw him walking down the street holding hands with his boyfriend and she told their mother. He was immediately kicked out. He made his way from the small town in Pennsylvania where he had grown up to San Francisco, because he had heard it was a good place to go if you're gay. The backpack with most of his belongings, including a sleeping bag and extra clothes, was stolen from him in the bus station when he arrived. He took this as a first indication that San Francisco isn't really a great place to be if you're living on the streets, whether you're gay or not. In fact, the local gay community has overall been less than welcoming to the young people who have found their way there.

Needs of LGBTQ+ Youth Experiencing Homelessness

Through their research, True Colors United (n.d.) provides insights into the needs of the youth. When describing their needs, they divide the youth into two groups: first, lesbian, gay, bisexual and questioning, and second, transgender, since some of the more pressing needs of transgender youth can be different from those who are cisgender.

For LGBQ youth, they explain: "The service providers we surveyed identified housing and identity-related supports as the two greatest needs for lesbian, gay, bisexual, and questioning youth experiencing homelessness" (True Colors United, n.d.). Other needs for LGBQ youth included acceptance, emotional support, employment, health care, and education.

For transgender youth, "housing was the most frequently cited need, followed by access to transition-related supports. Transition-related supports include access to legal support, name/gender marker change, access to healthcare specific to transgender youth, access to hormones, and emotional support" (True Colors United, n.d.). Other needs for transgender youth included health care, education, and employment—the same as for the LGBQ youth.

On the Streets

When the youth are on the streets, they experience discrimination, including being discriminated against for their age, socioeconomic status, survival skills, housing status, appearance, their very identities, their race, their history with the foster system, and/or the juvenile legal system. Experiencing homelessness is traumatic on a daily basis, and these forms of discrimination contribute to the trauma.

The following are examples of the kinds of signs (Figures 3.2 to 3.4) these young people (and of course all folks who are experiencing homelessness) see on the streets.

We must keep in mind that these are the experiences they've had already when you interact with them—every day is traumatic, including the trauma of feeling unwanted and pushed out. Therefore, it becomes even more important for libraries to create a welcoming and supportive environment, with clear indicators their presence is not simply tolerated but is embraced.

Figure 3.2 Sign in store window.

Figure 3.3 Sign on outside of building.

Figure 3.4 Sign on outside of building.

The outcome of the challenges on the streets for these young people can lead to self-medication, self-harm, death by suicide, and low self-esteem. It's extremely difficult to keep up positive self-esteem when your very existence is considered to be dangerous and stigmatized. As Thomas put it:

> I just get so frustrated because especially at night when I'm trying to sleep and there are people walking by me, I just feel so judged, like, they're looking at me and saying, oh this kid's an alcoholic, this kid's a drug addict, this kid's a drop-out, this kid's a loser, this kid's, you know, whatever . . . just looking at you like you're dirt. I used to think a lot higher of myself and now I have a lot of self-esteem issues and I'm like well, I don't wanna get in your way. Well, like, what? That never would've been me before, I was more assertive and more, self-positive imaged but recently I'm like uhh, I don't wanna get in your way, don't look at me . . . and it sucks. (2012, personal communication)

Thomas's story is a perfect example of what it feels like to be leading a life that is stigmatized. As mentioned in the quote in Chapter 1, people who are oppressed can lose control over the stigmatized images that are reflections of societal attitudes toward their lives. Nowhere in our society is there any indication it's acceptable to be experiencing homelessness or poverty.

Caution

There are many challenges in the lives of LGBTGQ+ youth experiencing homelessness, and we need to keep these challenges in mind as we think about ways we can best serve the young people in our libraries. However, it's also critical we emphasize that no statistics define the youth. They are not victims, and they are very clear that they don't think of themselves that way. When you talk to or about them, it's critical you use positive language as much as possible—language that doesn't stigmatize the young people or put their lives in a negative context, so it appears they have done something wrong or that they are to be pitied or patronized. As Josiah stated:

> And even though people say that we're victims and that we're from, we're this and that, you can't be a victim and vulnerable and survive on the streets, or be homeless. That there, there comes a little bit of self-sufficiency, and a little bit of direction that's of our own making for us to actually be at this point. (2012, personal communication)

We must always remind ourselves that each person is unique. We can discuss general issues that relate to this group as a whole, but as with any generalizations, it's important to remember we're talking about individuals.

In addition, although you may hear the term "at risk" applied to LGBTGQ+ youth, they are only at risk because of how society feels about their identity, not because they are innately at risk. For instance, a public space may put them at risk by having rules that exclude them. But the rules are what need to be changed, not the individual. In addition, we need to help remove the shame attached to the word "homeless" or the stigma of misrepresentations related to being LGBTGQ+, so that all individuals can be open about their lives wherever they are.

TRAUMA-INFORMED CARE (TIC)

What is a TIC agency/program?

When a human service program takes the step to become trauma informed, every part of its organization, management, and service delivery system is assessed and potentially modified to include a basic understanding of how trauma affects the life of an individual seeking services. Trauma-informed organizations, programs, and services are based on an understanding of the vulnerabilities or triggers of trauma survivors that traditional service delivery approaches may exacerbate, so that these services and programs can be more supportive and avoid re-traumatization. (SAMHSA, 2018)

Library staff can use a TIC approach in working with any of their library users. LGBTGQ+ youth experiencing homelessness benefit from this approach because it can help them feel respected and safe in the library, and so they can take advantage of your resources and the library space itself.

Some of the indicators a space is supported by a trauma-informed approach are the *absence* of the following:

- DO NOT signs—no loitering, no food and drink allowed, no sleeping, no large bags . . . NO, NO, NO on signs around the library and even at the entrance

- Barriers to receiving services (rigid requirements for registering for a library card, a lack of flexibility in serving library users)

- Public conduct policies that don't take into account the range of life experiences of the library users

Resilience, Grit, and Deserving

Resilience and grit are frequently applied to people as a way of avoiding the systemic and societal failures that force them to display "grit," instead of looking at the factors that create a need for it. Be cautious about applying these words to anyone experiencing homelessness, including the young people being discussed here. Instead, ask yourself why they have to have grit and what your library can do to address the reasons. Being resilient can serve a person well, but what if they're not resilient—is that a failure? Is that person not deserving or weak? And what systemic inequities or power differentials are forcing them to display resilience?

"Deserving" is another term that can be a subtext to descriptions of individuals. We may hear about someone who is being helped because they fit into some idea of someone who is deserving of our help—we approve of what they're doing, so they deserve our help. Or we don't approve—they didn't go into the shelter we found for them or they didn't show up for an appointment we made, so they're undeserving. Again, be cautious about taking this approach. Everyone deserves to have a safe and predictable place to lay their head at night—everyone.

Practical Needs

The practical needs for the youth are similar to the needs of all folks who are experiencing homelessness, including legal rights, health services, educational opportunities, employment resources, connections to social services, and of course housing. However, there are some ways in which these practical needs are different from unstably housed adults.

To begin with, legal rights for minors are limited compared to adults. The age for these rights can differ from state to state, but basically minors may be restricted in their ability to work, consent to health care, rent, apply for student loans, sign a legal document (such as a rental agreement), rent a car, rent a hotel or motel room, or even register for a library card. Being aware of the laws in your state and your community and sharing options and alternatives can make a difference to the youth as they try to navigate the barriers in their lives.

Health care can be a particular challenge for transgender youth. It's not uncommon for health care providers to be unsupportive or even hostile toward transgender patients. Helping a young person find a supportive clinic or doctor can make a huge difference to them and to their health. And in keeping with this, an all-genders bathroom would be another way of supporting transgender and gender nonconforming youth.

The next four graphics are examples of all-genders bathroom signs. Figure 3.5, from the Harvey Milk Terminal 1 at the San Francisco International Airport, shows an institutional commitment to offering an all-genders bathroom that can be used by anyone at the terminal.

Figure 3.6 is from the annual American Library Association June conference. This figure shows the potential for considering converting bathrooms at a one-time event like a conference.

Figure 3.7 is an example of a simple sign that can be found in buildings that support all-genders restrooms, but also in places that only have one

Figure 3.5 All-genders bathroom at Harvey Milk Terminal 1 at San Francisco International Airport.

Figure 3.6 Gender-neutral bathroom sign at American Library Association conference.

Figure 3.7 Simple graphic for all-genders restroom sign.

ALL GENDERS
RESTROOM

Figure 3.8   Student-made all-genders bathroom sign.
(Created by Priya Ford)

PLEASE JUST WASH
YOUR HANDS

restroom, and so everyone uses it. This may be the least likely to create concern from those who are uncomfortable with the concept of an all-genders bathroom.

Figure 3.8 is an example of a homemade sign created by student Priya Ford, a student.

As you can see, there are a range of possibilities for signage to indicate all-genders bathrooms, and each library should create one that best suits their community.

Emotional Needs

The emotional needs of LGBTGQ+ youth experiencing homelessness are similar to those of adults and they include: A place to just "be"; a sanctuary from the streets and the weather; a feeling of community and belonging; and, spiritual and/or philosophical books, resources, and programs. However, because we are talking about young people, there are the additional challenges of the emotional and developmental changes happening as they mature. Imagine a 14-year-old, living on the streets and without caring adults to provide emotional and physical support. Simply being that person when they come into the library can make a huge difference.

What Can Your Library Do?

Here are some ideas for ways to create a welcoming, supportive, and useful environment for all youth experiencing homelessness, including those who are LGBTGQ+:

- Consider your forms: Are they gendered? Could they be gender neutral? Example: Instead of he/her, use their, or instead of his/hers, use theirs.
- If you don't already have all-genders bathrooms, could you?
- Examine your signage: Is the wording positive or negative? Do they say "No, no, no"? Or do they state what is possible? Example: *Don't speak loudly* versus *speak softly*.
- Do you have indicators, such as rainbow flags, that this is a place where LGBTGQ+ youth are invited and welcome?
- State your pronouns and, if you are comfortable doing so, ask others for theirs. When you make a mistake, quickly apologize and correct yourself. If you make a practice of normalizing the sharing of personal pronouns—by having them on your name badge, by including them in your e-mail signature, by encouraging everyone to state their pronouns—you can help make your library welcoming to everyone.
- If you have photos/art work on the walls, make sure it represents everyone.
- Listen, listen, listen—and follow the lead of the youth
- Partner with LGBTGQ+ youth serving agencies, for training, for advice, for support, for inspiration.
- Be conscious of your language.
- Make sure your services and offices are truly accessible.

Suggestions from Youth

The youth in the NRS study (2010) were asked what improvements could be made by service providers. Overall, they were happy with the services they were receiving; however, they did offer these suggestions, which can be useful for guiding library staff as well:

- Treat youth with respect. They come from homes where they did not feel respected, and they do not feel respected on the streets.
- Be honest and direct. Do not be insistent, making your suggestions sound like something they must do. This is a turnoff to teens.
- Be sensitive to emotional situations and what youth are going through as it affects their behavior.
- Reduce "processing" requirements and ask for less information— youth on the street have trust issues.
- Better referral process. A long chain of phone calls trying to find the right people to help is not helpful.
- Make clear that youth will not be turned over to parents/authorities.

In the NRS research, many of the youth mentioned a lack of available information. As the report states:

> Many youth feel that lack of knowledge about what services exist, what those services can do for them, how to find services, and where to find them, are the biggest barriers to youth getting help. While numerous recommendations for posting information in public places ranged from hospitals and YMCAs to fast food restaurants and "teen hang-outs," such a scope is neither feasible nor likely to be highly effective. However, one point was reiterated by youth as a clear means of directing youth to helpful services and gets to the heart of the awareness issue was to create a centralized list of services to make them easily accessible. (NRS, 2010)

This suggestion could be adopted by a library and the list made available not only in the library, but also through other locations where the youth congregate, as well as online. It's important to keep in mind, though, that this list must be kept up to date or it is not only useless, but it can make the youth wary of trusting the library's resources and trusting library staff.

Language

Language shapes our thoughts, assumptions, and ideas. When speaking about the youth, one service provider pointed out the importance of using what she called "youth-focused" language. Her example was using the term "risk of exploitation" rather than saying "survival sex." With the youth and really with anyone experiencing homelessness, our language should show support. Language can be welcoming and respectful or it can be hostile, patronizing, or disrespectful. One of the best ways to understand what language a person uses is to listen—to their words, to their requests, to their conversations. How do they refer to themselves and their lives?

The words we use have a lot of power—we can subtly criticize, support, or even advocate by the language we choose to use. Learning to examine and question our language is a learning process. You'll make mistakes, and if you do, simply apologize and promise to do better next time. Sincere efforts by library staff to understand and be there for the youth go a long way toward helping them take control of their lives and reach out, create new connections, build trust, and move forward toward their goals.

CONCLUSION

In this chapter we have looked at the needs of those experiencing homelessness and we've highlighted examples of what is being done. Understanding what our community members need and the ways in which libraries can fill these needs can help us serve those who are unstably housed.

In Chapter 4, we look at how to assess your community's needs, create a vision statement, and create an action plan that will help you take action. We also cover how to make your case to your stakeholders and staff and how to address resistance.

REFERENCES

Beck, E., & Twiss, P. C. (2018). *The homelessness industry: A critique of US social policy.* Lynne Rienner.

The Brooklyn District Attorney's Office. (2018). *Begin again continues in 2018.* http://brooklynda.org/begin-again

Covenant House. (n.d.). *Teen homelessness statistics.* https://www.covenanthouse.org/homeless-teen-issues/statistics

Diaz, S. (2018, March 1). The effects of housing insecurity on health outcomes and costs. *Healthify.* https://www.healthify.us/healthify-insights/the-effects-of-housing-instability-on-health-outcomes-and-costs

Eberhardt, J. (2019). *Biased: Uncovering the hidden prejudice that shapes what we see, think, and do.* Viking Press.

Fisher-Borne, M., Cain, J. M., & Martin, S. L. (2015). From mastery to accountability: Cultural humility as an alternative to cultural competence. *Social Work Education: The International Journal, 34*(2), 165–181.

Human Rights Campaign (HRC). (n.d.). *Glossary of terms.* https://www.hrc.org/resources/glossary-of-terms

LA County Library. (n.d.). *Earn your diploma.* https://lacountylibrary.org/diploma

lavamae[x]. (2020a). *As the COVID-19 (coronavirus) Pandemic continues to escalate, we have some important updates.* https://lavamaex.org/coronavirus

lavamae[x]. (2020b). *COVID-19 prevention kits.* https://static1.squarespace.com/static/5dd47e90e2e27e5a2bbcaece/t/5e7b7108a894b9637f628b41/1585148174311/Coronavirus+Wishlist+_+Hygiene+Kit+Making.pdf

lavamae[x] San Francisco. (n.d.). *San Francisco schedule and locations.* https://lavamae.org/san-francisco

Marmot, M. (2011). Highlights from an Australian interview with Sir Michael Marmot and his recent Canadian presentation to health economists. *Epimonitor.* http://epimonitor.net/Michael_Marmot_Interview.htm

National Alliance to End Homelessness (NAEH). (2016). *Resources: Housing first.* https://endhomelessness.org/resource/housing-first

National Runaway Safeline (NRS). (2010). *Why they run: An in-depth look at America's runaway youth.* https://www.1800runaway.org/homeless-teen-research/why-they-run

PBS NewsHour Weekend. (2016, January 16). *How NYC is tackling 1.4 million open arrest warrants for "quality of life" crimes.* https://www.pbs.org/newshour/show/how-nyc-is-tackling-1-4-million-open-arrest-warrants-for-quality-of-life-crimes

Poudre River Public Library District. (n.d.). *Computer classes.* https://www.poudrelibraries.org/classes

powell, j. a., & Brooks, A. (2017, October 10). America can't fix poverty until it stops hating poor people. *Bloomberg CityLab.* https://www.bloomberg.com/news/articles/2017-10-10/a-bipartisan-plea-to-stop-othering-those-in-poverty

SAMHSA. (2018). *Trauma-informed care and alternatives to seclusion and restraint (NCTIC).* https://recoverymonth.gov/organizations-programs/national-center-trauma-informed-care-alternatives-seclusion-restraint-nctic

True Colors United. (n.d.). *Our issue.* https://truecolorsunited.org/our-issue

University of California Berkeley. (n.d.). Definition of terms. *Centers for Educational Justice and Community Engagement.* https://cejce.berkeley.edu/geneq/resources/lgbtq-resources/definition-terms

University of Wisconsin Milwaukee. (n.d.). Gender pronouns. *Lesbian, Gay, Bisexual, Transgender, Queer Plus (LGBTQ+) Resource Center.* https://uwm.edu/lgbtrc/support/gender-pronouns

Voices of Youth Count. (2017, November). Missed opportunities: Youth homelessness in America. *Chapin Hall at the University of Chicago.* http://voicesofyouthcount.org/brief/national-estimates-of-youth-homelessness

Warth, G. (2015, December 30). Libraries pitch in with homeless count. *The San Diego Union-Tribune.* https://www.sandiegouniontribune.com/lifestyle/people/sdut-homeless-count-county-libraries-2015dec30-story.html

4

Creating an Action Plan

INTRODUCTION

In Chapter 4, we look at our communities—who lives there, what are their housing and support needs, what services and housing are available to them, and the steps you can take to create an action plan that will help to address the needs you've discovered. We'll create a vision statement for the work you want to do, based on what you've found and then create an action plan that reflects that work. Also covered in this chapter is making your case to stakeholders and staff and addressing resistance.

COMMUNITY

Before we can talk about what the library and community can do, it's helpful to define the word "community." The following two definitions provide some insights into this word that has a range of meanings, depending on who is using it:

- "A group of people with diverse characteristics who are linked by social ties, share common perspectives, and engage in joint action in geographical locations or settings" (MacQueen et al., 2001).

- "Community is a body of people living in the same locality. . . . Alternatively, a sense of identity and belonging shared among people living in the same locality. . . . Also, the set of social relations found in a particular bounded area" (Dale, 1990, p. 562).

While participating in a webinar, online librarian participants offered their own definitions of the word "community." Their answers included:

- "All of the people who make up the world closest to me."
- "All those around me who make me feel a sense of belonging."
- "People whose fates are interconnected." (Personal communications, 2020)

It's interesting to note that community for these librarians meant a sense of connectedness, of belonging, of closeness. There are so many levels to what community can mean. For this book and this topic, we look at community as being the people—all the people—who are being served or who could be served by your library. Within that larger community, there will be subgroups who feel strongly about their close communities and their connections. There are families and friends and groups. There may be a school community, a community of artists, of scholars, library staff, those who are connected through sports, those who are living in tents, cars, and RVs and who have created a strong community, and so on. Yet, as we see in the second definition above, all of the smaller communities live in the same locality; that is, they share the same geographic area and are bound by the same regulations and laws, as well as the weather, the geography.

Ask yourself: How do you define community? And when you think of serving your community, when you talk about meeting the needs of your community and reflecting your community in your materials, displays, and resources—have you considered those who are experiencing homelessness?

If we turn this around and look at who is in the community of people experiencing homelessness, we will see the same pattern. There is geographic community, as well as the closeness a person might feel to those who share the same daily life challenges or who have been a part of their efforts to move forward in life or even to simply stay alive. The library is in many cases part of their community, as is expressed in an article on a controversy in St. Louis, Missouri, over the closing of a shelter that was located near the public library:

> Faye Abram, a social work professor recently retired from St. Louis University, says that it helps to bear in mind that even though homeless people don't have a home, they still have a home base. In this particular case, she says, the Central Library didn't *attract* the homeless so much as it was located within the community of the homeless. . . . "The library was part of their community," Abram said. "And the library because of its generally open policies and liberal hours was like a safe space." (Krull, 2017)

For this book, we are looking at the ways in which the library can be part of the caring community needed by those who are experiencing homelessness. It can be easy to assume people who are experiencing homelessness are simply using the library because it can provide some of their basic needs, like a bathroom, a place to charge their phones or laptops, a refuge that is temperate and relatively safe. We also need to understand how libraries not only provide resources and relevant materials and connections, but are part of their community, just as they are for your housed community members.

ASSESSMENT

The next step in addressing homelessness in your community is to have an idea of what's actually happening there. Doing an assessment of your community needs related to homelessness requires a multifaceted approach.

However, before we look at how to gather needed statistics, we will look briefly at what is called Asset-Based Community Development, or ABCD (Stuart, 2017).

Asset-Based Community Development

There are numerous articles about this topic, so this will be a brief overview of an approach that encourages us to look at a community through an assets lens, rather than a deficit lens. In previous chapters, we've looked at the challenges being encountered by people who are experiencing homelessness. These are challenges they encounter both inside and outside the library. As library workers we need to know who is experiencing homelessness and why.

But the ideas for what is needed to address the lives of our unhoused community members need to come primarily from those community members themselves. As Stuart (2017) explains:

> ABCD focuses on the half-full glass. The half-empty glass represents the notion that communities are deficient and have many needs. The half-full glass represents the notion that communities (and the people who live there) have many strengths, capabilities and assets. It is the half-full glass that gives us something to work with.

The basic precepts of ABCD include focusing on the strengths of a community and on relationships. As the library, it's essential we don't try to take charge and tell our unhoused community members what they need and how we can help. We can instead listen, create opportunities for people to have discussions about what is important to them, and what they would like to see in their future.

As part of these discussions, we also look at what is sometimes called "community mapping," in which community "assets" are brought together through relationships. For example, the shower program mentioned in

Chapter 3 was created by bringing together unhoused community members, church groups, a local activist group, and the school district. A need was identified by the people experiencing homelessness, and a few were actively engaged in creating a program that would use their assets—in this case, all of these organizations who were committed to taking action—to make it happen.

Another excellent example is a community member who lives in her van—Veronica (not her real name). Veronica joined her city's Homeless Task Force and became involved in creating a nonprofit organization that sued the city to try to prevent them from evicting a community of people who were using public land as their home. That community had been in existence for 12 years, and no one had tried to evict them during that time. This community worked together—had community meetings, helped each other build structures, transported water and food, cared for their members, created art—and supported each other through employment or work exchanges.

When the nonprofit ultimately lost their lawsuit, Veronica became an activist and raised awareness about the lives of her friends. In addition, she taught herself auto mechanics and now works both inside and outside her community. Veronica is a great example of a strengths-based approach. She was able to use her talents and enthusiasm to create change in her community and continues to do that every day.

Housing and Urban Development (HUD) Statistics

As you assess your community, you can use the HUD point-in-time (PIT) count to have a better understanding of your community's needs and the ways in which the library might help.

Every year on one day in January HUD performs a PIT count across the United States. This count "provides a count of sheltered and unsheltered homeless persons on a single night during the last ten days in January" (U.S. Department of Housing and Urban Development, 2018). The statistics gathered from this count are broken down into Continuum of Care (CoC) geographical areas, and so you are able to search this database by year and then by scope (U.S. Department of Housing and Urban Development, 2021a). Once you access this data at https://www.hudexchange .info/programs/coc/coc-homeless-populations-and-subpopulations -reports, you'll be given the choice to filter by year and scope. As of this writing, the most recent year available was 2020.

Scope includes a choice of:

• All states, U.S. territories, Puerto Rico, and District of Columbia.

• All states and District of Columbia.

- For a state.
- For a CoC.

If you choose CoC, you'll then be given the opportunity to select the state. After you've chosen the state, you can select the CoC, which are broken down into geographical areas. For larger urban areas, there may be one CoC, while for smaller suburban or rural areas, the CoC will be made up of several geographical areas. This is obviously a challenge if you are trying to gather specific statistics for your own small area. We'll look more closely at this challenge and rural homelessness later in this chapter.

Table 4.1 shows the first part of the 2020 CoC report for the Appalachian Region CoC in Tennessee.

The other statistic that is available is the Housing Inventory Count (HIC). As they note on the HUD website:

> Continuum of Care (CoC) Homeless Assistance Programs Housing Inventory Count Reports provide a snapshot of a CoC's HIC, an inventory of housing conducted annually during the last ten days in January, and are available at the national and state level, as well as for each CoC. The reports tally the number of beds and units available on the night designated for the count by program type, and include beds dedicated to serve persons who are homeless as well as persons in Permanent Supportive Housing. New for this year, the reports also include data on beds dedicated to serve specific sub-populations of persons. (U.S. Department of Housing and Urban Development, 2021b)

Table 4.1   HUD 2020 Continuum of Care Homeless Assistance Programs Homeless Populations and Subpopulations: TN-509 Appalachian Regional CoC

Point-in Time Date: 1/22/2020

Summary by household type reported:

	Sheltered		Unsheltered	Total
	Emergency Shelter	Transitional Housing*		
Households without children[1]	142	29	122	293
Households with at least one adult and one child[2]	14	10	0	24
Households with only children[3]	1	0	0	1
Total Homeless Households	157	39	122	318

Summary of persons in each household type:

Persons in households without children[1]	142	29	127	298
Persons Age 18 to 24	0	2	4	6
Persons Over Age 24	142	27	123	292
Persons in households with at least one adult and one child[2]	47	40	0	87
Children Under Age 18	30	23	0	53
Persons Age 18 to 24	2	1	0	3
Persons Over Age 24	15	16	0	31
Persons in households with only children[3]	1	0	0	1
Total Homeless Persons	190	69	127	386

Source: US Department of Housing and Urban Development "2020 Annual Homeless Assessment Report (AHAR) to Congress: Part 1: Point in Time Estimates of Homelessnesss, January 2021." Washington, DC. https://files .hudexchange.info/reports/published/CoC_PopSub_CoC_TN-509-2020_TN _2020.pdf.

When you go to the website at https://www.hudexchange.info/programs /coc/coc-housing-inventory-count-reports, you can use the same filtering method you used for the CoC, by selecting an HIC by CoC. Using the statistics, you may be able to tell where the biggest need is. For instance, you could decide you would like to provide a program that supports families with children, but when you look at your local statistics and the HIC, you find it is veterans who have the biggest need for housing and support.

Here are the four pages of an HIC from 2020 for the Appalachian Regional CoC in Tennessee—CoC Number TN-509. The first page is represented by Table 4.2, which provides a summary of all beds reported by this CoC. The second page is shown as Table 4.3, which lists all

Table 4.2   HUD 2020 Continnum of Care Homeless Assistance Programs Housing Inventory Count Report: Summary of All Available Beds Reported by Contiuum of Care. CoC Number: TN 509. CoC Name: Appalachian Regional CoC.

	Family Units[1]	Family Beds[1]	Adult-Only Beds	Child-Only Beds	Total Yr-Round Beds	Seasonal	Overflow / Voucher	Chronic Beds[2]	Veteran Beds[3]	Youth Beds[3]
								Subset of Total Bed Inventory		
Emergency, Safe Haven and Transitional Housing	34	192	238	3	433	36	2	n/a	18	3
Emergency Shelter	25	154	177	3	334	36	2	n/a	0	3
Transitional Housing	9	38	61	0	99	n/a	n/a	n/a	18	0
Permanent Housing	47	137	446	0	583	n/a	n/a	224	225	0
Permanent Supportive Housing*	29	77	393	0	470	n/a	n/a	224	187	0
Rapid Re-Housing	18	60	53	0	113	n/a	n/a	n/a	38	0
Grand Total	81	329	684	3	1,016	36	2	224	243	3

Source: US Department of Housing and Urban Development "CoC Housing Inventory Count Reports, January, 2020," p. 1. https://files.hudexchange.info /reports/published/CoC_HIC_CoC_TN-509-2020_TN_2020.pdf

Table 4.3   HUD 2020 Contiuum of Care Homeless Assistance Programs Housing Inventory Count Report: Emergency Shelter. CoC Number: TN 509. CoC Name: Appalachian Regional CoC.

Emergency Shelter

Provider Name	Facility Name	Family Units[1]	Family Beds[1]	Adult-Only Beds	Child-Only Beds	Seasonal	Overflow / Voucher	Total Beds	Chronic Beds[2]	Veteran Beds[2]	Youth Beds[2]
Abuse Alternatives	Abuse Alternatives	3	10	2	0	0	0	12	n/a	0	0
Change Is Possible (CHIPS)	Change Is Possible (CHIPS) F	1	6	6	0	0	0	12	n/a	0	0
Family Promise of Greater Johnson City (	Family Promise of Greater Jo	5	15	0	0	0	0	15	n/a	0	0
Family Promise of Greater Kingsport (For	Interfaith Hospitality Networ	4	14	0	0	0	0	14	n/a	0	0
Frontier Health	Link House 'Project Safe Plac	0	0	0	3	0	0	3	n/a	0	3
Haven of Rest	Haven House	1	8	0	0	0	0	8	n/a	0	0
Haven of Rest	Miss Dolly's House/Family H	1	8	0	0	0	0	8	n/a	0	0
Haven of Rest	Haven Men's Rescue Mission	0	0	38	0	0	0	38	n/a	0	0
Haven of Rest	Grace Home Women's Emerg	0	0	10	0	0	0	10	n/a	0	0
Hope Haven Ministries	Hope Haven Ministries Wom	1	10	0	0	0	0	10	n/a	0	0
Hope Haven Ministries	Hope Haven Ministries Men's	0	0	12	0	0	0	12	n/a	0	0
Johnson County Safe Haven, Inc.	Johnson County Safe Haven,	1	7	0	0	0	0	7	n/a	0	0
Opportunity House of Greene County	Opportunity House of Greene	2	24	0	0	0	0	24	n/a	0	0
River's Edge Fellowship Church	River's Edge Dream Center	0	0	8	0	0	0	8	n/a	0	0
Safe House	Safe House	1	12	0	0	0	0	12	n/a	0	0
Safe Passage	Safe Passage	1	10	6	0	0	0	16	n/a	0	0
Salvation Army - Johnson City	Salvation Army - Johnson Cit	0	0	45	0	18	0	63	n/a	0	0
Salvation Army - Kingsport	Salvation Army - Kingsport E	2	10	25	0	8	0	43	n/a	0	0
Salvation Army, A Georgia Corporation	Salvation Army - Bristol	1	7	25	0	10	0	42	n/a	0	0
Shepherd's Inn	Shepherd's Inn	1	13	0	0	0	2	15	n/a	0	0
Total		25	154	177	3	36	2	372	n/a	0	3

Source: US Department of Housing and Urban Development "CoC Housing Inventory Count Reports, January, 2020," p. 2. https://files.hudexchange.info /reports/published/CoC_HIC_CoC_TN-509-2020_TN_2020.pdf

emergency shelters reported by this CoC. The third page is represented by Table 4.4, which shows all transitional housing and permanent supportive housing from this CoC. The final page is represented by Table 4.5, which provides an inventory count of all rapid rehousing in this CoC. Altogether, these numbers offer a snapshot of the housing availability in this particular CoC. As you can see, this information may help library staff understand the scope of housing availability in their community.

As you compare these reports, what do you see? Where is the biggest need in this CoC? This kind of question helps a library understand their community and be able to focus their efforts on what is most needed.

Table 4.4   HUD 2020 Contiuum of Care Homeless Assistance Programs Housing Inventory Count Report: Transitional Housing/Permanent Supportive Housing. CoC Number: TN 509. CoC Name: Appalachian Regional CoC.

Transitional Housing

Provider Name	Facility Name	Family Units[1]	Family Beds[1]	Adult-Only Beds	Child-Only Beds	Seasonal	Overflow / Voucher	Total Beds	Chronic Beds[2]	Veteran Beds[3]	Youth Beds[3]
Friends and Neighbors, Inc.	Friends and Neighbors, Inc.	8	26	0	0	n/a	n/a	26	n/a	0	0
Haven of Rest	Haven Lighthouse for Men 1	0	0	16	0	n/a	n/a	16	n/a	0	0
Haven of Rest	Haven Lighthouse for Men 2	0	0	16	0	n/a	n/a	16	n/a	0	0
Haven of Rest	Grace Home Women's Transit	0	0	4	0	n/a	n/a	4	n/a	0	0
Hope House	Hope House	1	12	7	0	n/a	n/a	19	n/a	0	0
Salvation Army Johnson City	(VA) Grant Per Diem	0	0	18	0	n/a	n/a	18	n/a	18	0
Total		9	38	61	0	n/a	n/a	99	n/a	18	0

Permanent Supportive Housing

Provider Name	Facility Name	Family Units[1]	Family Beds[1]	Adult-Only Beds	Child-Only Beds	Seasonal	Overflow / Voucher	Total Beds	Chronic Beds[2]	Veteran Beds[3]	Youth Beds[3]
Appalachian Regional Coalition on Home	ARCH PSH 2	0	0	12	0	n/a	n/a	12	12	0	0
Appalachian Regional Coalition on Home	ARCH PSH 1	0	0	14	0	n/a	n/a	14	14	0	0
Bristol Tennessee Housing & Redevelop	HUD-VASH	0	0	10	0	n/a	n/a	10	0	10	0
Fairviewhousing Management Corporatio	The Manna House	0	0	31	0	n/a	n/a	31	31	0	0
Fairviewhousing Management Corporatio	Appalachian Family Housing	10	31	0	0	n/a	n/a	31	31	0	0
Horizon Community Development corpor	Heartland Residence, Inc	0	0	9	0	n/a	n/a	9	9	9	0
Horizon Community Development corpor	Unaka Residence, Inc.	0	0	8	0	n/a	n/a	8	8	8	0
Johnson City Housing Authority	HUD-VASH	0	0	160	0	n/a	n/a	160	0	160	0
Kingsport Housing and Redevelopment A	CoC Grant	9	25	94	0	n/a	n/a	119	119	0	0
Kingsport Housing and Redevelopment A	HOPWA	10	21	55	0	n/a	n/a	76	0	0	0
Total		29	77	393	0	n/a	n/a	470	224	187	0

Source: US Department of Housing and Urban Development "CoC Housing Inventory Count Reports, January, 2020," p. 3. https://files.hudexchange.info /reports/published/CoC_HIC_CoC_TN-509-2020_TN_2020.pdf

Table 4.5   HUD 2020 Contiuum of Care Homeless Assistance Programs Housing Inventory Count Report: Rapid Rehousing. CoC Number: TN 509. CoC Name: Appalachian Regional CoC.

Rapid Re-Housing

Provider Name	Facility Name	Family Units[1]	Family Beds[1]	Adult-Only Beds	Child-Only Beds	Seasonal	Overflow / Voucher	Total Beds	Chronic Beds[2]	Veteran Beds[3]	Youth Beds[3]
ASafeHarborHome, Inc.	ASafeHarborHome CoC RR	3	9	6	0	n/a	n/a	15	n/a	0	0
Change Is Possible (CHIPS)	CHIPS ESG Rapid Re-Housi	2	6	1	0	n/a	n/a	7	n/a	0	0
Fairviewhousing Management Corporatio	Manna House ESG RRH	5	18	11	0	n/a	n/a	29	n/a	0	0
Family Promise of Greater Kingsport (For	Family Promise of Greater Ki	0	0	0	0	n/a	n/a	0	n/a	0	0
Kingsport Housing and Redevelopment A	KHRA GKAD ESG RRH	3	13	11	0	n/a	n/a	24	n/a	0	0
Volunteers of America Mid-States	Volunteers of America Mid-S	5	14	24	0	n/a	n/a	38	n/a	38	0
Total		18	60	53	0	n/a	n/a	113	n/a	38	0

Source: US Department of Housing and Urban Development "CoC Housing Inventory Count Reports, January, 2020," p. 4. https://files.hudexchange.info /reports/published/CoC_HIC_CoC_TN-509-2020_TN_2020.pdf

Rural Homelessness

In smaller and rural communities, the numbers you find through HUD may be much less helpful. Rural homelessness can and usually does look quite different from urban and even suburban homelessness. During a presentation to my University of Tennessee, Knoxville library school class, "The Role of Libraries in Addressing Homelessness and Poverty," Pamela Twiss, a social work professor at California University of Pennsylvania, noted some of the challenges for the PIT count in rural areas:

- It's a very cold day in January.
- Volunteers count those "on the street."
- Rural count teams emphasize cities/towns.
- No teams search vast acreage.
- No helicopters look for campers.

As she pointed out, this means the focus is more on the urbanized areas of rural and very rural counties (personal communication, 2020).

Davidson et al. (2016) explain that homelessness "is pervasive in rural communities due to high rates of poverty, lack of affordable housing, and inadequate housing quality, unemployment/underemployment, and geographic isolation (Abstract, p. 3). In their study for the National Health Care for the Homeless Council, they found there were issues related to how homelessness was defined, which led to undercounts, a lack of services, and a lack of knowledge about existing services.

This study included three groups. The first group was made up of participants who were currently experiencing homelessness, who had previously experienced homelessness, or who were precariously housed. The second group was made up of staff of local organizations, and the third group included local government officials and affiliates.

It is vital to understand the barriers rural areas are encountering related to housing and homelessness. In their "Rural Strategies Workshop," Homebase (2019) outlines the barriers and strengths for rural Continuum of Care (CoC. See Glossary in Appendix A). The barriers they list include:

- Geography and access to services.
- Community misconceptions.
- Limited resources and low capacity.
- Client isolation. (p. 7)

These are the same barriers libraries experience as they begin addressing homelessness in rural areas. Geography and access to services are a challenge in urban areas, but in rural areas it can be extremely difficult for people to access employment opportunities or employment itself, receive medical care, attend school, access the Internet, receive free or low-cost food, look for housing, and other tasks that will help them survive and begin to move out of homelessness.

For the CoCs, community misconceptions include undercounts in the annual PIT count, raising awareness in the communities about who is experiencing homelessness, and leveraging nontraditional partnerships. Again, all of these apply to libraries. Limited resources and low capacity can describe not only rural CoCs, but also rural libraries. Client isolation can be a major factor in rural homelessness, especially for those who are alone.

Getting to know your rural area and who is serving (or not serving) those who are unhoused will help you as you move forward on your action plan. We can learn from the way these CoCs are approaching these barriers, by using creative approaches and taking advantage of partnerships. In Chapter 5, we'll talk more about rural partnerships and what they can look like.

In rural areas, as well as large urban and suburban areas, one step you can take is to reach out to agencies, organizations, and institutions that interact with people who are unstably housed. Some examples include:

- Local YMCA/YWCA.
- K–12 schools.
- Colleges and universities.
- The faith community.
- The local police/sheriff's department.
- Hospitals and local medical professionals.
- Transportation agencies, such as local transit districts.
- Restaurants/cafés.
- Social services.
- Library staff.
- Community service organizations.
- Other community agencies/organizations/volunteer organizations.
- Local motels and hotels.

By reaching out, you can learn more about the work that's being done, the needs that are being expressed, what barriers are being encountered, and how your library could play a role.

Gathering information about people experiencing housing insecurity can be challenging for many reasons. People may not identify as homeless, so finding other terms to use can be useful. Are they looking for housing? Are they staying in motels/hotels or doubled up with friends or family? In either case, they may not be sure how long they will be able to do that. Their housing therefore may be tenuous, so while they are not literally sleeping on the streets, they can't relax and know they have a place to go that is dependable and reliable.

Homelessness takes many forms, and so we must learn to recognize its many guises. For each adult, each family, each child, each youth, we can ask our community and the organizations that serve them: Does everyone have a safe, predictable, affordable, and habitable place to sleep every night? If not, what are the barriers? And how can we help? We can also ask ourselves: What can we do as library staff? That leads us to assessing our libraries.

Assessing Your Library

To gain a better understanding of what your library is able to offer in addressing homelessness, you must also assess your library. This assessment includes looking at staff, budget, programs, resources, collections, key stakeholders, community support, and partnerships.

A good place to start is by looking at your assets. What does your library have that will help you? Examples include:

- A supportive and active Friends group.
- Current partnerships.
- Strong budget.
- Supportive community.
- Supportive administration.
- Supportive staff.
- Staff training.
- Staff member or volunteer who can write grants.
- Community connections with those who are experiencing homelessness.
- Meeting room space.
- All-genders restrooms.
- Public access computers with Internet connection.
- Laptop computers that can be checked out.
- Hot spots that can be checked out.
- Free legal services.

- Bus/public transportation services and information.
- Programs already in place that can actively serve all community members—for example, a résumé writing workshop, one-on-one computer tutoring, and weekly or monthly discussion groups. All of these and many more can include your community members who are experiencing homelessness.

Another way to assess your library and its assets is to use the following assessment tool, adapted from the WebJunction "Serving Spanish Speaking Communities Checklist" (Cuesta, 2012) and used in the 2019 Infopeople class "Library Services for Patrons Experiencing Homelessness" (Winkelstein, 2019). This checklist can also be found as a separate document in Appendix I.

LIBRARY SELF-ASSESSMENT CHECKLIST

Serving community members experiencing homelessness requires the entire library be behind the effort and that an awareness of the reality of homelessnes be integrated into every aspect of the library's services and operations.

Planning: Services to community members experiencing homelessness should be an integral part of all library planning efforts. The library's mission, goals, and objectives should specifically address services to these folks.

- ☐ Library director and library board are involved and committed to serving community members experiencing homelessness.
- ☐ Services to community members experiencing homelessness are included in the library's long-range/strategic plan.
- ☐ Library management and staff understand why serving community members experiencing homelessness is important.
- ☐ Library staff are provided opportunities to learn more about the complex nature of homelessness, the challenges in addressing it, and library services to community members experiencing homelessness.
- ☐ Library staff across all departments and classifications are involved in planning services to community members experiencing homelessness.
- ☐ Library staff have revised existing policies and procedures that impact delivery of services to community members experiencing homelessness.

Community Involvement/Connections: Effective libraries are heavily involved with community members experiencing homelessness. They make sure that community representatives are involved in the design and evaluation of library activities.

☐ Library staff meets with key community leaders and groups that represent community members experiencing homelessness on a regular basis to review and revise the service plan.

☐ Library staff have identified public relations activities with which community leaders and groups, and so on, from the community of those experiencing homelessness can assist.

☐ Library staff have participated in one or more events or programs related to homelessness.

☐ Library staff have developed a list of current and potential homelessness community partners and collaborators.

☐ Library staff have developed a process for tracking homelessness community connections made and a schedule for following up and staying in touch.

☐ A schedule/process is in place for library staff to participate in programs and services related to community members experiencing homelessness.

Facilitating Access and a Welcoming Environment: Access to library services by community members experiencing homelessness includes delivery systems and bibliographic processes that reflect cultural and economic differences.

☐ Signs directing people experiencing homelessness to the library can be found at shelters, food banks, free-food services, churches, and other popular spots.

☐ Culturally sensitive posters, art, and displays help create a welcoming environment.

☐ Library is open at hours convenient to all segments of the community.

Collection: The library's collection should reflect the needs, culture, and lives of all community members, including members who are experiencing homelessness.

☐ A collection development policy related to homelessness and poverty has been written.

☐ Library has a schedule/process in place for ongoing community input to homelessness and poverty collection development.

☐ Relevant collection displays and materials are in areas in the library where people gather.

Programs/Services Offered: Effective services to the community members experiencing homelessness must include a wide variety of programs that meet the specific needs and interests of the entire community.

☐ Programs/activities are offered in the library (e.g., finding and interviewing for a job, healthy eating on the streets, knowing your rights on the streets, how to apply for housing).

☐ Library programs/activities are offered in the community (e.g., library booth at a health or job fair for those experiencing homelessness, community events, visits to schools, speaking to concerned community groups).

☐ Staff are culturally responsive to those experiencing homelessness (e.g., eye contact, smiles, level of communications, respectful vocabulary).

☐ Additional activities of interest to those experiencing homelessness are available (other programs and/or grants).

☐ Methods for tracking programs and number of attendees are in place.

☐ Library delivers services in the community at local gathering spots for those experiencing homelessness (e.g., migrant camps, tent communities, public parks)

☐ Library coordinates/collaborates library services/programs with other agencies working with community members experiencing homelessness.

☐ Library programs encourage/facilitate participation by community members experiencing homelessness.

☐ Library has schedule/process in place for ongoing input from community members experiencing homelessness.

Internal Communications: Effective libraries make sure that staff, volunteers, Friends, and Trustees are informed and/or involved in the design and implementation of library plans to serve community members experiencing homelessness.

☐ Library staff, volunteers, Friends, and Trustees are aware of the plan and its impact on library services, staffing, promotion, and budget.

☐ Library staff, volunteers, Friends, and Trustees have been asked for input on how to best to implement the plan.

☐ Contributions and achievements of staff and volunteers in helping to establish and implement the plan have been recognized.

Staff Recruitment and Development: Effective libraries actively recruit staff at all levels that mirror the demographics of the homelessness community. They provide encouragement and opportunities for staff to develop and update skills in serving community members experiencing homelessness.

- ☐ A schedule/process for providing cultural humility, person-centered and trauma-informed training for all staff is in place.
- ☐ A schedule/process for encouraging staff to participate in activities in the homelessness community is in place.

Board Recruitment and Development: Effective libraries actively recruit board members who mirror the demographics of the community members experiencing homelessness. They provide encouragement and opportunities for board members to develop and update skills in representing and serving community members experiencing homelessness.

- ☐ A process for recruiting board members who mirror the demographics of unhoused community members is in place.
- ☐ A schedule for providing training that includes cultural humility, person-centered interactions, and trauma-informed care is in place.

Publicity and Media Relations: Effective libraries develop and maintain connections with media contacts in organizations and agencies that work with community members experiencing homelessness, as well as with the community members themselves. They monitor the impact of their marketing activities to unhoused community members.

- ☐ Library staff have developed a thorough list of social services and homelessness media contacts.
- ☐ Library staff have met with each homelessness media contact at least once to begin the relationship.
- ☐ Library staff, volunteers, Friends, and trustees are aware of homelessness promotional strategies.
- ☐ The library website includes content appropriate to the lives of those experiencing homelessness.

As you review this checklist, you can look for actions your library is already taking and find some suggestions for ones you have yet to begin. Which items were you able to check off? Which ones might be possible? Which ones are out of reach? Keep in mind that each community, each library, each staff is different—not only because of the range of needs, but also expertise, time, budget, and willingness to take on this topic.

CREATING A VISION STATEMENT

A vision statement is an overarching statement that succinctly sums up what your library would like to accomplish. Your library may already have a vision statement, and if so, that would be a good place to start. For instance, the Denver Public Library—where there is a well-established social worker program—simply has as their vision "A Strong Community Where Everyone Thrives (Denver Public Library, n.d.).

A vision statement for this work is similar: It describes what you'd like your library to do to address community homelessness. It should be about the community members and not about the library. That is, it shouldn't include language that implies or even states that unhoused people are a problem at your library. Homelessness and poverty are social problems that affect people's behavior, as well as their mental and physical health. The social issue is the problem, not the people. Maybe the vision statement will be the same as the one for your library, maybe it will be different. If you're not sure how to create one that describes the work you're doing, there are many sites online that provide guidance. For example, Jessie Lyn Stoner (2011) offers three concrete steps toward creating a vision statement:

What all great visions have in common is they provide an answer to these three questions:

1. Destination: Where are we going?
2. Purpose: Why do we exist? What greater good do we serve?
3. Values: What principles guide our decisions and actions on our journey? (Stoner, 2011)

Stone also encourages a collaborative approach to creating a vision statement, and if possible, this would help library staff and administration (and possibly your Friends group, Library Board, and other stakeholders) work together to create a shared vision that would help guide and inform all who are involved with the library.

CREATING YOUR ACTION PLAN

Once you have an idea of who is experiencing homelessness in your community, what needs are being met and which aren't, and what your library has to offer, you can create your own action plan. An action plan helps you create a concrete plan for an action you'd like your library to take that will meet a specific need related to homelessness. Your idea should be based on the information you've gathered about your community, rather than simply something you'd like to do. Ask yourself: What are the needs? What role can my library play in addressing these needs? It doesn't have to be an expensive, large, or far-reaching action. In fact, you may want to start with a simple plan that can be put into place without extensive funds or broad staff involvement.

Some examples of actions include:

- Hosting at your library a one-time fair of local service providers/organizations who provide information, support, and services to people experiencing homelessness.
- Selecting one organization/school/agency in your community and inviting them to meet with you to talk about partnering.
- Writing a small grant that will cover the cost of providing free feminine hygiene products in your restrooms.
- Reaching out to a local shelter to take a library laptop regularly to the shelter, to help shelter residents register for library cards, and clear any financial holds on their account.
- Creating a food pantry at your academic library.
- Provide free tutoring in your public library for students who are unstably housed.
- Bring together local veterans and veteran services to help with applying for services and benefits.
- Provide a one-time storytime at a shelter for families with children. Include a way for families to register for library cards.
- Reach out to a local synagogue/mosque/church. What are the needs of their unhoused members? What role could your library play in addressing these needs? How could you work together?
- Partner with the local DA and your law library to create a Community Court.
- Partner to help with the Point-in-Time (PIT) count.
- Create voting resources specifically for people who have no permanent address.
- Start a weekly discussion group that includes both housed and unhoused community members.
- Partner with a local organization to offer a "Know Your Rights" workshop/training. Invite someone who has experienced homelessness to talk about rights on the street.
- Offer a workshop about how to receive and use a Section 8 Voucher.
- Reach out to a local homelessness agency and ask to hold a focus group to discuss with unhoused community members what they need and how they think the library could help.

- Create a library advisory board made up of community members who have the lived experience of homelessness.
- Organize a "National Homeless Person's Memorial Day" (National Coalition for the Homeless, 2018).
- Create and post a list of recommended terms for staff to use. Include terms related to people with disabilities, the LGBTGQ+ community, mental health, and, of course, those who are unhoused.

These are just a few examples of the many ways libraries can be part of the caring community for people experiencing homelessness. If you aren't sure what would be appropriate, consider contacting local agencies and asking them what would help them in their work. Or, as we discussed with ABCD, if you have relationships with folks who are unstably housed, meet with them and offer your support. Ask them what this support would look like. As we've discussed, you won't necessarily be able to solve their most pressing need, which is probably housing, but there are many other daily obstacles for them.

Here's the template for your action plan (Table 4.6). You can also find it in Appendix B.

Details

In the first column, there is one box in which you list a need unique to this population. The second column gives you space to articulate how your library can help meet this need. The next column asks for any assets your library already has that could help (e.g., a partnership, a supportive library board, funds). The following three columns help break down your plan into action steps. First, think of three steps your library could take. Then, identify three potential barriers that could arise as your library begins to take these steps, and list strategies you will use for addressing those barriers.

The final three columns are practical details about this plan: a proposed time line, possible budgetary needs, and where you'll obtain any needed funds, and finally, ways you will evaluate your plan.

Assets

As you can see, once you have an idea, the next step is to look at how you can use your library's assets to move your idea forward. Are you thinking of holding a weekly discussion group and you have a large meeting room where that could be held? Do you already have a relationship with the League of Women Voters so you can help unhoused community

Table 4.6   Action Planning Tool

Need	
Your Action	
Library Assets	
Steps	1. 2. 3.
Potential Barriers	1. 2. 3.
Strategies	1. 2. 3.
Time Line	
Budget	
Evaluation	1. 2. 3.

members vote? Do you have staff who are passionate about addressing social needs, such as participating in the PIT count? Is working with traditionally underserved populations part of your strategic plan?

Steps

After you have identified how the library's assets will help with your plan, you can next break the plan down into steps. How exactly will you go about putting this plan into practice? For instance, for the discussion group, you might have someone in mind who would be an excellent leader for the group. So, Step 1 might be to reach out to this person. Or if you decide to participate in the PIT count, reaching out to your local HUD office or local officials who are in charge of the count. Or post a question to a library listserv, looking for other libraries who are doing the same. Step 2 could be to figure out the logistics: How will you be involved? Will it be at the library for the actual count? Or will your library gather donations for new clean socks, gloves, and hand warmers—items that can be given to those who are counted. Will library staff be directly involved?

Step 3 could be to put the plan into action: Reserve a room or provide training for library staff or put out a barrel to gather donations.

Potential Barriers

Barriers can be anything that could get in the way of carrying out your action plan. For example, there may be reluctance on the part of library staff to directly engage with people experiencing homelessness. Or the administration may be concerned this will bring in more people who are experiencing homelessness, and there have already been complaints from housed library users. Or there may not be a library staff member who can help coordinate your efforts.

Addressing the barriers can be challenging, but identifying them in advance will make a difference. For instance, a strategy to provide specific information and statistics about unstably housed people may help break down some of the stereotypes and fears staff members or administration may have. You could bring in a service provider who can offer insights at an all-staff training or offer a weekly tip for staff members. Or invite someone who is experiencing homelessness to a staff meeting—to talk about themselves, if they are comfortable doing that. Stereotypes and fears are powerful deterrents to taking supportive actions, so the more information you are able to provide, the more it will help with your plan.

Time Line

Once you've filled out the first six columns, you can move on to creating a time line that will help you stay on track and be realistic about what you are able to accomplish and when. The initial steps you take should be tied into this time line. If your project is a one-time event, you can set a date. If it's a more long-range project, like a weekly discussion group, then figuring out when you want to start will give you a target date as you put all the pieces together.

Budget

What you need for your budget and where the money will come from depends of course on what action you'll be taking. If it's a program, your Friends group may be able to cover the costs for speakers and refreshments. If you decide to be involved in the PIT count, there may be no direct costs, but there will probably be staff time. The amount of funds you have available may be a factor in what you decide to do. There are many small steps you can take that have no financial implications, but all will require staff time of some kind, even if it's simply contacting local service agencies and providing fliers for existing programs or attending one of their meetings.

For a more ambitious plan, such as hiring a social worker, the budget can initially come from a grant and, if the program is considered successful, can later be included in the library budget itself. Types of grants include both LSTA (Library Services and Technlogy Act) and IMLS (the Institute of Museum and Library Services). For example, the rural Niles District Library in Michigan received LSTA funds to support one master's of social work position, as well as stipends for social work interns (Niles District Library, 2018). On their website they provide a link to their application documents, as well as their grant award letter. Looking at what other libraries have done, as well as reaching out to local partners, can help you figure out what funds you'll need and how to obtain them. Funding in libraries can be tight, so this is an excellent example of how partnerships could play a role.

Evaluation

Finally, evaluation. As with any of your programs, evaluation is essential for gaining an understanding of what went well, what could be improved, whether you met your stated goal, and whether or not you will continue. In your evaluation you'll also be looking at outcomes—what you hoped to accomplish and what actually happened. For instance, you may have created a one-day event that revolved around providing employment information, and while that information was well received, the best outcome was the positive feedback from your unhoused community members about how they felt having an event specifically for them. Outcomes can surprise you, and they are a good way to discover what is needed and appreciated.

A critical part of evaluation is determining why you're doing it. Is it a requirement as a part of your funding? Are you wondering if you accomplished your goal? Is it worth continuing or doing again? Do you want to hear more about the impact on your community members? Would you like to make some improvements?

If your plan includes people experiencing homelessness, it's critical to keep in mind that in-person feedback is probably the most direct and useful information. Using an online form may be difficult or even impossible for some people, unless it's easily accessible through the library computers and there are library staff available to assist.

If you use surveys, either paper or online or both, decide what kinds of questions you're going to ask. Will they be open-ended, where participants fill in a blank line or box? Or Likert style—using only specific choices? Will you ask demographic questions, and if so, do you have a reason for that? For demographic questions, I suggest using simple questions with a blank line for gender, race, and ethnicity, rather than a long list of options. If you do provide options, be sure not to use the word "other," but instead offer a line that says something like "prefer to self-identify." A combination of simple Likert-style questions and open-ended questions can work well. In addition, keep the survey as short and concise as possible, to increase the chance people will take the time to fill it out.

Small focus groups can also be a good way to hear reactions and responses. As with any of your library users, make sure the evaluation is in line with your audience. Also, numbers, as you know, while relevant for some programs, aren't everything. Sometimes the simple interactions with a few people can be life changing. Therefore, you should be clear on what you're looking for in the evaluations. A rubric may help guide you. For example, you could weight the answers using this rubric:

- 10%: Number of people who attended/were involved
- 25%: Reached intended audience
- 25%: Personal stories about impact
- 15%: Feedback from staff
- 15%: Feedback from partners
- 10%: Value for money/staff time spent

This is simply an example and should be adjusted depending on the program/action.

Other components of evaluation include:

- **Observation:** Were participants engaged? Were staff comfortable providing the program? Were there surprises?

- **Interactive feedback:** If participants are comfortable, you can ask questions before and after the event, to assess whether you accomplished your goal. For instance, at a staff training, you could survey staff about homelessness, including vocabulary, stereotypes, statistics, fears, and so on. Then after the training, have a post-training survey, asking the same questions.

- **In-person one-on-one interviews:** Using a paper survey as a start, you could ask participants if they're willing to answer some questions about the event. What did they like about it? Did they learn something or gain something? What would make it better?

- **Look at the reasons for your action plan:** Did your event address those? Did you accomplish what you hoped to accomplish? Were your assets useful? Were you able to overcome barriers?

- **Budget:** Did you allocate enough funds? Not enough? Too much? Were the funds used well—that is, are you satisfied with the outcome, and did you feel it was worth the cost?

However you decide to evaluate your program, taking notes can also be useful later.

Evaluation is a tool, and when used to encourage frank and personal responses, it can help you with future plans.

DREAM PLANS

Sometimes a big plan—one you don't think you can necessarily put in place—can help you understand what you, your library, and your community would like to see if there were no limitations, if anything were possible. Appendix D provides information and a template for creating your own dream plan.

MAKING YOUR CASE TO STAKEHOLDERS AND STAFF

Stakeholders

Making the decision to create an action that will support your community members who are experiencing homelessness will probably need some groundwork—in particular, being clear about why you're proposing this and why it's appropriate for a library. We discussed this in Chapter 2, looking at the Universal Declaration of Human Rights (United Nations, n.d.), the updated ALA policy B.8.10 "Addressing Poverty, Inequality and the Responsibilities of Libraries" (ALA, 2019), the fact that libraries are in theory for everyone, the community's health, and the reality that poverty and homelessness are in our communities and libraries can play a crucial role in addressing them, through resources, connections and safe supportive spaces. But knowing you may encounter resistance, making a strong case to begin with will help.

In their book, *Whole Person Librarianship: A Social Work Approach to Patron Services*, Zettervall and Nienow (2019) offer a librarian's quote that speaks to this issue:

> Public libraries are connectors to the community. What if what a person needs is a connection to the community organization or anything else the community has to provide? We can be the expert in that too. And that's a hundred percent our role as much as finding physical or digital materials for someone. (Bella, homelessness and poverty librarian, p. 11)

This quote fits in well with clearly expressing your specific goal. As one library social worker pointed out, it's not about equality, it's about equity. Providing services, resources, connections, bathrooms, a safe space—all of these contribute to addressing homelessness and poverty. Because the community is unequal in opportunities, we need to not look at providing everyone the same service, but instead look at what our library users need. If a library user wants information about preschools in the area, we don't have to make sure we provide the same information to everyone we serve—that wouldn't make sense. The same holds for our community members who are unhoused—we fit our reference services to meet their needs. And again, to reiterate an earlier point, we are providing resources not solutions. We absolutely cannot solve anyone's problems, but we can do our best to make sure they leave the library feeling we've met their information and resources needs to the best of our ability.

Another concern that may come from stakeholders is tax monies. You may hear statements such as "Libraries should be for people who pay the taxes to support them." This view can come from a "them" and "us" approach to community. "We" pay taxes and "they" don't. It can be challenging to move people away from this approach, but there are a few points you can make. To start with, libraries are most of all for the entire community and even those who are passing through the community. Internet guest passes are common in public libraries and can be used by travelers who need to check their e-mail, print boarding passes, look for local resources, keep in touch with friends, and so on. They may pay taxes somewhere, just not in your community.

Another point that can be made is that many people who are unhoused *do* pay taxes. They are not unemployed; they are underemployed. The common misconceptions that people experiencing homelessness are lazy, unemployed, resistant to work, unreliable, and dishonest—all these adjectives and more—create an atmosphere of distrust and stigma that can be difficult to overcome. This could be a great first action plan for your library—demystifying and destigmatizing homelessness to raise community and staff awareness and provide a forum for people with the lived experience of homelessness to share insights into their lives.

In addition, we serve everyone in our libraries because this is what libraries do. This public-spirited approach is the backbone of public libraries. By providing safe spaces, resources, connections, and more, we are helping people move forward in their lives. With our help, many people who are currently unemployed and unhoused will be able to find both housing and employment. By serving everyone, we are investing in our communities.

Making the Case to Staff

It's not difficult to find complaints about people who appear to be unhoused and who are using libraries. In addressing these complaints, a good first approach is to avoid conflating homelessness with specific behaviors, such as the overuse of drugs, mental health challenges, and lack of hygiene. Although people who are unhoused may have these life challenges, so do housed people. It's critical we don't make assumptions about people experiencing homelessness. As library social worker Susan Voss-Rothmeier, LCSW, expressed in an informal survey of social workers and what they would like library staff to know:

> It's important for staff to understand that people who are experiencing homelessness are unique individuals and none are the same. I sometimes hear our society refer to people in a lockstep manner as if all people with similar circumstances think and act in the same way. People who are unhoused are not any more similar to each other than people who are housed may be to each other. So I encourage staff to refrain from phrases such as "homeless people think or do or need x." Instead, I encourage staff to get to know their patrons over time and understand their individual needs and preferences. (Personal communication, 2019)

Jean Badalamenti and Elissa Hardy, social workers at the DC Public Library and Denver Public Library, respectively, offer related suggestions for library staff in their article "Supporting Autonomy While Setting Clear Boundaries" (Badalamenti & Hardy, 2019). As they write:

> "How do we address homelessness . . . in our libraries?" Essentially, when we ask this question we are already categorizing groups of people into

behaviors we associate with those groups. By doing this we stigmatize, generalize, and marginalize people. What we should be addressing is behavior alone, while recognizing the resiliency and humanity of the customer. Successfully addressing behavioral challenges is based on a framework that maintains dignity and respect, yet sets clear boundaries and expectations. (Badalamenti & Hardy, 2019)

As they point out, library staff need to be cognizant of the role that trauma can play in the behavior of library users, no matter their housing status. Using a respectful and trauma-informed approach can help library staff as well as community members.

Making this point to staff and stakeholders can help them understand the importance of the work libraries can do to address homelessness and poverty in their communities, by not only providing resources, but also by expanding the social connections at the library, which can lead to greater understanding as well as bringing in voices who may not have been listened to in the past. Diversity in its myriad forms makes us stronger.

Making the case to staff also includes listening to their concerns and being clear about what they are. One way to do this is to create a staff survey, which allows staff members to express their concerns, ideas, suggestions, and thoughts related to addressing the topic of homelessness at their library. Appendix C includes an example of such a survey.

Pressley (2017) reports on her survey of library staff about "serious mental illness" and library users who are perceived to be experiencing homelessness. In her results, she highlights the request from library staff for training and information related to mental health life experiences, as well as their concerns about their own safety and the safety of other library users. In her conclusion, she points out that:

People who have serious mental illness should receive courteous, thoughtful service from the people who work in the library and access to the programming that the library offers, with assistance if need be in the manner that any other user who has a disability would be served.

This goal—to treat those with visible mental health conditions—with "courteous, thoughtful service" is one that should be kept in mind. Providing training that can help alleviate any anxieties about safety is a great way to approach common fears based on stereotypes, especially if there is the assumption the library user is also experiencing homelessness.

Another reason for creating programs and resources to meet the needs of unhoused people is the partnerships and community connections libraries are able to create through this work. We talk more about trainings and partnerships in Chapter 5.

ADDRESSING RESISTANCE

As we discussed in Chapter 2, there are multiple reasons for addressing homelessness in our libraries. Resistance to this idea can be met with explanations like the ones presented in that chapter. But resistance is frequently prompted by fear, with the stigma and assumptions about unhoused people precipitating that fear. Public education campaigns, bringing in speakers with the lived experience of homelessness, partnering with social service agencies, volunteering or creating programs so staff members and library users have direct and personal interactions in a shared setting, without a power differential, can all make a difference. Chapter 6 offers many examples of programs that have successfully lowered resistance and increased a feeling of shared community.

CONCLUSION

In Chapter 4, we have looked at how to create your action plan, using assessment as a tool. In Chapter 5, we look at partnerships, staff training, and funding—all critical parts of moving forward with your plan.

REFERENCES

ALA. (2019). ALA Policy Manual: Section B. *Addressing poverty, economic inequality, and the responsibilities of libraries.* American Library Association. http://www.ala.org/aboutala/sites/ala.org.aboutala/files/content/Section%20B%20New%20Policy%20Manual-1%20%28REVISED%2011_4_2019%29.pdf

Badalamenti, J., & Hardy, E. (2019, February 19). Supporting autonomy while setting clear boundaries. *Public Libraries Online.* http://publiclibrariesonline.org/2019/02/supporting-autonomy-while-setting-clear-boundaries

Cuesta, Y. (2012). Serving Spanish speaking communities success checklist. *WebJunction.* https://www.webjunction.org/materials/webjunction/Serving_Spanish_Speaking_Communities_Success_Checklist.html

Dale, S. (1990). *Controversies in sociology. A Canadian introduction* (p. 562). Copp, Clark and Pitman.

Davidson, C., Murry, V. McBride, Meinbresse, M., Jenkins, Darlene M., & Mindrup, R. (2016, April). Using the social ecological model to examine how homelessness is defined and managed in rural East Tennessee. *National Health Care for the Homeless Council.* https://nhchc.org/clinical-practice/homeless-services/special-populations/rural-populations

Denver Public Library (DPL). (n.d.). *Mission & strategic plan.* https://www.denverlibrary.org/content/about-dpl

Homebase. (2019). *Rural strategies workshop.* https://www.homebaseccc.org/post/strategies-for-rural-communities

Krull, R. (2017, October 16). What's a library to do? On homelessness and public spaces. *The Millions.* https://themillions.com/2017/10/whats-a-library-to-do-on-homelessness-and-public-spaces.html

Library Research Service (LRS). (n.d.). *Library user survey templates & how-tos.* https://www.lrs.org/library-user-surveys-on-the-web

MacQueen, K. M., McLellan, E., Metzger, D. S., Kegeles, S., Strauss, R. P., Scotti, R., Blanchard, L., & Trotter, R. T. (2001). What is community? An evidence-based definition for participatory public health. *American Journal of Public Health, 91*(12), 1929–1938.

National Coalition for the Homeless. (2018). *Homeless Persons Memorial Day.* https://nationalhomeless.org/about-us/projects/memorial-day

Niles District Library. (2018). *Social workers in rural and small libraries.* https://sites.google.com/nileslibrary.net/swirsl

Pressley, T. (2017). Public libraries, serious mental illness and homelessness: A survey of public librarians. *Public Library Quarterly, 36*(1), 61–76.

Stoner, J. L. (2011). Jessie Lyn Stone on leadership: The key to visions that work. *Seapoint Center for Collaborative Leadership.* https://seapointcenter.com/vision-statements

Stuart, G. (2017). What is asset-based community development? *Sustaining Community.* https://sustainingcommunity.wordpress.com/2013/08/15/what-is-abcd

United Nations. (n.d.). *The Universal Declaration of Human Rights.* http://www.un.org/en/universal-declaration-human-rights

U.S. Department of Housing and Urban Development (HUD). (2018). *Balance of state continuum of care toolkit.* https://www.hudexchange.info/resource/5735/balance-of-state-continuum-of-care-toolkit

U.S. Department of Housing and Urban Development (HUD). (2020a). CoC homeless populations and subpopulations reports. *HUD Exchange.* https://www.hudexchange.info/programs/coc/coc-homeless-populations-and-subpopulations-reports

U.S. Department of Housing and Urban Development (HUD). (2020b). CoC housing inventory count reports. *HUD Exchange.* https://www.hudexchange.info/programs/coc/coc-housing-inventory-count-reports

Winkelstein, J. A. (2019). Library services for patrons experiencing homelessness. *Infopeople.* https://infopeople.org/content/infopeople-past-online-training

Zettervall, S. K., & Nienow, M. C. (2019). *Whole person librarianship: A social work approach to patron services.* Libraries Unlimited.

5

Partnerships, Funding, and Staff Training

INTRODUCTION

In this chapter, we look at partnerships, funding, and staff training. For partnerships, we will define them, discuss how to create them, and determine why they are vital to this topic.

Funding can definitely be a challenge, so examining the many paths to funding and what funding you may actually need is discussed.

Finally, staff training is a great start to the work we're talking about.

PARTNERSHIPS

As part of the "We Are Santa Monica" effort, we've emphasized three simple words of advice for those who want to be part of the solution: *donate, advocate* and *volunteer*. There's a fourth dimension that's also making a difference: *partnering*. (Cole, 2020)

The above quote is from an article about Santa Monica, California, and homelessness. Cole (2020) provides an overview of homelessness in that city and how it's being addressed. His emphasis on partnerships is one that can't be stressed enough. As library staff we provide connections and resources, but as partners we can provide so much more.

We start by defining partnerships. When you think of being a partner, what comes to mind? Wildridge et al. (2004) provide a range of definitions of partnerships, based on their thorough literature review of articles written about this topic. Common themes they list include:

- Arrangements between organizations, groups, individuals.
- Shared aims, vision, mission. or interest.

- Trust.
- Collaborative value.
- Informal or formal. (pp. 4–5)

In the introduction to their article, the authors state they are using this review to demonstrate that:

- Partnerships are not a soft option but hard work.
- Partnerships take time to develop.
- Partnerships must be realistic and aim for what can be achieved, not be set up to fail by being too ambitious.
- Partnerships can, if successful, achieve more than individual agencies working alone. (p. 4)

Wildridge et al. (2004) also talk about the "partnership lifecycle." As they say, there are five key stages:

1. **Connecting:** how potential partners can get to know each other and plan their future activities together.
2. **Contracting:** how to negotiate and decide roles, rules, and funding.
3. **Conflict:** how to manage the inevitable conflict between partners.
4. **Collaborating:** how to keep the momentum going when the partnership is working well.
5. **Closing:** how to end a partnership, or to end one partner's involvement. (Wildridge et al., 2004)

How can we apply this information about partnerships to our work as libraries addressing the many challenges related to homelessness?

We begin with the advantages of partnerships. If you already have partnerships, what are some of the advantages? Stricker (n.d.) provides a list of some of them, including:

- Sharing expertise.
- Innovation—coming up with creative ideas together.
- New audiences.
- New opportunities—for example, presenting at each other's conferences.
- To help further your goals.

Other advantages include:

- Using each other's spaces.
- Increased opportunities for grant funding.

- More people involved means more accomplished.
- Expands the library's connections.
- Breaks down barriers created by stereotypes.

Partnerships can take many forms. They can be short term or long term. They can bring together entities of similar sizes or completely different sizes. What you contribute as the library and what your partner contributes can be vastly different. Partnerships don't mean each partner puts in the same amount of work or hours or tangible goods. What they offer is a chance to enhance what you can offer as a library and do the same for your partner.

For example, Wardrobe for Opportunity (n.d.) is an organization that provides employment support services, including professional-looking clothing for all people, housed or not, who are looking for employment. One way they collect this clothing is by partnering with banks, who have a closet where they have set aside space for donations. This allows them to make it as convenient as possible for people who want to donate, while continuing to increase their stock of clothing. If the library has a small room or closet, it could set up a clothing rack and offer to be one of the drop-off points.

This partnership would highlight the role libraries can play in collaborating to address the needs of their community members, it may bring in new library users, and it supports an organization that may also be interested in working together in other ways.

As you consider creating a partnership, do your homework and learn as much as you can about them. Keep these questions in mind:

- Do your vision and mission statements align?
- Are they financially viable?
- Do they have good communication skills?
- Are they able to work collaboratively?
- Do you know why they want to partner with the library?
- Are they willing to meet regularly?
- Are they open to new ideas?
- Do they have an understanding of libraries?
- Do you have an understanding of their work? (Stricker, n.d.)

One way to approach using library partnerships to address homelessness is to look at partnerships you may already have and build on those relationships. Have you worked with the local YMCA to provide programs? Or perhaps you offer free summer lunches for children through a partnership with your state library or a local school district? Or you have a program that offers free legal advice or tips on résumé writing, or you offer your community room for a local book group to meet. Or maybe there's a local agency that provides support at your library unofficially. There are myriad ways libraries partner—some that require little time or funds from the library, others that require more, and some that are initiated by libraries and are, as the authors point out, definitely hard work.

If you have already created relationships like these, you probably know more than you realize about how to forge a partnership. Perhaps it started with a chance conversation with a local organization—they were looking for a room to hold their monthly staff meetings and you have the space.

For instance, a local organization that is comprised of people with a range of disabilities was looking for an accessible meeting place in a small town in California. The public library there has a large meeting room that is wheelchair accessible and large enough so people using wheelchairs can form a circle as they engage in conversation. You may not think of this as a partnership—after all, the library only provided the space—but this definitely worked to the advantage of both the group and the library.

For the library, the group brought in people who might not have normally visited or realized it was so accessible. The group caught the attention of community members and brought in new members. And this simple beginning could lead to presentations about accessibility for all library users or recommendations from the group for expanded accessibility or collection development suggestions. If a library staff person attended one of the group's meetings, they could hear about the challenges being encountered and talk about ways the library could play a larger role.

This last point is perhaps one of the most imperative in partnerships or in considering partnerships: actively listening to your community and thinking about ways the library could play a role in the work they do or the challenges they face.

One way to listen to your community is by encouraging your staff to be involved in local boards and committees that are addressing social issues like homelessness. Library director Todd Stephens from Spartanburg Public Library in South Carolina encourages his library staff to "serve on local nonprofit boards, homeless shelters, and other human service agencies. Spartanburg staff are now on 36 nonprofit boards" (Lynch, n.d.).

Of course, if your library is in a rural area or smaller town, there may not be 36 nonprofit boards or even 10. But it is worth looking at who is doing the human services work in your area to see how a staff member of the library could be involved. As we've discussed, rural homelessness can look quite different from urban or even suburban homelessness. You may have to be creative about volunteering and creating connections. Find out who is serving families, youth, and individuals who are experiencing homelessness. Does the school have a McKinney-Vento (see Glossary in Appendix A) person you can talk to? Is there a group serving veterans? Is there a YMCA? A Rotary club? Maybe a local clinic or hospital? How about the faith community? Many churches, synagogues, and mosques are already involved in supporting their congregants who are experiencing homelessness.

For example, the Tennessee Valley Unitarian Universalist Church (TVUUC) in Knoxville, Tennessee, works with more than 20 other local churches to take turns delivering bags of food and other household items (like soap and toilet paper) to families in the area (TVUUC, n.d.). One year a local PhD student from the University of Tennessee library school provided children's books to go along with the food bags. Maybe a staff member from the library could be present at a local food pantry, to talk about the library, to hand out donated books, to make connections with families who may not be comfortable using a library.

FoodBanks.net (n.d.) is one place where you can find out if there's a local food bank.

Other potential partners for libraries include:

- The local adult LGBGTQ+ community.
- Local government and citizen groups, such as:
  ○ Kiwanis
  ○ Rotary Club
  ○ Red Cross
  ○ Planned Parenthood
  ○ City government groups
- Local advocacy groups.
  ○ NAACP
  ○ ACLU
  ○ League of Women Voters
  ○ Groups addressing reintegration of people who were incarcerated
- The faith community.
- Schools/universities/colleges/adult schools.
- Senior groups/centers.
- Legal aid agencies.
- Local clinics.

There are many, many examples of partnerships related to homelessness. Chapter 6 offers in-depth examples of what libraries are doing, so in this chapter we've only included one—a partnership between a public library and an emergency shelter for transitional aged youth (ages 12–24).

Partnership Example

The young adult librarian from the local library, in tandem with a local librarian volunteer, maintains a small library at the shelter, as well as providing an opportunity for the youth to clear their library records and obtain a library card, using the shelter as their address. The two librarians try to visit during the community meetings held at the shelter, because these meetings offer an opportunity for them to introduce themselves, as well as to hear the challenges being experienced by the youth.

One evening the youth were talking about a job flyer they had received the previous day. The online applications were due the following day, and they had no ready access to Internet computers. The two librarians discussed this quietly, and the YA librarian offered to reserve a bank of computers at her library, so the youth could have the time to fill out the applications and technology support from library staff if needed. This small act meant 10 youth were able to successfully fill out job applications. It also meant the staff at the shelter became aware of the possibilities embedded in partnering with the library. Staff at the library realized addressing youth homelessness didn't have to be a huge action—they could start with something simple, which wouldn't require extra funds.

Many of the youth were already spending time at the library during the day—to get out of the constant public gaze, to be warm or dry or cool, to use the resources. But they were reluctant to reach out to library staff for many reasons: They didn't want to draw attention to their housing situation, they weren't sure they would be treated with respect, they were afraid they would be kicked out. This simple one-day program let them know the library supported them and cared and could make a difference in their quest to find jobs, housing, educational opportunities, health-related resources, and more.

As you consider partnerships, think about what your library has to offer and make a list. This list of "assets" will help you realize the potential your library has for contributing to the work that's being done in your community. Some examples include:

- Meeting rooms.
- Public restrooms (and possibly all-genders restrooms).
- Comfortable seating.
- Resources (print, electronic).

- Internet computers.
- Subject expertise.
- Local connections/partnerships you have already created.
- Programs/webinars/trainings.
- Reading materials.
- A supportive community.
- Location—Are you centrally located? Is there public transit?
- Accessibility for people with disabilities or mobility challenges.
- Familiarity for people who are comfortable using libraries.
- Nonjudgmental: Ideally libraries treat everyone equitably and without judgment.
- Library staff who are knowledgeable, helpful, and excited about partnering.
- What else? What are services, resources, and assets your library can provide in a partnership?

Creating a list like this can help you when you reach out to potential partners.

Smaller Libraries

As we've discussed, if your library is in a rural area or if you have a smaller library, your list of assets may be a little shorter. For example, you may not have a separate meeting room, or there may not be public transit for potential library users to access your library easily. But this doesn't mean there aren't possibilities for partnerships. For instance, your library has computers, informed and concerned staff, access to resources, a safe space, bathrooms, community, and probably state or even national connections, subject expertise, and more. Smaller and rural libraries may have to be more creative about their partnerships, but that doesn't mean they can't create them. In fact, if you're in a small/rural library, you are probably already doing that.

Reaching Out

Once you have decided you'd like to address some aspect of homelessness and that reaching out is the next step, how do you do that? There are some specific steps you can take, depending of course on which partner you have chosen.

The first step is to ask yourself: Why this partner? How did you decide? What does my library have to offer them? How would their work contribute to the library?

For example, maybe you've noticed that the staff at your library are concerned about having to interact with people who appear to have a mental health challenge that is untreated or undertreated. These library users may talk quietly to themselves or be reluctant to engage in conversations with library staff. They may seem socially uncomfortable and are not behaving like library users are expected to behave. You'd like to see these staff members—and, in fact, all staff members—receive support. One idea you have is to reach out to a local mental health organization. Maybe they could offer an in-service function for staff that would provide information, role playing, opportunities for discussions, and shared experiences. Library staff is enthusiastic about this idea and administration is supportive, as long as it doesn't require funds, which are tight right now.

Second: How are you going to approach this organization? Should you call? E-mail? Make an appointment? Simply show up?

Of course, there's no correct answer for this question, since it depends on the organization, your time, and their time. If you already have a connection, then that would be a great place to start. If not, calling is more personal than an e-mail. Inviting them to come to the library for a tour and a conversation could also work well. If they are already in your library, perhaps using it informally—that's an excellent opportunity to reach out in person.

Another possibility is to reach out to them through partnerships you already have. Social service agencies and other community-support agencies tend to have many connections and partnerships already. For instance, maybe you've been working with the local YMCA, and they already have a connection to a community mental health organization. Could someone at the YMCA introduce you to a staff member at the mental health organization?

One thought to keep in mind is the need to *persist*. Unless they clearly express that they're not interested, don't be discouraged or put off if there is no response to your initial inquiries, however you reach out. People are busy, and the stereotype of a library not being relevant to their work can create a reluctance to take the time to respond. Persistence means that in a polite and friendly way you don't give up. If one method doesn't work, you try another.

Maybe you personally know someone who has connections at an agency or organization you'd like to contact. Could they provide an introduction? People who work in social services, public health, and other direct service organizations are likely to be as busy as you are at the library. They may not see the value of working with a library, so you may need to convince them.

So a second suggestion is: *Be prepared.* Be prepared to answer questions, to be clear about what you're looking for, to state what the library can offer, to share what you know about them. Maybe this organization would like more visibility in the community—a library could help with that. Maybe they'd like more opportunities to engage with community members—a library could help with that. Maybe they'd simply like to provide trainings to more people—training library staff would help with that, and also staff could recommend their trainings. Local organizations like this and libraries have the same goals: to support people as they pursue their own goals and help them navigate any barriers.

Once you've made contact, if possible, arrange a face-to-face meeting with someone from your potential partner organization/agency. Share your mission and vision statements with them, and tell them why the library is interested in partnering with them. Offer some examples of what the library would bring to a partnership, and provide examples of partnerships you've had or ones other libraries have had. Ask them to talk about their mission statements, their goals, and their needs. Be prepared to tell them what you've learned about them and why you think they would be a good partner for the library. Leave with a concrete task for each of you and an appointment to talk again. Follow up the meeting with a brief e-mail or personal note, to thank them for their time, and tell them you're looking forward to working together.

A partnership takes time to develop, so this means you'll also need *patience.* But know that it's well worth the time—your unhoused community members, your staff, your library, your community, and your partner will all benefit.

Partnerships as a Marketing Strategy

One of the aspects of partnerships we don't talk about enough is their role as part of our marketing. Marketing our libraries is one of our biggest challenges, because of the persistence of the stereotype of what a library does. When we partner, we not only create meaningful relationships, we also introduce our partners to the concept of what we actually do and our interest in supporting the community. When we create partnerships, we create a natural word-of-mouth campaign that offsets common misconceptions about libraries.

In addition, if we are working with an agency or organization for an event, for example, flyers and other kinds of notices will be distributed not only by the library, but also by the agency—so we increase our visibility and the interest in who we are and how we are invested in meeting the needs of our community members.

Funding

The funding you will require for working with your partners on homelessness in the community will depend on what you'll be doing. If you're going to provide storytimes at a local shelter for families with children, the investment will be mainly of staff time. If you also want to provide free new books to shelter residents, you may find that a small grant from a local chain store, like Dollar General, will cover the cost. You could also reach out to local bookstores for donations and even for advanced reading copies (ARCs).

Larger projects, like creating a social worker program at your library, will require regular and reliable funds. For example, the Denver Public Library (Colorado) started their social worker program with funds from the city of Denver, because the library and the city shared the goal of addressing homelessness. With the initial success of the program, it was later expanded and made permanent (IFLA, 2017). The Elmhurst (IL) Public Library social worker program is funded through the city library budget, while the Toronto (Canada) Public Library started their program with a smaller temporary budget funded by the library foundation. Their program is now part of the library operating budget.

Examples of where to obtain funds include:

- The library's budget.
- The city's budget.
- Social service agencies.
- A special grant from a private foundation.
- A special grant from a city, state, or national government agency.
- Contributions from local community NGOs (nongovernmental organizations) or agencies—for example, the United Way.
- Funds from a library support group, such as the Friends group or a library foundation (IFLA, 2017).
- IMLS/LSTA grants.
- Grants from state library associations.
- Working with the local business community.
- Working with a national business organization.

Applying for grants with partners will increase the possibilities for the kinds of grants you can apply for and also your chances of receiving the grants. Don't forget about in-kind support as well—this kind of support may be easier to obtain and could also bring in other partners. For instance, if you need to make copies of flyers, posters, or banners, reaching out to a local graphic artist, copy shop, or sign shop can not only help you, but can also bring awareness to these local businesses. Maybe you'd like to regularly provide a social worker or health worker in the library, but you don't have the funds. Hosting a public health or social work intern by partnering with a local university or school can help both of you without needing additional funds.

Staff Training

Another vital component of addressing homelessness in your library is staff training. We've already talked about one example of staff training—partnering with a local service agency to provide support and information about mental health challenges, including some tips on how to interact in a respectful and supportive way.

There are numerous possible topics for staff trainings, but it would be helpful for you to have an idea of the kinds of questions library staff would like to have answered. What are their biggest concerns? What would make them more comfortable? What would they like to know? Appendix C has examples of a survey you can use for library staff, so you can be sure to address their questions and concerns, as well as providing information they may not have considered asking.

Another aspect of staff training to consider is the inclusion of professionals, such as social workers, public health workers, McKinney-Vento liaisons, shelter managers, representatives from the faith community who are working with their unhoused congregation members, police officers, community service officers, EMTs, clinic workers, volunteers, and library staff from other libraries who have created programming. In addition, including people with the lived experience of homelessness can have a huge impact on both the library staff and the speakers, by creating connections and addressing the built-in power imbalance between staff members and unhoused library users.

Example of Staff Training

An example of a staff training related to libraries and homelessness was the staff training offered by the National Network of Libraries of Medicine New England Region (NNLM NER) to staff at the Bangor (Maine) Public Library. The training included a representative from the local public health agency, staff members from a local youth shelter, and a professor of psychology from the University of Southern Maine. After presentations, everyone got together for "brainstorming" sessions. As reported by one attendee, Margo M.:

Participants examined ways in which the library could support Shaw House and Hope House, as well as how these organizations could support the library. Outreach staff from Shaw House offered to stop into the library to check on high-energy youth. They encouraged library staff to contact them before situations escalated to the 911 level. Library staff offered to schedule the computer lab for Hope House. Hope House staff would have dedicated time and space to help those needing to fill out applications for housing and jobs.

Throughout the training, I heard staff from Bangor Public Library, Shaw House and Hope House say "I didn't know that you did that!" From my vantage point, I saw the power inherent in bringing everyone together. I was gratified that funding from NNLM NER supported a starting point for future collaboration. (M., 2018)

These kinds of opportunities—to get to know each other, to share concerns and offer suggestions, to think creatively about how to work together—are the positive and powerful outcomes of investigating and creating partnerships.

An outstanding illustration of hearing from those with the lived experience of homelessness were the "walking tours" at the "Coming Up Together" conference on youth homelessness held at the University of Ottawa, Canada. As part of the conference, attendees could sign up for youth-led walking tours given by youth who had experienced homelessness in Ottawa (Coming Up Together, 2018). Each tour was led by a different young person, so the tours were personal and individual. The group the author attended included:

- Learning how to be hit by a car (tip: jump onto the hood if you think you're going to be hit).
- The best places to ask for money (tip: not too close to a bank entrance, but not too far away either).
- The long list of the way public space has been criminalized and how to cope with that (sitting, lying down, asking for money, and camping are all illegal).

The leader of one group, Charlotte, commented on her involvement in this conference and the walking tours:

I never thought something that caused me so much trauma would lead to something so beautiful. Working with youth as a Peer Researcher (peer first and researcher second, as I like to say) has allowed me to transform my past experiences of youth homelessness into tools for public awareness, community building and more. (Personal communication, Charlotte E. Smith, 2020)

Hearing from people like Charlotte who are able to talk about the experience of homelessness can provide personal insights that help library staff create programs and resources that are relevant.

Other possible topics for staff training include:

- Trauma-informed care: what it is, what it looks like in the library.
- Vocabulary and language related to homelessness and poverty.
- Creative programming inside and outside of the library that is related to serving community members who are experiencing homelessness.
- Step-by-step tips for creating partnerships.
- Compassion fatigue/burnout: What is it? How do you recognize it? What helps?
- In-depth and accurate information about homelessness, including its definition, its causes, its impact, and life on the streets. This would also include addressing common stereotypes/myths about people experiencing homelessness. For example, an unhoused person is much more likely to be a survivor of violence than a perpetrator.
- What is respectful language and how to use it.
- De-escalation techniques.
- Common triggers and how to avoid them. For instance, if you have security guards at your library, explore whether they could wear street clothes rather than uniforms, which can be triggering for unhoused people, expecially youth.
- Training on using naloxone (Narcan).
- Looking at rules/policies/procedures, with input from both library staff and unhoused community members.
- How to get the word out about what the library is doing.

Library staff will probably have other concerns they would like to see addressed, so using a survey like the one in Appendix C can help ensure the library provides training that is relevant and of interest.

CONCLUSION

In Chapter 5 we have looked at creating partnerships, where to find funding, and what staff training looks like. In Chapter 6, we look at many examples of programs and partnerships libraries have created.

REFERENCES

Cole, R. (2020, January 24). A homelessness: A challenge we can only solve together. *City of Santa Monica.* https://www.santamonica.gov/blog/Rick -Homelessness-a-challenge-we-can-only-solve-together

Coming Up Together. (2018). *Coming up together: Conference 2018.* http://www .coming-up-together.ca

FoodBanks.net. (n.d.). *Find a food bank.* https://www.foodbanks.net

IFLA. (2017). *IFLA guidelines for library services to people experiencing homelessness.* IFLA Library Services to People with Special Needs. https://www.ifla.org/publications/node/12642

Lynch, J. (n.d.). Spartanburg Public Library, homeless patrons, and the golden rule. *TechSoup for Libraries.* https://www.techsoupforlibraries.org/spotlight/spartanburg-library-homeless-patrons-and-the-golden-rule

M., M. (2018, December 8). Focused outreach to Bangor (ME) Public Library. *NNLM NER.* https://news.nnlm.gov/ner/2018/12/08/focused-outreach-to-bangor-me-public-library

Stricker, M. (n.d.). Building effective and innovative partnerships. *New Jersey State Library and LibraryWorks.com.* http://www.libraryspot.net/Webinars/BuildingEffectiveandInnovativePartnerships.zip

Tennessee Valley Unitarian Universalist Church (TVUUC). (n.d.). *Calendar.* http://tvuuc.org/calendar

Wardrobe for Opportunity. (n.d.). https://www.wardrobe.org

Wildridge, V., Childs, S., Cawthra, L., & Madge, B. (2004). How to create successful partnerships—a review of the literature. *Health Information and Libraries Journal, 21,* 3–19. https://onlinelibrary.wiley.com/doi/full/10.1111/j.1740-3324.2004.00497.x

6

Traditional and New Programs and Services

INTRODUCTION

In Chapter 6, we look at traditional and new library programs and services that address homelessness in all its many aspects. We will discuss both short-term and long-term actions, because both of these can be useful as you decide what works best for your community and library.

Because homelessness is an intersectional social issue, there are a large range of opportunities for programs, depending on which aspect of homelessness you'd like to address. This may be your first foray into including the library in the caring community around those experiencing homelessness, in which case you may want to start with a short-term action. Maybe you've created smaller projects already, and you'd like to move forward with a larger one. Either way, there is always an action your library can take, and I hope the following examples will provide some ideas for you. I also want to stress that people who are unhoused don't only need to meet their basic survival needs. In addition, they should be encouraged to be part of the larger community, where they are listened to, where they can share their experiences, ideas, thoughts, and suggestions. None of us want to be reduced to simply being defined by our housing status or any other relevant descriptors. We are all complex human beings, no matter where we lay our heads at night.

SHORT-TERM ACTIONS

Short-term actions include:

- One-time events.
- A series of events with an end date.

- Actions that are small and may not continue.
- Actions that address immediate needs.

Short-term actions can be an excellent way to start addressing some aspect of homelessness without a large commitment of staff time or funds. They can also lead to long-term actions, through connections that are created or because of positive reactions to the program or action.

EXAMPLES OF SHORT-TERM ACTIONS

What is a short-term action your library could take? This could be an action initiated by a local organization that invites the library to be involved. It could be an action that evolves naturally as you are discussing ways to address challenges in your library or your community.

A good example of a short-term action is involving your library in the HUD point-in-time (PIT) count. One way to be a part of this count is to start by hosting trainings and drop-off points for related donations, like "socks, blankets, hygiene kits, first aid kits, hand warmers, packaged food, and/or bottled water" (Branch, 2020). For the PIT count in 2020, the **Pierce County and Tacoma County Public Libraries** (in Washington) were both training and drop-off sites for this critical count, which provides statistics on who is experiencing homelessness so appropriate funds can be allocated. (There's more about the PIT count in Chapter 1.)

Some branches of the **San Diego County Library** in California were the sites for the actual interviews for the count. Dolores Diaz, the executive director of the Regional Task Force for the Homeless, approached the library. Knowing that many local unhoused community members spent time at the library, a partnership with them made sense to her (Warth, 2015).

These two examples give you an idea of the range of ways your library could be involved in the PIT count. They also offer ways you can create positive connections to people experiencing homelessness, as well as local agencies. In an online survey of public and academic libraries, out of the 816 respondents, 95 libraries were involved in the PIT count (Bales & Winkelstein, 2018).

EMERGENCY/UNPREDICTABLE SITUATIONS

As mentioned in Chapter 1, this book is being written during what will probably be called the "2020–2021 Pandemic," although as of this writing, we can only hope it is over by the end of 2021.

Dealing with both the impact of the pandemic on the daily operations of a library and the housed community, most libraries have yet to take on how they can address the pressing needs of their unhoused community members. In a brief one-question survey on library listservs, prompt responses included the main step libraries are taking to address the needs of their entire communities is to keep their wi-fi on 24 hours a day. One library provides a protected outdoor space where people can use their devices, but with a physical distance requirement in many places of at least 6 feet, this space won't accommodate many people.

Two libraries are lending out their laptops to a few users, for use in their parking lots, and this will make a significant difference to those who don't have a device (personal communication, 2020). Across the country in rural or smaller communities:

> Some libraries are setting up technology labs in homeless shelters or are loaning out laptops and Wi-Fi hotspots to shelters so guests have access to technology and internet. Libraries that have bookmobiles or mobile libraries with Wi-Fi capabilities are setting up in central locations in the community so individuals can connect to wireless networks. (Personal communication, 2020)

Another library offered this response:

> For those without Internet or phone access, we are doing the old-fashioned messaging way of posting on the front door of the Library, daily updates from the City re. COVID-19 as well as posting information on local shelters and food banks. This helps not only those unhoused but also seniors and others that don't have access to phones/Internet. . . . We are also offering phone/email/chat services 60 hours/week and people can request items to be checked out. We pull the item(s) (up to 5), check items out with a valid library card and set outside to be picked up by appointment only. (Personal communication, 2020)

A specific example of a bookmobile acting as a wireless hub during the pandemic was the **Rockingham County Public Library** (North Carolina) bookmobile, which set up in Walmart parking lots to "provide wireless access for anyone with a device," from 9 a.m. to 3 p.m. on specific dates. The bookmobile only provided wi-fi and was "not open for public entry" (Rockingham Now, 2020).

Another short-term activity by libraries during the COVID-19 pandemic was using their 3-D printers to make personal protective equipment (PPE). Across the country, library staff took home the printers and made face shields and other parts, such as ear hooks, bands for face shields, and adjustable straps (Lissau, 2020). In fact, according to a Public Library Association (PLA) survey of more than 2,500 library systems, asking about the impact of COVID-19 on their libraries, PLA found that 12% were "using makerspace equipment to create medical supplies" (Public Library Association, 2020).

By the time this book is published, there may well be other ways in which libraries are taking on this challenge.

One specific suggestion for an action that libraries could take during a national emergency like the 2020–2021 COVID-19 pandemic is to reach out to a local organization that works with people experiencing homelessness, ask them what they need, and then let the housed community know what the needs are and how to help. Most if not all public libraries are staying in touch virtually with their library card holders, as well as providing information on their websites. Adding information and a link to positive concrete action community members could take will not only provide much-needed resources to agencies and organizations, but would also highlight the importance of taking care of all of our community members.

In addition, the library itself may be able to fill some of those needs. For instance, lending a laptop or tablet to a shelter along with a wi-fi hot spot. An excellent example of this kind of supportive partnership is the Nordstrom "Working Together in Our Communities" blog posting. As they state: "These are uncertain times and we hope you and your loved ones are all staying well. . . . During this challenging moment in time, we are looking at unique ways to help in our communities and highlighting how others can join together to make a difference" (Nordstrom, 2020). They include direct links to various partners, such as YouthCare and the Hetrick Martin Institute, both of which work with unhoused or marginally housed youth. The partners have lists of needed items, which makes it easy for those who can afford to help.

In response to the pandemic, organizations held webinars specifically for service providers and others who are addressing homelessness in their communities. For example, the National Alliance to End Homelessness (NAEH) provided a webinar series called the "NAEH COVID-19 Webinar Series," which included webinars like "Protocols for Addressing Sheltered and Unsheltered Homelessness" and "Serving and Supporting Unsheltered People During COVID-19" (NAEH, 2020a, 2020b).

Point Source Youth, an organization dedicated to ending youth homelessness, also provided a series of 15 webinars, "Free COVID-19 Weekly Webinars" (Point Source Youth, 2020). The first one, "The Impact of COVID-19 on the Youth Homelessness Crisis," included a panel of three speakers: Emily Mosites, from the CDC (Centers for Disease Control and Prevention), Jeff Schlegelmilch, deputy director for the National Center for Disaster Preparedness, and Charles G. Prober, professor of pediatrics at Stanford University. Attendees represented various agencies from across the United States.

The webinar provided insights into the challenges service providers are encountering and ideas for what to do. Some of the points that were made could apply directly to libraries:

- Use the term "physical distancing" rather than "social distancing," to encourage people to maintain social connections, which are crucial during a crisis and particularly important for community members experiencing homelessness.

- Ask the youth for suggestions on what needs to be done and how to do it, especially using the online environment.

- Be the voice for those who are needing support but aren't being listened to.

- Provide portable handwashing stations and even portable toilets if possible (Point Source Youth, 2020)

One example is a library/community center that was closed during this time, so they provided a portable toilet and handwashing station. This simple act makes a huge difference to the community of people who had previously been using the toilets and sinks in the building.

Figure 6.1 is a photograph of a portable toilet and handwashing station in the parking lot of the Albany (California) Community Center and Library. This setup serves not only those who are unhoused, but also any

Figure 6.1   Portable toilet and handwashing station in the parking lot of the Albany California Library and Community Center.

community member who needs either a toilet or a place to wash their hands.

Attending webinars and presentations like this are ideal opportunities for libraries to learn more and also to make their presence and interest known.

One topic that came up again and again during the pandemic was concern about how people who were unhoused, living in rural area, or experiencing poverty could access the Internet without a device or without wi-fi or both. Because schools as well as libraries were all closed, learning and connections were created online, which automatically impacted students who have limited or no access and who also may be helping their families. As one school librarian, Martina Martinez Siegert, posted:

> I think one of the things that concerns me so much as a school librarian is the elitist idea that everybody has Internet access or devices to participate in e-learning, remote learning or virtual learning. Or even the time. We have some students who are taking care of their younger siblings because their parents are working still or working from home. We have families whose only internet access is their phones data plan. We have families in rural areas that have no internet access and devices might be limited depending on the needs of the family. And, yes, there are some programs out there for free internet access, but there are some serious flaws with these programs. Our lower- and middle-class working families who are on a tight budget, or even a tighter budget now, can't afford the Internet or the larger phone data plan at the moment. (YALSA, 2020)

This school librarian's post and the many other comments posted during webinars drew attention to the already fragile state of those who do not have digital equity for numerous reasons. During this pandemic, it was as if the lid was removed from a pot of concerns, inequities and oppression that are historic and impactful. In this case, putting public school classes online widened the digital gap, besides taking away access to free breakfasts and lunches, opportunities to shower, social connections, quiet and safe places to study, and all the other ways public libraries and schools address homelessness and poverty.

Although many libraries and schools did their best, the result was on the whole a large number of people, including unaccompanied youth, families with children, survivors of domestic abuse, people with disabilities, veterans, the LGBGTQ+ community, and communities of color, were put at an even greater disadvantage. As we've discussed, there are many factors that lead to homelessness, and those very factors are at play during emergencies like this pandemic.

A sobering example of this was the higher rate of death among communities of color during this time. As Scott (2020) described in his

Washington Post article, "4 Reasons Coronavirus Is Hitting Black Communities So Hard," reasons for the disproportionate impact include:

- Higher rates of underlying health conditions, and less access to care—this is historically true, with health disparities, more hospital closures, and worse quality of health care.

- Black Americans hold a lot of "essential jobs"—which put them in harm's way during the pandemic.

- Insufficient information, including "bad and inconsistent information" from state and local governments.

- Housing disparities—unhealthy, older buildings "that harbor fecal matter and rodent infestations," community members living in "densely packed areas," which increases "the risk and prevalence of respiratory and pulmonary diseases." (Scott, 2020)

In his article, Scott cites an analysis of early data done by the *Washington Post* that found that "majority black counties have three times the rate of infections and nearly six times the rate of deaths as majority white counties" (Scott, 2020).

As discussed in Chapter 1, this kind of inequality of impact is reflected in statistics related to homelessness as well. As we address homelessness, we must remain aware of the historical and current racism that affects the health of our communities.

VOTER REGISTRATION AND VOTING

"The cornerstone of our democracy in the United States of America is the right of citizens to make their wishes known through the election process, yet low income voters, and particularly persons experiencing homelessness, are consistently one of the most poorly represented blocks when it comes to voter turnout, historically having faced numerous barriers across the country which have limited their participation in the election process. Many potential homeless and low income voters may not have the appropriate identification documents required by some states to register or to vote. Furthermore, individuals who are experiencing homelessness may lack the resources to educate themselves about candidates or may not be able to get to the polls on Election Day. Many individuals, homeless or otherwise, aren't even aware that no state requires residents to have a traditional residence in order to vote in elections" (Hustings et al., 2018).

Making sure everyone, no matter their housing status, registers to vote and is able to vote is a short-term action that can have long-term ramifications. In the United States, there are many state and national organizations that help people register to vote and actually vote.

One of the simplest ways for a library to be involved is to provide paper registration forms, as well as an online link for online registration. Some libraries also offer a place to drop off registration forms, as well as mail-in ballots. For instance, **Sacramento Public Library** (California) began serving as a place to drop off ballots in 2014 and as of 2020 has added 11 voter service centers where voters can register, change their address, and perform other tasks related to voting (personal communication, 2020). All of this is related to registration and voting, no matter a person's housing status.

But what about people who want to vote and don't have a permanent address? Can they register? Can they vote? This is the kind of information you can provide to your unhoused community members, to make sure they are informed and supported so they can participate in elections.

Here are some basic facts about voting and homelessness:

- According to Nonprofit Vote, "persons experiencing homelessness can register and vote in all 50 states" (Nonprofit Vote, n.d.).
- For an address: If possible, people should use a shelter address or somewhere they can receive mail. However, "homeless registrants may denote a street corner or a park as their residence, in lieu of a traditional home address. The federal voter registration form and many state forms provide a space for this purpose" (Nonprofit Vote, n.d.).
- The "You Don't Need a Home to Vote" campaign from the National Coalition for the Homeless (NCH) provides a manual to help individuals and organizations ensure housing status isn't a barrier to voting. This manual is invaluable for libraries who want to gain an understanding of the barriers for voters who are unhoused and suggestions on how to lower or remove these barriers (Hustings et al., 2018).
- The introduction (quoted above) provides insights into what libraries could do:
  - Help unhoused voters get the necessary IDs, by partnering with an organization such as VoteRiders (2020), which educates people on state requirements for IDs and helps people afford IDs.
  - Help unhoused community members gain access to required documents, by providing information and connections.
  - Provide educational resources about local, state, and national elections and make sure they are accessible to all community members.

○ Work with local organizations, such as the League of Women voters and other volunteer organizations, to find or fund transportation to the polls.

○ Help address the need for an address to receive a vote-by-mail ballot. Could you offer your library's address? Could you find a local partner who could help with this? Can unhoused community members pick up mail at the local post office or a local business? This is the kind of information your unhoused voters need to know.

○ If your library provides services to local jails or juvenile detention centers, in some states inmates can register to vote while incarcerated. A good example of this is the "Voting in California Jails: A Community Toolkit" (Let Me Vote, 2020). Library staff in these institutions can provide accurate voter registration information, as well as online registration forms. They can also reach out to potential partners, such as the public defender's office or a social services agency.

In our efforts to address the immediate necessities of community members experiencing homelessness, it can be easy to forget other aspects of people's needs. Voting offers the opportunity to make positive and meaningful changes, as well as the social inclusion that comes with being a part of our democracy. Although there may be the misapprehension that people who are unhoused aren't interested in voting, this isn't true. As they say in the NCH manual:

> Low income people are no more or less interested in politics than anyone else. Please don't let your attitude be a barrier. Our clients are often disconnected from community life. Voting helps them reconnect with their community in a positive way. (Hustings et al., 2018)

Many of the so-called quality-of-life laws in communities are created through local elections. These laws impact many unhoused community members directly. Everyone needs to have a say in the creation of these laws, including those who are most affected.

In the recommended resources, you'll find a short list of organizations dedicated to making sure everyone who qualifies to vote is able to do that.

Another useful resource is the GODORT libguide: "The Voting and Election Toolkits" (GODORT, n.d.). Again, this resource isn't designed specifically for unhoused community members, but the information applies to all of us, housed or unhoused. This toolkit includes a wide range of resources divided into sections. These are:

• Hotlines.

• Voter Registration & Election Day Resources.

- Population-Specific Information & Resources.
- Voting Rights: Laws, Cases, Policy.
- Voter Engagement.
- Voter Education.
- Campaign Finance/Funding Information.
- Primary Sources, Lesson Plans, & Exhibits.

Resources like these make it easier for libraries to help all their library users participate in voting.

HUMAN/LIVING LIBRARY

Creating a Human Library is a great and low-cost way to provide space and listeners for community members who are experiencing homelessness. The Human Library concept was initiated in Denmark in 2000 in response to hate-based violence. The basic idea is that the library is made up of people instead of books, and it offers "readers" a chance to talk directly with someone who represents a stereotype or bias the reader may hold. As they say on their website: "Every human book from our bookshelf, represent (sic) a group in our society that is often subjected to prejudice, stigmatization or discrimination because of their lifestyle, diagnosis, belief, disability, social status, ethnic origin etc." (Human Library, n.d.).

Sturgeon (2017) describes a human or living library held at the **Fredericton Public Library** (New Brunswick, Canada) where the human books were unhoused community members. Interviews with two of the human books highlight the importance of allowing unhoused people to share their stories and lives with housed community members.

A human library requires careful planning, but the rewards are great. The author has helped plan two human libraries, and both were enthusiastically received by both the books and the readers. The Human Library website offers guidance on creating such a library, and there are also related resources, including links to webinars, on the WebJunction website (Peterson, 2016).

As described in Chapter 1, homelessness among people who were previously incarcerated is unfortunately all too common. The "JustUS Voices Living Library" hosted five formerly incarcerated women who could be "checked-out" by attendees. This kind of event can help connect community members who may not normally be connected and can break down stereotypes and stigma about incarceration (A New Way of Life Reentry Project, 2017). Holding a Living Library like this at your library would be a great way to bring community members together and provide insights into the challenges of coming out of incarceration.

RESOURCE FAIRS AT THE LIBRARY

Across the United States, libraries are hosting resource fairs that focus on services for people experiencing homelessness. For example, the **Danville Public Library** in Danville, Illinois, hosts a get-together of local resource organizations and people experiencing homelessness. The event, started in 2016, is called "Project Uplift," and the goal is to "connect homeless, or home insecure, persons and families and those who love them with information and resources within the Danville community" (Bailey, 2020). In 2020, they had about 20 organizations involved and besides the resources, they provide a meal, gift bags, door prizes, and a musical presentation by library staff (Bailey, 2020).

In May 2019, the City of San Diego held a Mental Health Resource Fair at the **San Diego Central Library**. This 9-hour-long fair featured information from San Diego area health care and mental health organizations. The daylong program schedule included:

- CalFresh Workshop.
- Meditation.
- Reptile petting and art program.
- "Check your mood" screenings.
- Suicide prevention training.
- A choir performance.

The list of partners for this event is impressive and an outstanding example of the variety of partners that can work together with the library. Included in the list of partners were:

Community Health Improvement Partners (CHIP).
County of San Diego Behavioral Health Services.
Courage to Call.
ECS Friend to Friend Program.
Family Resource Center at Hannah's House.
Father Joe's Villages.
Feeding San Diego.
Hannah's House.
Healthy Adventures.
Homeless Empowerment Through Art & Leadership (HEAL).
LiveWell.
McAllister Institute.
Mental Health Systems.

National Alliance on Mental Illness in San Diego (NAMI San Diego).

Roadmap to Recovery.

San Diego County Health & Human Services.

San Diego Youth Services.

Sharp.

Think Dignity.

2-1-1 San Diego.

UC San Diego Health.

Union of Pan Asian Communities.

Vista Hill: Parentcare—Central.

Volunteers of America (City of San Diego, 2019).

Smaller and rural libraries don't have the opportunity to work with so many partners, but this list can give you an idea of the possibilities for partnerships.

A program that would work well for both smaller and larger libraries would be one like the "Stories and Experiences of Homelessness" held at the **King County Library** (Washington). In partnership with the Homeless Speakers Bureau from Real Change, the library invited people with the lived experience of homelessness to share their stories with the community (King County Library, 2017).

LONG-TERM ACTIONS

Long-term actions are just that—programs that are in place for an extended period of time. These can be weekly get-togethers, regular outreach, specific materials to be checked out, programs that address a particular need, and others. Many of these are provided to the public through community partnerships, an ideal way to increase the library's potential for meeting the needs of their community members, as well as securing funds, such as grants.

EXAMPLES OF LONG-TERM ACTIONS

The Central Branch of the **Sonoma County Library** (California) offered a weekly drop-in art program called "Seen and Heard." This program was held while the library was closed, and it offered community members who were experiencing homelessness an opportunity to create art together. The program was initiated by librarian Rebecca Forth, in an effort to create more personal connections and positive visibility for the local unhoused community. Funded by local and federal grant money, the program drew a range of artists (Taylor, 2014).

As part of their "Programs for People in Need," **Seattle Public Library** (Washington) circulates wi-fi hot spots for people experiencing homelessness. In their online report "Services and Programs for People in Need in 2018," they reported they had 675 wi-fi hot spots that had circulated 8,254 times, with "157 additional Wi-Fi hotspots circulated to residents in tent cities and shelters in 2018" (Seattle Public Library, 2020).

The **Public Library of Cincinnati and Hamilton County** (Ohio) has made "a conscious decision to be welcoming to homeless people," committing themselves to asking: "How can we help your quality of life?" (Rossen, 2019). Besides the usual resources, such as Internet computers, this also includes bringing in social services organizations, free faxing, printing out Greyhound bus tickets, and providing reference services to inmates before they are released from incarceration (May 2019).

The **Denver Public Library** (DPL) (Colorado) has shown an ongoing commitment to addressing homelessness with multiple programs. These programs include:

- The Hard Times Workshop, which is a partnership between the Lighthouse Writer's Workshop and the library. This popular program is for anyone "going through a hard time" and serves both housed and unhoused community members (Pankrat, 2017).

- A partnership with Bayaud Enterprises, a nonprofit organization that helps people find and maintain employment in Denver. Bayaud has a laundry truck that stops at the library several times a month. As they say on their website: "The laundry truck provides free services for those in need. Drop off your laundry and it will be washed, dried, and returned to you the same day" (Bayaud Enterprises, 2020; Pankrat, 2017).

- Coffee Connections: An informal twice-a-month get together of library staff and community members experiencing homelessness. Attendees enjoy "snacks, crafts and games" (Denver Public Library, 2020; Pankrat, 2017). Elissa Hardy, a social worker and community resource manager at DPL, commented on the power of the connections created at these get-togethers:

   A few months ago a customer came up to me and thanked me for having this program. He stated, "Before you all did this I wasn't sure you wanted us here. Now I know we're welcome here." That customer then started engaging with our team and just voluntarily went to a substance treatment program, knowing we're here to support him. (Personal communication, 2020)

- A peer navigator program, in which people with the lived experience of homelessness help people who are currently unhoused. This program is overseen by the social workers at DPL, and the peer navigators help unhoused community members connect with resources for jobs, food, and housing (Henning, 2019).
- Social workers in the library (more about this in the social worker section).

The **Washoe County Library**, in Reno, Nevada, offers a "community court docket," which provides a "less intimidating place for those who have been cited for minor infractions and also reduce recidivism" (Bonaparte, 2020). The community court functions the same way as a regular courtroom, including a prosecutor, a defense attorney and a judge, but in the library, rather than the courthouse. The court is for so-called quality-of-life crimes, which includes many of the infractions people who are experiencing homelessness are cited for, such as asking for money, sitting or lying down on a sidewalk, trespassing, and camping. This is an excellent example of partnering to address an aspect of the lives of those who are experiencing homelessness. As they note in the article:

> Those cited appear to court at the library and complete an assessment. The assessment is to pinpoint what they need help with. 22 providers are there ready to provide them with services. That could be finding housing, getting an ID and medical services.
> They go to court and negotiate a sentence that could involve signing up with programs they offer and community service. No fines or jail time are involved. (Bonaparte, 2020)

This idea of community courts is happening in other city libraries. One of the first was the "Community Court" in Spokane, Washington, which opened its doors at the **Downtown Spokane Public Library** (Washington) on December 8, 2013 (Spokane Public Library, n.d.). As it says on the Spokane Public Library website, the Community Court is:

> A cooperative collaboration that has resulted in low barrier access to social service providers of every variety. The Spokane Municipal Community Court seeks to reduce and properly address quality of life offenses in the downtown area by utilizing a collaborative, problem-solving approach to crime. (Spokane Public Library, n.d.)

This concept is a welcome antidote to the triggering, rigid, and unfriendly nature of the usual court proceedings, as well as an opportunity for unhoused people to have ready access to social services. One of the particular points the Spokane Library website emphasizes is their strong partnerships with local resources. Their list of partnerships includes:

- Health care/insurance.
- SSI/disability assistance.
- Education and job training.
- Clothing.
- Behavioral health.
- Housing.
- ID cards.
- Food.
- Library services.
- Crime victim assistance/advocacy.
- Trauma therapy.
- Veteran programs.
- DSHS assistance.
- Nutrition education.
- Payee assistance.

This impressive list offers insight into the power of partnerships and the range of possibilities as libraries look beyond using public conduct policies and rules to control access. Creating a Community Court at your library or partnering with a Community Court that is held at another location outside of the courthouse means libraries can make a difference as people experiencing homelessness move forward in their lives.

The **Charlotte-Mecklenburg Library** (North Carolina) offers several programs geared particularly toward people experiencing homelessness, as well as programs that address the needs of both unhoused and housed community members. "Write Like You Mean It" is a program for adults, described on their website as:

> Take a creative leap into the unknown. Explore the world of writing with fun prompts, field trips, guest speakers and supportive listeners. This group is open to anyone who enjoys writing. (Charlotte Mecklenburg Library, 2020)

This writing group emphasizes that "everyone is a writer" simply by writing and encourages attendees to write in response to a prompt and then share their writings if they are comfortable doing that. As McGivney (2019) describes the group in her article:

> Conversations and greetings blend accents from New York, Tennessee, India, and Eritrea. Under the table, by attendees' feet, sit the bags they carried in: purses, backpacks, grocery bags, duffels. The type of bag (and

whether the person spent the previous night sleeping on the street, in a shelter, or in a home) and the type of accent (and whether the person was born in this country or on another continent) is irrelevant. Diversity isn't this group's goal; creativity is.

This group is a wonderful example of the writing and/or conversation library groups that bring together folks with different life experiences, varied living situations, and a shared interest in writing and telling their stories. This is the kind of group that helps to break down stereotypes and assumptions and creates community.

Another program at the **Charlotte Mecklenburg Library** (North Carolina) is "Turning Pages," a book discussion group specifically for people who are unhoused or in housing transition. Members of this group discuss a range of titles, chosen by the group, and share conversation, coffee, and snacks (McGivney, 2019).

HELPING PEOPLE TELL THEIR STORIES

With the financial support of an LSTA grant, the **Fresno County Public Library** worked with unhoused community members to create a documentary, *Our Lives*. The interviews were conducted and filmed by the unhoused community members, and then the footage was edited and put together by a partner in the project, the Community Media Access Collaborative (CMAC) (Bentley, 2015). There were two public showings of the film, with surveys following the showings. The surveys showed that 96% of the respondents indicated they were "more likely to make contact and improved their desire and willingness to assist in ending homelessness" (IFLA, 2017).

Another way to tell stories is through photographs or "photovoice." **Humboldt State University** (HSU) (California) created the "Humboldt County Homeless College Student Photovoice Project," led by HSU social work professor Pam Bowers and funded by a $4,091 Humanities for All Quick Grant from California Humanities. This project provided cameras to students who were attending college while experiencing homelessness (Humboldt State University, 2018).

To quote from the HSU website:

Photovoice is an empowerment research strategy first developed in the 1990s by University of Michigan's Caroline C. Wang and Ford Foundation Program Officer Mary Ann Burris, who used it to create and discuss photographs as a catalyst for personal and community change. Since then, many fields such as public health, social work, and education have implemented the process.

Libraries are perfect venues for a photovoice project. For instance, a library could host a photovoice project that provides cameras to community members who are experiencing homelessness, post the photographs in the library, and host a reception where the photographers could discuss their work. This would provide social connections, as well as offering housed community members the opportunity to understand what homelessness looks like in their community.

COFFEE AND CONVERSATION

One of the best-known programs in libraries is the **Dallas Public Library's** (DPL) (Texas) long-running "Coffee and Conversation" program, started in September 2013. This program brings together housed and unhoused community members for discussing a particular topic, engaging in a joint activity, or hosting a guest speaker. On the ALA Public Programming Office's "Programming Librarian" website, Jasmine Africawala from DPL offers a detailed explanation of the program, including tips on advance planning, marketing, budget, day-of-event activity, program execution, and advice. The advice in particular is worth noting here:

- Talk to your customers first and get to know their names, then personally invite them to the first program. This should not be required after the program gets started and word-of-mouth spreads.

- Find the right staff person to lead the program. The staff person should be engaging and usually considered someone "who could talk to anyone" or "the life of the party" in order to keep conversations going and prevent potential awkwardness.

- The program should be set up with coffee and in a comfortable space for people to converse. Conversation is just as integral to the program as the coffee. (Africawala, 2015)

Other libraries that offer similar programs include the **Multnomah County Library** in Oregon, the **DC Public Library**, the **Pima County Public Library** (Arizona), and the **Broward County Library** (Florida). The account of the program at the **Broward County Library**, called "Coffee and Conversation With a Librarian," includes a description that highlights the importance of this kind of programming:

> It offers an opportunity for persons experiencing homelessness and other customers to informally meet with a librarian and social service providers to discuss topics or concerns over a cup of coffee. Coffee and Conversation with a Librarian significantly benefits the community by providing people

experiencing homelessness with a safe, comfortable place they can go to share information and get assistance. It reaches a traditionally underserved population in a non-traditional way by creating a judgement-free, informal atmosphere where everyone is treated equally and with dignity. It fills a gap in community services by working with attendees in both small groups and one-on-one to build trust and help with issues of importance to people experiencing homelessness. (National Association of Counties, n.d.)

A coffee and conversation type of programming has the added benefit of being low cost and adaptable to many kinds of libraries, from urban to suburban to rural. The program at **Pima County Public Library** is called "On the Streets," and as Pima County librarian Kate DeMeester put it: "The best way to build relationships with the people who frequent the library is by talking to them" (Brean, 2019).

Coffee and conversation types of programs also provide an antidote to the power of stereotypes in our society. As mentioned in Chapter 3, in a quote from Walter Lippmann, stereotypes can have a powerful impact on our assumptions (Eberhardt, 2019, p. 219). By creating close relationships through casual conversations, shared meals, discussions, and more, unhoused and housed community members can move past stereotypes of each other and instead create understanding and appreciation.

HEALTH

Health related to homelessness is another topic that is being addressed by libraries. In partnership with the City of Vancouver (Canada), the **Vancouver Public Library Foundation** sponsors an annual "Alley Fair," which includes free meals and health resources for community members experiencing homelessness and poverty (Downtown Eastside Neighborhood House, 2020). The fair "brings together over 35 heath agencies that serve the poor. The fair feeds 1500 people and offers resources directly on the street, tests for AIDS, Hep C, offers haircuts, etc. It is coordinated with community partners" (IFLA, 2017).

Many libraries host health fairs, although they are not necessarily (or usually) geared toward community members who are experiencing homelessness. However, there's no reason you can't include their needs in your health fair, since so many of them overlap. For example, health screenings, such as blood pressure checks, apply to all community members. Supplemental information so all community members are served could include:

• Representatives from local free/low-income clinics that include dental, physical, and mental health.

- Representatives from a government agency that can provide information about applying for health (and other benefits, such as SSI and SNAP) for people with little or no income.
- Healthy eating on the streets.
- Dealing with daily trauma.
- A representative from a social services agency.
- AIDS testing.
- Local free resources for showers and laundry.

As you get to know your unhoused community members, you can also ask them what would be helpful to them. Appendix E includes tips on how to create health fairs or other kinds of fairs.

Another aspect of health and homelessness are mobile youth clinic vans. Examples of these can be found across the United States, including Nevada, Arizona, and California. The Teen Health Van in the San Francisco Bay Area has been in operation since 1996, and it's a project of the Lucile Packard Children's Hospital Stanford's Community Partnership program. Services provided to unstably housed youth by the van team include:

- Comprehensive treatment, including immunizations.
- Complete physical exams.
- Acute illness and injury care.
- Pregnancy tests.
- Pelvic exams.
- Sexually transmitted disease testing and treatment.
- Family planning.
- HIV counseling and testing.
- Health education.
- Social services assessment and assistance.
- Referrals to community partners and agencies.
- Substance abuse counseling and referral.
- Mental health counseling and referral.
- Risk behavior reduction counseling.
- Nutrition counseling. (Stanford Children's Health/Lucile Packard Children's Hospital Stanford, 2016)

However, these vans provide more than simply health care. Because of their precarious, unstable, and traumatic lives, the youth being served are not used to trusting other people. But for the youth who take advantage of the van's resources, medical advice, and treatments, this van has come to feel like a safe and reliable place where they are really seen and appreciated for who they are. As Dr. Seth Ammerman states about the youth: "These kids have strengths. . . . And by focusing on their strengths, it can really make a difference. Because strength builds strength. And success builds success" (Romero, 2016).

Libraries could partner with these health vans, by arranging for the library to be one of the stops for the van health team to provide their services. A good place to start is with the Children's Health Fund website at https://www.childrenshealthfund.org. This website is rich with information about the health of children and teens experiencing homelessness and poverty and includes resources, research, and links to participating programs in various states. For instance, one link takes you to a program in rural North Carolina that provides telemedicine at local schools for children and families without health care (HealthESchools, n.d.). Reaching out to the Children's Health Fund or simply exploring their website could lead to a potential partnership that would broaden their reach and serve your unhoused families with children. Figure 6.2 is a photograph of the Nevada Children's Health Project mobile van.

Figure 6.2   Nevada Children's Health Project mobile van.
(Photograph by Randal Christensen)

OTHER SERVICES FOR UNACCOMPANIED YOUTH

Unaccompanied youth are youth who are unhoused, between the ages of 12 and 24, and unaccompanied by a parent or guardian. These young people are living without the emotional and physical support provided by a home as well as by caring adults, and this affects their lives in myriad ways.

Unhoused youth tend to make an effort to remain invisible, so if they are using your library—and they very likely are doing that—they will probably not let you know their housing status unless you get to know them. And even then, they will probably not use the term "homeless" and in fact, will not respond to efforts to engage them by calling them homeless. So it is up to us, as library staff, to create an environment where youth feel comfortable and safe sharing information about their lives.

There aren't many library programs specifically for this age group, but here are a few examples.

The **Seattle Public Library** (Washington) offered:

- Staff training on LGBTQ+ youth homelessness.
- Weekly drop-in to connect youth with services.
- Queeraoke/Open Mic parties at two branches.
- Safe Space Program—youth who have left home are connected to services.

The **Richland Public Library** (South Carolina) held community forums on youth homelessness. The **Nashville Public Library** (Tennessee) partnered with a local shelter that serves transitional aged youth (TAY) and the **Hennepin County Library** (Minnesota) partners with a local agency that serves TAY. The **Charlotte Mecklenburg Library** (North Carolina) works with a local agency to help youth find temporary shelter so they can attend school (IFLA, 2017).

EMPLOYMENT

Another kind of program offered by libraries to their unhoused (and housed) library users are programs related to finding employment. Libraries offer a range of employment resources, as well as computer assistance, links to job sites, help with writing résumés and applications, Internet access so community members can apply for the jobs, and more. Unhoused community members can take advantage of these resources and letting them know—through personal connections, by sending relevant information to local shelters and social services agencies—will make a difference. One of the barriers to access for those without a permanent address can be the inability to qualify for a library card, which means they can't use a library computer. Some libraries are removing this barrier by offering daily one-time log-ins, allowing people to use a shelter address to get a library card, and offering limited cards, such as the **Berkeley Public Library** (BPL) (California) "Easy Access Card." As explained on the BPL website:

> An Easy Access Library card is available to California residents who have picture ID and who cannot currently provide address verification. Patrons with this type of card may use library Internet computers, in-house laptops, and have full access to all online databases and services. Easy Access cards also allow for the checkout of up to three physical items. Up to three holds may be placed with Easy Access cards. Easy Access cards expire after one year. (Berkeley Public Library, n.d.)

This kind of card helps community members use the library's resources, including the computer for employment searches.

Most libraries have a limit on the amount of time a person can use the Internet computers. Many also use a computer reservation system, so library users can be sure to have access to a computer. Depending on the time limits, these may not be long enough to apply for employment, so libraries that extend the time can make a difference to those seeking employment.

The **Richland County Library** (South Carolina) has created a program, the New Hope grant, to help people experiencing homelessness find jobs. Funded by the United Way, the program "helps people with job applications, learning computer skills, how to finance, and many other things to get them out in the work force" (Jones, 2018).

The **Charlotte Mecklenburg Library** (CML) of North Carolina received $25,000 in LSTA funding to bring the "knowledge, skills, abilities, and resources of the **Job Help Center** (JHC) of the CML to the **Urban Ministry Center** (UMC) of Charlotte, where about 600 homeless or disadvantaged individuals receive services daily" (State Library of North Carolina, 2014). This program was a partnership between CML and UMC, by using the expertise of the JHC to bring computer and job skills classes directly to the people experiencing homelessness, rather than them having to travel to the library, because transportation is frequently challenging for unhoused community members. This kind of program can also create positive relationships between service agencies, the clients they serve, and library staff.

Partnerships with local agencies or organizations can play a key role in addressing employment needs through libraries. For example, as part of their "Education and Employment," Larkin Street Youth Services (LSYS) in San Francisco (California) offers what they call the "Larkin Street Academy" for ages 24 and under. Included in the LSYS Academy services are "[j]ob readiness, college readiness, computer classes, job placement and retention, internships, tutoring, GED tutoring and classes, secondary and post-secondary school enrollment and support, mindfulness, visual and performing arts" (Larkin Street Youth Services, n.d.). They also provide drop-in employment services, which include "Resume and cover letter assistance, mock interviews, job search assistance, career guidance" (Larkin Street Youth Services, n.d.).

Reaching out to an agency like LSYS, letting them know what you offer at your library, and asking how the library could support the work they're doing could lead to a positive relationship and much-needed support for their clients and also potentially fill some gaps for the library, as well.

EDUCATION

Another type of program that can make a difference in the lives of your community members are programs and resources related to education. There are many aspects to education, depending on the unhoused community members' needs. This includes information about:

- Getting a GED.
- Studying for and taking required exams.
- Selecting colleges/universities to apply to.
- Financial aid.
- Collecting the needed documents.
- Filling out applications, including writing essays.
- Having access to an e-mail address.
- Having access to a computer.
- Transportation.
- Letters of recommendation.
- Tutoring.
- Access to textbooks/required readings.
- A quiet, safe, private space to study.

Your library may provide many of these already and so, similar to the employment resources, it's a matter of letting unhoused community members and social services agencies know about your resources and how to access them. This is again a time when local partners can make a difference, by working with them to understand the needs of the clients they serve. Also, reach out to the schools, as well as the community members themselves: Both of these can help inform what you do to help and support educational efforts.

For instance, although it's not specifically geared toward people experiencing homelessness, the **Los Angeles County Library** (California) offers a way to earn an online accredited high school diploma for free. As they write on their website:

> No high school diploma? Get a second chance to finish what you started. You can earn an accredited high school diploma for free online in just 18 months or less through LA County Library and the Career Online High School program. You'll also receive a career certificate and personalized online career coaching. (LA County Library, n.d.)

Creating a program like this and then letting local shelters, social service agencies, and other places where unhoused community members may meet or live could lead to a successful and meaningful partnership.

Another possibility would be to reach out to an organization that is already providing educational support and offer your computers for Internet access and writing, your quiet study rooms, your access to textbooks—whatever support would help with their program. The LSYS mentioned earlier would be a good contact for this as well, since they are covering employment as well as education.

Maybe you already offer a résumé writing or job interview workshop at your library. With their guidance, it could be expanded to include unhoused youth or adults. Or maybe they provide resources and programs but are short on computers. Does your library have a computer lab or a bank of computers that could be reserved regularly to support the work they're doing? Investing time in learning about their work and then approaching them directly could create opportunities for you and your new partner.

HOUSING

Housing is, of course, the biggest challenge for community members who are experiencing homelessness. How can libraries help with housing?

Many libraries already provide resource lists and information about local housing, including lists of local resources. Library staff and social workers in libraries also include housing in their resources and through personal connections, outreach, knowledge of local housing opportunities, federal, state, and local programs. There are no simple or quick solutions to housing, although there are federal programs, like Section 8 (see Glossary in Appendix A). However, once a person actually gets on the Section 8 waiting list, they can wait for years for housing to be available. In addition, applications are usually processed more quickly if a person applies online instead of submitting a paper application (Affordable Housing Online, 2020).

This is one way libraries could help—by letting their unhoused community members know they can use the library computers to fill out these online applications and by bookmarking the link to the applications.

Here are other ways libraries could help with housing:

- Reach out to local agencies who help connect people with housing.
- Provide support and computers for people to fill out housing applications. One possibility is to have volunteers who help answer questions about the technical aspects of applying online. The volunteers could include people who have the lived experience of homelessness themselves.
- Invite local, state, or federal housing agencies or experts to speak at the library.
- Highlight local resources on bulletin boards and on the library's website.
- Partner with local groups that are working on alternatives to traditional housing, such as host homes or tiny houses.

An example of a tiny house project is the "Tiny House Village" at Youth Spirit Artworks (YSA) in Oakland, California. The goal of this project is ultimately to build 26 tiny houses that will be part of a plan to house 100 of the 1,700 unhoused youth in Alameda County (California). The tiny house village will include:

- Twenty-six secure 8′ ×10′ tiny houses with
  - Murphy beds.
  - Windows.
  - Skylight.
  - Storage.
  - Electricity.
  - Furnishings.
  - Heated floors.
- On-site, clean communal bathrooms and showers.
- A kitchen yurt for residents to cook weekly communal meals and securely store their own food.
- Community gathering space for meetings.
- Associated jobs training program through YSA.
- Associated social services through YSA.

- Restorative justice (see Appendix A Glossary) covenant and community process.
- On-site resident assistants who live in the community. (Youth Spirit Artworks, 2020)

This project is supported by multiple volunteers, the faith community, the youth themselves, and a range of funders and contributors, including contributions from over 25 congregations, as well as individual donors. YSA itself was founded by Sally Hindman in 2007, with a goal to be a place "where homeless and at-risk youth could come to create and sell art, learn job skills, and contribute to their neighborhoods through community revitalization art projects" (Youth Spirit Artworks, n.d.).

A library could help with a project like this by hosting work parties, offering a program on tiny houses, which can be found across the United States, or even simply inviting an organization to park one of their tiny houses on the library's property, to draw attention to it. The Unitarian Universalist Church of Berkeley (UUCB) has done just that, as can be seen in Figures 6.3 and 6.4.

Figure 6.3 Front of Youth Spirit Artworks tiny house at UUCB.

Figure 6.4 Back of Youth Spirit Artworks tiny house at UUCB.

PROGRAMS FOR FAMILIES WITH CHILDREN

Libraries are offering programs for unhoused families with children. For example, the **Queens Public Library**, in collaboration with the New York City (NYC) Department of Homeless Services and two other library systems—the **New York Public Library** and the **Brooklyn Public Library**—created a pilot program in NYC family shelters to provide support and resources to support reading and literacy skills for children and their caregivers (Terrile & Vilardell, 2017). This program is a perfect example of library partnerships with agencies that have shared interests. It included:

> A weekly story time for toddlers and preschoolers at one shelter; a parent book club at another shelter; library card registration drives for back to school and summer reading; summer reading arts and crafts programs at three shelters each summer, along with book collections purchased for those sites. (IFLA, 2017)

The **Queens Public Library** also uses its bookmobiles to provide library services to shelters for families with children. The Queens Library

Mobile Library brings books, DVDs, and free wi-fi to shelter residents in Queens. They help residents get library cards, so they can use the other more spacious libraries in their borough. The library partners with social service agencies and works closely with family shelters (Bruinius, 2019).

Youth services librarians at the **Mercer County Library** in Lawrenceville, New Jersey, provide "weekly programs at a large, multi-service family shelter in their community" (IFLA, 2017). The **Multnomah County Library** in Portland, Oregon, provides volunteer "book talkers" who visit parks, apartment complexes, and places where families are living in vans and cars (IFLA, 2017). The **Columbus (Ohio) Metropolitan Library** has a "Ready to Read Corps" that visit "family shelters with their Bookmobile and provides programming and resources" (IFLA, 2017).

As you can see, there are many possibilities for reaching unhoused or unstably housed families with children. Creating partnerships and finding volunteers are both helpful approaches to serving this population well. It is essential you begin by reaching out and gathering information about the needs in your community—by communicating with local social service agencies, by communicating directly with the people you interact with in your library, by creating opportunities for library staff to be out in the community talking with family members about their needs. The schools can be another place to find out more about what is needed, especially if you are able to connect with the local McKinney-Vento (see Glossary in Appendix A) school officer. Serving the reading, literacy, and social needs of unhoused families with children is a critical part of meeting the library needs of all your community members.

LIBRARY PROGRAMS/PARTNERSHIPS FOR VETERANS

Some libraries are directly addressing veteran homelessness and housing instability by creating programs and partnerships. For instance, at two of their branches, **San Diego Public Library** (California) provides "trained volunteers" to help veterans and their families find resources and connect to benefits they may be entitled to (City of San Diego, 2020). Their "Veteran's Resources" web page also includes a list of links to various resources, including:

- Education.
- Health.
- Housing.
- Employment.
- General benefits.

- Hotlines.
- State and federal resources.
- San Diego organizations.

The American Library Association has created a document that highlights what libraries are doing to work with veterans in their communities. "Libraries Help and Honor Our Veterans" offers examples, suggestions, and recommended resources for libraries and those who are interested in working with libraries (American Library Association, n.d.). Although the focus isn't on homelessness, this four-page document provides examples of what libraries across the United States are doing to meet the needs of veterans and their families. One specific example of how libraries are working with unstably housed veterans and their families includes the **Seattle Public Library** (Washington), which "offers drop-in help for low-income or homeless Veterans" by providing space for a local organization to meet with veterans and their families (p. 2).

Another example of libraries partnering to address veteran homelessness is the Boots on the Ground (BOG) program at the **Kansas City (Missouri) Public Library** (KCPL). Although this van service is provided by the Salvation Army, Vietnam Veterans of America, Catholic Charities, and the Department of Veteran Affairs, they have a regular monthly stop at the KCPL Central Library, as well as occasionally other branches. They provide resources and services related to housing, benefits, legal aid, assistance with forms, and much more (Kansas City Public Library, n.d.).

If you are thinking about working with unhoused veterans, there are plenty of examples of the services and support they receive from organizations outside of the library. For instance, the "Criteria and Benchmarks for Achieving the Goal of Ending Veteran Homelessness" provides a list of criteria to end veteran homelessness. Included in this list are the need for "resources, plans, partnerships" (United States Interagency Council on Homelessness [USICH], 2017a). Libraries can offer both relevant resources and partnerships.

USICH also offers "10 Strategies to End Veteran Homelessness" (2017b). Although some of these are beyond the reach of libraries, there are relevant suggestions as well. Number 7 on the list is "Identify and Be Accountable to All Veterans Experiencing Homelessness" (p. 3). As safe and nonjudgmental spaces, libraries can be spaces where unhoused veterans can be identified and provided with relevant resources and connections. Numbers 9 and 10 are also relevant to libraries: "Increase Connections to Employment" and "Coordinate with Legal Services Organizations to Solve Legal Needs." As library staff, we already provide connections to employment opportunities, as well as related programs, such as filling out an application, writing a résumé, and practicing interview skills. Many libraries provide legal resources, and some have free regular lawyer services. For example, the Albany Library (a branch of the Alameda County Library system), in Albany, California, provides a monthly "Lawyer in the Library" service, where a volunteer lawyer meets one on one with community members for 15 minutes. Similar services are offered at the **King Library** in San Jose (California) and the **Dallas Public Library** (Texas) (IFLA, 2017).

Another example of tips that can be adapted for libraries is the article "Inside the Push to House San Antonio's Homeless Vets" (Marks, 2016). Although the article isn't about what libraries can do, it offers examples that could provide models for libraries. For example, there is a description of the interaction between two people: Shane Browning, an unhoused veteran, and Teresa Estrada, a case worker "navigator," employed by a local nonprofit, Family Endeavors. As the article notes:

> They're seated across from each other in a small, drab cubicle. Browning produces various documents, checking boxes and initialing blank spaces on a seemingly endless number of forms, while Estrada asks questions about his credit history and monthly income. (Marks, 2016)

This "small, drab cubicle" could instead be a study or meeting room in a larger library, or simply a table in a smaller library. The kinds of services supplied by Family Endeavors would work with the community-oriented resources provided at a public library, including "housing, employment, medical assistance and anything else they need to stay off the street" (Marks, 2016). Family Endeavors and nonprofit organizations like them frequently are able to find funding and support through various grants and city, state, and federal funds. Providing a space at the library, relevant resources, and possibilities for future programming and collaboration would be a great idea for a library that wants to address veteran homelessness.

SERVING UNHOUSED OLDER ADULTS

Many public libraries provide services, programs, and resources specifically for older adults. For instance, **Brooklyn Public Library (BPL)** (New York) offers "inclusive programming and services tailored to our patrons over the age of 50, including lectures, films, performances and educational programs that reflect the wide interests of today's older adults," as well as "reading and viewing materials to older adults in nursing homes, senior centers and adult day-care centers" (Brooklyn Public Library, n.d.).

To find out what the older adults in their rural service area would like from the library, **Perry Memorial Library** in Henderson, North Carolina, partnered with two local services organizations, Meals on Wheels and ACTS (Area Christians Together in Service) House, to "deliver surveys along with meals to learn what books and resources are of interest to these senior patrons" (Melko, 2020). For seniors not living independently, they also consulted with the local county Department of Senior Services.

Neither of these are programs specifically for older adults who are experiencing homelessness, but they are good examples of the kind of work that could be done to address this particular population: tailoring programs to their needs, creating partnerships, and asking the community members directly. Some older adults are living in shelters or doubled up or literally on the streets. As with any unhoused community members, it's essential to learn more about their lives and needs and how the library could help. It's difficult to find examples of specific library programs for unhoused older adults, and yet as previously mentioned, older adults are at an increasing risk of experiencing homelessness. Of course, many of the programs—such as social workers in libraries, programs for veterans, "easy access" cards, connections to local resources, and partnerships—will include seniors. However, as with senior services for housed seniors, unhoused seniors could benefit greatly from programs, resources, and services designed specifically for them. Maybe your action plan could address this need!

SOCIAL WORKERS IN PUBLIC LIBRARIES

Across the United States (and Canada), libraries are hiring social workers or hosting social work interns. Leah Esguerra, at **San Francisco Public Library** (California), is credited with being the first social worker in a public library where she started in 2009. As time has passed, her job has evolved, so she now connects library users with mental health services, and helps them find jobs, legal support, and even housing. She can do assessments and connect library users with available community services, such as clinics, mental health services, or a doctor (Dwyer, 2019).

Since then, this idea has spread, and there are multiple examples of these programs and variations on the funding and the services provided. One crucial function of the social worker concept is not only helping community members, but in addition supporting library staff. Social workers in libraries can provide training for library staff to help them support library users who are experiencing homelessness.

The list of libraries with social workers is long and getting longer. Here are some examples:

- The Long Branch Free Public Library (New Jersey)
- DC Public Library (Washington, DC)
- Denver Public Library (Colorado)
- Georgetown Public Library (Texas)
- Seattle Public Library (Washington)
- Brooklyn Public Library (New York)
- Oak Park Public Library (Illinois)
- Central Arkansas Library System
- Newark Public Library (New Jersey)
- Delaware Libraries
- Chicago Public Library (Illinois)
- Jefferson County Public Library (Colorado)
- Richland Library (Columbia, South Carolina)
- Kansas City Public Library (Missouri)

In their online survey of academic and public libraries, Bales and Winkelstein found that 114 out of the 816 respondents had on-site social workers (2018). One way to find out more about social workers in libraries is through the Public Library Association "Social Work Interest Group" on ALA Connect. This group provides information, webinars, discussions, answers to questions, and more. As they note: "This community is for anyone interested in learning more about social work in public libraries. The PLA Social Worker Task Force will use this space to discuss issues facing public libraries, provide a space to connect with others, generate and share best practices and resources" (ALA, 2019).

There are numerous articles and resources online about social workers in libraries, and many are listed in the Appendix G, Recommended Resources. If you are considering adding a social worker or social work intern to your library, it's worth hearing from those who are doing the work or whose libraries are engaged in providing these services.

Another source of information about social workers in libraries is the blog for "Whole Person Librarianship," created by Sara Zettervall and Mary Nienow. Started with a focus on the connection between social workers and library workers, the blog "has shifted to educate librarians and library staff on relevant social work concepts and tools" (WPL, n.d.). In addition to the blog, WPL has a "Community of Practice Google Group," where library staff, social work interns, and social workers in libraries exchange ideas, suggestions, questions, and support (WPL, 2020). You have to join the group to be able to read the forum and receive regular e-mails, but the information is well worth it. There are ongoing discussions and helpful answers that touch on a range of issues, from hosting a social work intern to questions about foster youth to new articles and interviews.

One example of a posting was a response to a query in April 2020 from another WPL member, who was asking about writing a proposal for a library social worker. Helen Malinka, from Berlin-Peck Memorial Library in Berlin, Connecticut, posted her proposal from her library. With her permission, that proposal can be found in Appendix N.

Appendix L includes some answers from social workers about their work in libraries. Reading through their answers offers insights into the challenges, rewards, suggestions, and lessons learned by being a social worker in a library setting.

An example of hosting social work interns is a program through the University of Maryland School of Social Work (SSW). This program, called Social Worker in the Library, began in 2017 at four library branches of the **Enoch Pratt Free Library**. It "brings graduate student social work interns into library branches to help customers address issues such as poverty, food insecurity, homelessness, and addiction" (SSW Communications, 2018). The success of this program is a testament to the power of partnerships—it brings together the University of Maryland and the Enoch Pratt Free Library, with grant funds from IMLS, the PNC Foundation, the Bunting Family Foundation, and other key donors (SSW Communications, 2018).

PEER NAVIGATORS

Another aspect of social workers in libraries is what are called "peer navigators," as mentioned earlier in reference to the **Denver Public Library**. Peer navigators or peer providers are using their lived experiences with such life occurrences as mental health challenges and homelessness to counsel and guide others with similar experiences (SAMHSA-HAS, n.d.). Peer navigators in libraries are able to personally identify with the experiences of unhoused community members and create connections as well as offering relevant resources.

The **San Francisco Public Library** (SFPL) calls their peer navigators "Health & Safety Associates," or HASAs. As Esguerra describes:

> The team tries to see if the patrons also need a free place to eat, shower, store their belongings, apply for public benefits etc. If the patron is willing to engage further, we try to encourage them to connect with a primary care provider as many of them have not seen a doctor in years. (Esguerra, 2019)

The **Brooklyn Public Library**, the **DC Public Library**, and the **Denver Public Library** also have peer navigators, as does **Kalamazoo Public Library** (KPL) in southwest Michigan. In an interview with the local television station, WWMT, the peer navigator at KPL, Anthony Sorrentino, describes his own life and how he now gets to be the "person that I always needed." The KPL peer navigator program is a partnership with the Recovery Institute of Southwest Michigan, which provides the library with peer navigators and resources (Berdine, 2019). This is an outstanding example of a partnership that benefits both the library and their partner.

GOING FINE FREE

Although libraries may not be specifically considering their community members who are experiencing homelessness when they go fine free, this approach has a positive impact on unhoused adults, youth, and families with children. Being unstably housed can make it difficult to keep track of materials like library books, and in addition, transportation is frequently a challenge. Having flexibility in return dates and not charging fines when items are late, means community members can be comfortable checking out much-needed books and other materials. For example, families with children will be more willing to check out books for their children, knowing that if the materials are returned late, they won't be charged late fees. As of this writing, the Urban Libraries Council maintains a "Fine Free Map" of U.S. libraries. As they say, "Across North America, many library systems are going 'fine free,' ceasing or limiting their use of overdue materials fines to reduce access barriers. ULC has created the below interactive map to help you understand and learn from libraries that have gone fine free" (ULC, 2020).

HONOR SHELVES

Libraries of all sizes have created honor shelves that provide books and sometimes magazines that aren't catalogued and are available for both housed and unhoused community members who don't have library cards. The expectation is that the materials will be returned at some point, although there is no official way of keeping track of them, and no one follows up. The main goal of an honor shelf is to meet the needs of unhoused community members. In their online survey of public and academic libraries, Bales and Winkelstein found that 138 out of the 816 responding libraries offered honor shelves of some kind (2018).

If you create an honor shelf, provide books in excellent condition that would be of interest to your unhoused community members. The best way to find out what is of interest is to ask: either directly or by creating a suggestion box or hanging a clipboard and pen near the shelf, so people can request particular topics or genres. Many libraries use books that have been donated to the library, for example, for book sales.

An honor shelf is one way to work around policies that prohibit library users without a permanent address from checking out materials. This kind of policy acts as a barrier to access, and it is a policy worth reconsidering. However, in cases where that can't happen, an honor shelf tells your unhoused library users you are concerned that they, too, have relevant reading materials.

BOOK BIKE PROGRAMS

An interesting twist on honor shelves are "book bike" programs, which directly meet the needs of community members who are experiencing homelessness, as well as seniors, families with children, and others who don't have the transportation to get to the library or don't have the required ID for getting a library card. For instance, the **Tempe Public Library** (Arizona) Book Bike travels "along city bikeways, visiting parks, community centers and other public areas. Routes adapt to the needs of the community and the weather" (Tempe Public Library, n.d.). The book bike offers up to three books to community members, as well as relevant resources about city programs and local organization.

The Tempe book bike program is "supported by the Arizona State Library, Archives and Public Records, a division of the Secretary of State, with federal funds from the Institute of Museum and Library Services [IMLS]," in partnership with the Homeless Outreach Program Effort (HOPE) and the Arizona Coalition for Military Families (Tempe Public Library, n.d.). These are good examples of both funding sources and partnerships.

Other examples of book bike programs can be found at **Austin Public Library** (Texas) and **Heights-Cleveland Heights Public Library** (Ohio). The **Pima County Public Library** (Arizona) provides more information about creating your own book bike program with a research paper written by Katrin A. Abel, called "Public Library Book Bikes: History and How-To" (2015).

SOCIAL CONNECTIONS

Creating social connections is critical for community members who are experiencing homelessness. We've looked at some ways libraries are contributing to these social connections, such as the coffee and conversation model or the Living Library. How else could the library help create these connections? As noted in Chapter 3, these social connections help a library be all-inclusive—welcoming and anticipating all community members.

If your library already has programs, such as storytimes, speakers, knitting groups, craft programs, book groups, and other interactive events, one way to include unhoused community members is to make sure they are invited and welcomed. You can send the information to shelters, service agencies, the faith community, schools, clinics, food banks, and so on—places where unhoused community members could learn about what you are offering at the library. By reaching out, you are letting people know you want them to be part of your library programs.

If you specifically reach out to shelters, for example, a family shelter, you could also include a small map that shows the location of the library in relation to the shelter. Small gestures like this can go a long way toward demonstrating your library is a welcoming space for all.

Feeling safe and welcomed are essential parts of serving your community members who are experiencing homelessness. Another way to create positive social connections at the library is to create an environment that feels supportive for all. Calling out negative and stereotyped language, by respectfully asking library users and staff members to be aware of the words they use and the impact of those words, can mean that unhoused community members, including those who are LGBTGQ+, know the library is on their side. Library staff must make sure they don't call people "the homeless guy" or say someone must be "off their meds" or other derogatory language that creates an atmosphere of intolerance, ridicule, or insensitivity. By not tolerating this kind of language, a library can let unhoused community members know this is potentially a nonthreatening place to spend time. In Chapter 1 we talked about trauma-informed care and ways to be guided by this approach. Reducing trauma by being respectful and welcoming will make a difference to your unhoused library users and has the potential to reduce incidents of behavior that may be alarming to library staff. We all have our ways of reacting to trauma and need a safe space to lower our guard and be our most responsive and relaxed selves.

REALLY LONG TERM

As of this writing, the **Charlotte-Mecklenburg Library** in Charlotte, North Carolina, has unveiled a plan for building a new library, scheduled to be open in 2024. McGivney (2019) describes the programs that currently exist in the library, as well as the considerations that have gone into creating a vision for the new library. It is heartening to see the way in which people who are unhoused or unstably housed seem to have been considered in the design of the building. McGivney offers examples of the current programs that provide opportunities for unhoused community members to create personal connections and to be engaged at the library. These programs, described in previous sections of this chapter, are highlighted in McGivney's article and add to the narrative of a city that is committed to creating a library space that serves all of its library users. As Lee Keesler, CEO of Charlotte-Mecklenburg Library, states:

> The new library will continue its commitment to the homeless and those in housing transition. Additional writing and reading groups will join Write Like You Mean It and Turning Pages, film screenings will offer daytime entertainment, and new classes will offer personal and professional enrichment. A social worker, and possibly a health professional, will work in the new library to offer help. "We care about these folks a lot," Keesler says. "(Main Library is) an important part of the homeless ecosystem." (McGivney, 2019)

Incorporating the needs of your unhoused community members into your library's vision, mission and future plans can seem intimidating. One approach is to take it slowly. If you're not building a new library or if you have limited funds, you can still look at your library and ask yourself the questions we talked about at the beginning of this book: Who are you trying to serve? How can you serve all community members? What is getting in your way? What could you do about that?

PROGRAM/PARTNERSHIP IDEAS

Below are some ideas for programs and/or partnerships your library could consider. A good place to begin is to look at what's happening in your community and across the country, both in libraries and in organizations and agencies that work with people experiencing homelessness.

• Organize a "National Homeless Persons' Memorial Day."

This event is organized annually on December 21, the longest night of the year. As it says on their website:

> The National Coalition for the Homeless, the National Consumer Advisory Board and the National Health Care for the Homeless Council encourage communities to host public events on or near December 21 remembering your neighbors who have died homeless in the past year. (National Coalition for the Homeless, 2019)

An organizing manual for this event can be downloaded from their website. They point out that anyone can coordinate an event, including "advocates, service providers, homeless and formerly homeless individuals/families, religious leaders, city representatives, students and concerned citizens" (National Coalition for the Homeless, 2019). It's interesting to note that, like many organizations who work with people experiencing homelessness, they don't mention libraries.

- A related event would be to show the *The INN Between*, an amazing film about the INN Between in Salt Lake City (Utah), whose mission is "to end the tragic history of vulnerable people dying on the streets of our community by providing a supportive and safe haven for those who have nowhere to live during a medical crisis" (INN Between, 2020). In the trailer for the film, one of the doctors, Jeffrey McNally, emotionally describes how most of the people talk about feeling safe there. The INN Between is a place where people can go to die without being judged, ridiculed, and watched—where they can die with dignity and respect (INN Between, 2020).

- Research the possibility of offering lockers for unhoused community members to store their belongings while they're at the library. Out of 816 survey respondents, 15 libraries provided storage lockers (Bales & Winkelstein, 2018). For example, Georgia Tech Library in Atlanta, Georgia, provides both short-term and long-term lockers of various sizes for their students (Georgia Tech Library, n.d.). Through a charity organization, ACA, Lisbon, Portugal, provides 48 "solidarity lockers" to unhoused community members. Lisbon City Hall covers 60% of the cost, and the remainder is covered by donations. As they explain, the lockers not only provide storage, but they also provide connections to ACA's street team members, who help them "obtain documents, get medical treatment, secure a state pension or find housing" (Silva, 2016).

- Bring together local organizations and agencies to create an event similar to the events and resources offered by I-Dignity, which helps people gather the paperwork needed for getting an ID. As they note on their website: "[r]estoring dignity and hope by providing identification" (I-Dignity, 2020). The I-Dignity website would be a good starting place for an event like this. The lack of an ID is a significant barrier for many people who are experiencing homelessness.

- Reach out to local youth shelters by contacting them directly and visiting if possible. Ask them what would be helpful to them, and let them know what you can offer. For example: provide tours of the library for the youth and staff, maintain an honor shelf at the shelter, check out a wi-fi hot spot to the shelter, reserve a block of computers for the youth to use at a specific time, offer to exhibit the youth's writings and art work, host a "meet the artist" evening so the youth can meet with housed community members, ask the youth to join your Teen Advisory Board, bring authors to the shelter, take a laptop to the shelter so youth can get library cards and clear their records, invite the youth to the library to talk about what they'd like the library staff and the community to know about their lives.

- Invite a local human-trafficking organization or expert to offer a program at your library so community members can learn more about this topic, recognize signs, and create positive actions that can be taken. For instance, the Community Coalition Against Human Trafficking (CCAHT) are passionate advocates about this topic and can provide resources and support for creating a program like this. Their values include:

  ○ We choose love first.

  ○ We approach our work with humility and a spirit of service.

  ○ We create innovative solutions to complex problems.

  ○ We believe in the power of community.

  ○ We serve with the understanding that healing takes time (CCAHT, n.d.).

- Create a community forum, where community members, both housed and unhoused, come together to hear from housing experts, service providers, and unhoused community members, and talk about what needs to be done in the community and what a first step would be.

- Host an informational panel and discussion about Host Homes or a similar program in your area. Host Homes provide temporary housing or permanent housing for youth and adults, depending on the program. For example, there are Host Homes that provide temporary housing in someone's home for unhoused LGBTQ+ youth (SF LGBT Center, n.d.) and Host Homes that provide permanent housing in someone's home for adults with disabilities (Lutheran Social Service of Minnesota, n.d.). Host Home programs can be found in cities and towns across the United States, and they offer opportunities for stable housing and meaningful connections. An excellent example of a rural Host Home program can be found on the Point Source Youth web page, "Host Homes: Empowering Youth Through the Housing They Need." There you can watch a video of one young person who was hosted in rural Pennsylvania (Point Source Youth, n.d.).

- Offer a program on Community Land Trusts (CLTs). As they say on their website: "Community land trusts are non-profit, community-based organizations designed to ensure community stewardship of land" (Community-Wealth.org, n.d.). The website for this organization is a rich resource for information about this concept, which is primarily designed to help create affordable long-term housing.

- Offer a program on "Direct Cash Transfers." Direct cash transfers are just that: giving money directly to people experiencing homelessness. Going against what one might assume, direct cash transfers actually save money for "local authorities, by reducing the need for emergency services" (Williams and Zhao, 2020). Even better, people who received enough cash in one study experienced an increase in "housing stability, food security, selective well-being, cognitive function, savings,

Figure 6.5 Photograph of support tower at "Searching for Home. History Colorado Exhibit, 2016."
Reprinted with permission.

assets and slight improvements even in employment" (Williams and Zhao, 2020). GiveDirectly (2020) offers research on cash transfers and like the previous study, they saw effects on monetary poverty, education, savings, and empowerment. A program like this could not only educate housed community members, but also could help dispel the common stereotypes we've talked about.

• Partner with a local store or Planned Parenthood to provide free menstrual products in all your bathrooms. These products are expensive yet necessary, and having access to free ones could make a huge difference to women who menstruate.

• Create an interactive exhibit about the importance of relationships. In 2016, the History Colorado Museum created an emotional and educational exhibit about homelessness called "Searching for Home" (2016). The exhibit included an opportunity to build a Jenga-type support network, to highlight the impact of strong community and personal relationships on a person's ability to survive and thrive. Museumgoers were encouraged to build their own support towers and then remove the blocks one at a time. Figure 6.5 is a photograph taken at that exhibit. Libraries could create a similar exhibit, so housed community members could understand the importance of these connections.

RESOURCE LISTS

Whether or not you are able to have a social worker in your library, you can still have a list of resources for people who are experiencing homelessness or are unstably housed. Many libraries are providing lists like this. Out of 816 respondents in an online survey of public and academic libraries, 473 libraries provided a resource list (Bales & Winkelstein, 2018).

Examples of the kinds of resources to include:

• Connections to housing information
• Health resources, such as free or low-cost clinics, including both mental and physical health
• Low-cost or free food—preferably food that is healthy
• Access to clothing
• Connections to employment resources
• Educational resources
• Places for free or low-cost entertainment
• Information about local ordinances

- Legal information
- Connections to the faith community and the supports they may be providing
- Information about local McKinney-Vento liaisons
- Information about free or low-cost transportation
- Volunteer opportunities
- Local charging stations and free Internet when library is closed

There are a few points to keep in mind as you're creating these lists:

- A paper copy, as well as an online list, will make it easier for those who don't have regular access to the Internet.
- The lists must be kept up to date. If you create a list, there must be library staff who are willing to commit to checking it frequently and updating the information. An out-of-date list can be discouraging and difficult, especially if the community member had to go a distance to access the resource.
- A "warm handoff" (see Glossary in Appendix A) is always better than simply handing someone a piece of paper. This is a great example of how useful it can be to have created partnerships with community agencies and organizations. If you can tell your library patron: "Ask for so-and-so" or if you can call your contact and say: "I'm sending Chris to see you," that can make all the difference to whether or not your patron follows up and whether they feel welcome and connected when they do.

Appendix H provides a model of a resources flyer from the Central Arkansas Library System, created by AmeriCorps member Jordan Johnson (Johnson, 2020).

OTHER ACTIONS

Across the United States, libraries are providing personal services tailored to the needs of their unhoused community members. In their online survey of public and academic libraries, Bales and Winkelstein (2018) noted a range of actions being taken by the respondents. These included:

- Help with transportation, for example, free bus passes (52 out of 812 respondents).
- Food pantries, free meals, and snacks.
- Hygiene packs.
- Monthly meetings with local service providers.
- Charging stations (494 out of 812 respondents).

- Free feminine hygiene products.
- Programs and special events for: people experiencing homelessness, service providers, and housed community members on the topic of homelessness.
- Vouchers for local hotels/motels and showers.
- One-on-one computer tutoring.
- After-school snacks for K–12 students.
- Laundry vouchers.
- Staff training.
- Free seed library and community garden.
- Vaccination days.
- Warming/cooling centers.
- Free use of the library's phone.
- Off-site shelter visits (79 out of 812 respondents).

Academic libraries also create libguides for their students who are experiencing housing and/or food insecurity. Good examples of these are:

- Palm Beach State College (Florida) "Community Resources: Housing Insecurity/Homelessness & More: Home" (Palm Beach State College, 2019).
- Queensborough Community College/CUNY (New York) "Student Basic Needs Supports: Home" (Queensborough Community College, 2020).
- University of Pittsburgh (Pennsylvania) Library System "Pitt and Community Assistance Resources" (University of Pittsburgh, 2020).
- Troy University (New York) "What Is Food Insecurity?" (Troy University, n.d.).

These libguides include local resources, definitions of terms, recommended books, statistics, and more. For instance, Troy University provides a photograph of a food insecurity display at their Dothan Library.

These are all examples of not only how libraries are listening to their communities and acting on what they hear, but also of what great partners libraries can be.

COLLECTION DEVELOPMENT FOR YOUNG PEOPLE

Another way to care for your unhoused community members is to make sure your materials, especially your children's and young adult books, are respectful and don't include stereotyped and disempowered images of those experiencing homelessness. Appendix M offers guidance in selecting these books. It is easy to find books that are stereotyped; it is much more challenging to find those that families and youth will embrace as being supportive.

ASSET-BASED COMMUNITY DEVELOPMENT (ABCD) (SEE GLOSSARY IN APPENDIX A, AND CHAPTER 4)

Guided by ABCD, invite your unhoused community members to meet with a facilitator at the library to discuss what is most important to them. A good guide in this work is this description from Graeme Stuart:

> We do address needs by focusing on what communities and individuals already have (their strengths and assets) in order to create the change they want to see.
>
> Rather than using language that reinforces problems and needs, we use language that reinforces potential, change and strengths. There is a difference in speaking about the priorities of a community and the needs of a community. In the first they are in control and setting the agenda. The second can often suggest they need outside support to meet their needs. (Stuart, 2017)

Using an ABCD approach, a library could:

- Provide a space and a facilitator trained in ABCD.
- Offer the library as a source of resources, meeting spaces, outreach, partners, volunteers, connections, and funds—whatever your library is able to offer as support to community members experiencing homelessness.
- Make it clear they are not leading but are there for support when asked.

ADVOCACY AND PREVENTION

At the beginning of this book we talked about homelessness itself. Quoting from *The Homelessness Industry* by Elizabeth Beck and Pamela Twiss (2018), we emphasized the need to always keep in mind: Why is this necessary? What created the need for this book?

Homelessness is a confluence of multiple societal factors, including racism, homophobia, transphobia, ableism, classism, poverty, lack of health care, underemployment, unemployment or a lack of meaningful employment, inadequate housing supply, lack of affordable health care, and more. We can address the outcomes of these factors by providing much-needed services, connections, and resources, but unless these societal challenges are addressed, this is forever.

That's not to say we shouldn't be doing all we can—I strongly believe we should. Some of the services and resources we provide have the potential to make a difference in the long term—early childhood literacy, connecting community members to employment, housing and educational opportunities—all of these and others help people move forward in their lives and can have a lifelong impact. But it is also necessary to look at advocacy and prevention: How can libraries help change the landscape of homelessness and poverty, so the public isn't dependent on institutions like libraries and schools to provide a bridge over the existing huge divides?

The definition of advocacy being used for this book is: "Efforts by those who have power, place and privilege to address the social inequities that underlie societal challenges such as homelessness and poverty." Libraries have all of these, and so any work we do has the potential to change lives. As nonpartisan institutions, libraries cannot take political stands, but we can offer resources, programs, and materials that support community members who want to address the underlying societal factors we've talked about in this chapter and in this book.

The global pandemic of 2020 and 2021, which was happening as this book was written, is a perfect example of why we need more than good ideas, great programs, and committed staff. All across the United States right now, libraries are closed. Gone are the social connections, the Internet access, the charging outlets, the free lunches for children, the bookmobiles, conversation programs, libraries as safe places with bathrooms, the social workers in the libraries, the much-needed resources, and so on. Library staff are being as creative as they can, particularly using online connections to offer storytimes, e-books, access to databases, connections to museums and other cultural institutions, and similar programs.

Many of the library social workers are adapting their work to this new situation. Some are trying to make sure there are handwashing stations, portable toilets, and clean water available, as well as providing ways to help the community quarantine in place if they are without homes (personal communication, 2020). Some are continuing to work with their clients, through various noncontact ways. For example, with the help of the social worker, the **Richland County Library** (South Carolina), in partnership with the United Way of the Midlands, created a document called "COVID-19 Updates," which includes information about shelters, health and health care, transportation, education and recreation, food and other personal needs, finances, legal, legislation, and links for updates about the virus. The document is geared toward professionals and is updated daily (Richland County Library and United Way of the Midlands, 2020).

However, for community members who are experiencing homelessness, there isn't a lot the libraries are providing, which makes sense because libraries aren't really designed to address the daily lives of unhoused community members. They are not the default library users: Safely housed folks with devices, electricity, and protection from the elements are the targeted audience, and libraries serve them well. This is not to say that libraries aren't concerned about their unhoused community members—they are. However, in general, the underlying assumptions about who is being served on a daily basis places the emphasis on those who are stably housed. There are libraries across the United States that are working hard to address everyone's needs, but the majority find it much more challenging to meet the needs of people who don't have the basics, like electricity, devices, and toilets. It's a challenging situation for everyone, including library staff.

In an article in the *Denverite*, Stevie Pinkerton talked about how the closing of the library will impact him: "That'll be a huge inconvenience," said Pinkerton, who has been experiencing homelessness for three years. "I imagine peeing in a lot of alleys" (Bryson, 2020).

So on to advocacy and prevention. What can we do? As Beck and Twiss (2018) tell us, there are three key areas for structural change—the kinds of change we need to advocate for if homelessness and poverty are to truly be addressed and prevented. These three areas are:

- Housing.
- Employment and wages.
- Health and mental health care. (pp. 240–241)

All three of these areas are complex, and there are no easy fixes for any of them. But you could look at each of them—learn more about what is happening locally, statewide, and nationally, and choose one aspect that fits with your library, your staff, and your community. For instance, what are the housing policies in your area? Is there a lack of affordable housing, as there seems to be all over the United States? If so, could you hold a community forum on housing, looking at the barriers to creating enough housing for everyone? That is, could your library help prevent homelessness?

Or perhaps your library could sponsor a community reads program and read a book like *The Color of Law: A Forgotten History of How Our Government Segregated America* by Richard Rothstein and then invite local housing advocates and community members to talk about how to address the results of past government policies.

Does your community have regulations about sitting or lying down in public or handing out food in parks? To raise awareness, you could hold a community forum to discuss why these laws exist and their impact on some community members.

Advocacy could also mean reaching out to local, state, or even national organizations, and ask what their priorities are. How are they advocating? How could the library, as a nonpartisan but concerned institution, play a role in their campaigns? For example, the Western Regional Advocacy Project (WRAP) advocates for a range of issues and offers various resources on their website, including legal research (WRAP, n.d.). Their reports and resources could provide information for creating a libguide on legal issues related to homelessness or even a workshop or community forum.

In addition, if a library is listed as a partner on the websites and published resources created by these organizations, it can bring attention to the work being done and the challenges libraries are addressing. Libraries can advocate by simply being partners, both in name and in action.

Another kind of advocacy is the basic word-of-mouth, personal one-on-one connections we can all make in our daily lives. If we bring up what pediatrician and University of California Berkeley Public Health professor Colette (Coco) Auerswald calls "housism" (personal communication, 2020), we can draw attention to the lopsided way our society views homelessness. The assumption that everyone worthwhile has a home, while those who don't are somehow inferior, contributes to the ongoing inequities that are experienced every day. Using cultural humility as a tool, we can examine our own attitudes and assumptions, then call out ones we see around us, in both our home and work lives.

As we've discussed in this book, stigma and stereotype are powerful and tenacious. But we can be vigilant and proactive and offer a different story, one that supports all of our community members and erases these false assumptions. With one story, one interaction, one book, one film, one conversation, one library display, one polite correction at a time. We can do this. Because that's what advocacy looks like. And with powerful advocates like libraries, maybe we can prevent homelessness before it even begins.

CONCLUSION

In Chapter 6 we looked at short-term and long-term actions a library can take to address the myriad ways community members experience homelessness. There are no correct answers to what a library can do, and there are many ideas, programs, connections, and resources being provided at libraries that we never hear about. In this chapter I've highlighted some examples so you can see the range of ways you could approach taking action. There is no action too small to start this journey. One conversation with a service provider or an unhoused parent or a young person who has been at your library every day for months but has never engaged with library staff or a volunteer at a shelter or . . . who else? Maybe you decide to show a film about homelessness or transgender youth or food deserts or telehealth, and you bring in a panel that includes people with lived experience as well as other local experts and local agencies or organizations. Who knows what could come out of this one event? This chapter and this book are about creating those connections, one partner at a time, so your library can become part of the caring community surrounding those who are experiencing homelessness in our cities, our towns, our states, and our country.

REFERENCES

Abel, K. A. (2015). Public library book bikes: History and how-to. *Pima County Public Library.* https://www.library.pima.gov/blogs/post/public-library-book-bikes-history-and-how-to

Affordable Housing Online. (2020). *What happens after applying to a Section 8 waiting list?* https://affordablehousingonline.com/guide/section-8-vouchers/what-happens-when-I-apply

Africawala, J. (2015, April 24). *Program models: Coffee and conversation.* https://programminglibrarian.org/programs/coffee-conversation

American Library Association (ALA). (n.d.). *Libraries help and honor our veterans.* http://www.ala.org/news/sites/ala.org.news/files/content/ALA-Veterans-2016Nov10.pdf

American Library Association (ALA). (2019). PowerPoint from ALA 2019 PLA preconference: Librarians and social workers: Partnerships that work for connecting people in need. *Social Work Interest Group.* https://connect.ala.org/pla/viewdocument/powerpoint-from-ala-2019-pla-precon?Community Key=5c2df085-e960-4608-87e7-fc132b3a43d9&tab=librarydocuments

Bailey, J. (2020, January 21). Project Uplift in 4th year connecting homeless with resources. *Commercial-News.* https://www.commercial-news.com/news/project-uplift-in-th-year-connecting-homeless-with-resources/article_6880ee84-3956-11ea-aceb-8b86cad3bc13.html

Bales, S., & Winkelstein, J. A. (2018). [Libraries and homelessness]. Unpublished raw data.

Bayaud Enterprises. (2020). *Bayaud's laundry truck.* https://www.bayaudenterprises.org/community-individual-services/mobile-services/laundry-truck

Bentley, R. (2015, April 9). Library produces "Our Lives," a documentary on Fresno's homeless. *The Fresno Bee.* https://www-1.fresnobee.com/entertainment/movies-news-reviews/article19648353.html#

Berdine, A. (2019, October 6). Kalamazoo's Public Library peer navigator program offers resources to those in need. *WWMT West Michigan.* https://wwmt.com/news/local/kalamazoo-public-librarys-peer-navigator-program-offers-resources-to-those-in-need

Berkeley Public Library. (n.d.). *Your card.* https://www.berkeleypubliclibrary.org/library/your-card#Easy_Access_Card

Bonaparte, V. (2020, February 11). Different approach to court proceedings. *2News.* https://www.ktvn.com/story/41689553/different-approach-to-court-proceedings

Branch, Z. (2020, January 13). Volunteers needed for homeless Point-in-Time Count. *South Sound Magazine.* https://southsoundmag.com/volunteers-needed-for-homeless-point-in-time-count

Brean, H. (2019, December 30). Library program offers meals, food for thought to homeless patrons. *Tucson.com.* https://tucson.com/news/local/library-program-offers-meals-food-for-thought-to-homeless-patrons/article_a5ca2db4-e9fb-5e71-adb7-0612e518b885.html

Brooklyn Public Library (BPL). (n.d.). *Services for older adults.* https://www.bklynlibrary.org/outreach/older-adults

Bruinius, H. (2019, October 31). Books on wheels: When the library comes to the homeless shelter. *The Christian Science Monitor.* https://www.csmonitor.com/USA/Education/2019/1031/Books-on-wheels-When-the-library-comes-to-the-homeless-shelter

Bryson, D. (2020, March 16). Denver is working on a coronavirus plan for people experiencing homelessness, but so far has few details to offer. *Denverite.* https://denverite.com/2020/03/16/denver-is-working-on-a-coronavirus-plan-for-people-experiencing-homelessness-but-so-far-has-few-details-to-offer

Charlotte Mecklenburg Library. (2020). *Write like you mean it.* https://cmlibrary.org/event/125375-write-you-mean-it

City of San Diego. (2019). Mental health resource fair. *San Diego Public Library.* https://www.sandiego.gov/mentalhealthfair

City of San Diego. (2020). *Veteran's resources.* https://www.sandiego.gov/public-library/services/outreach/vrc

Community Coalition Against Human Trafficking (CCAHT). (n.d.). *We are a force for change.* https://growfreetn.org/about

Community-Wealth.org. (n.d.). *Community land trusts (CLTs).* https://community-wealth.org/strategies/panel/clts/index.html

Denver Public Library. (2020). *Upcoming events: Coffee connections.* https://www.denverlibrary.org

Downtown Eastside Neighborhood House. (2020). *Alley health fair.* https://dtesnhouse.ca/?p=1149

Dwyer, C. (2019, July 17). Your local library may have a new offering in stock. *NPR.* https://www.npr.org/2019/07/17/730286523/your-local-library-may-have-a-new-offering-in-stock-a-resident-social-worker

Eberhardt, J. L. (2019). *Biased: Uncovering the hidden prejudice that shapes what we see, think and do.* Viking Press.

Esguerra, L. (2019, January 4). Providing social service resources in a library setting. *Public Libraries Online.* http://publiclibrariesonline.org/2019/01/providing-social-service-resources-in-a-library-setting

Georgia Tech Library. (n.d.). *Lockers.* https://www.library.gatech.edu/lockers

Give Directly. (2020, December 22). *Research on cash transfers.* https://www
.givedirectly.org/research-on-cash-transfers

Government Documents Round Table of ALA (GODORT). (n.d.). Voting and
election toolkits. *American Library Association.* https://godort.libguides
.com/votingtoolkit/home

HealthESchools. (n.d.). Caring for your child's health just got easier. *Center for
Rural Health Innovation.* http://health-e-schools.com

Henning, C. (2019, January 7). Former homeless help current homeless through
peer program at Denver Public Library. *4CBS Denver.* https://denver.cbs
local.com/2019/01/07/denver-public-library-homeless

History Colorado Museum. (2016, April 11). *Searching for home.* https://www
.historycolorado.org/story/exhibits/2016/04/11/searching-home

Human Library. (n.d.). *Human Library: Unjudge someone.* https://humanlibrary
.org

Humboldt State University. (2018, February 9). Homeless students' photography
to show life and strength. *Humboldt State Now.* http://now.humboldt.edu
/news/homeless-students-photography-to-show-life-and-strength

Hustings, M., Leomporra, A., & Chavez, H. (2018). You don't need a home to
vote manual. *National Coalition for the Homeless.* http://nationalhomeless
.org/campaigns/voting

I-Dignity. (2020). *Restoring dignity and hope by providing identification.* https://
idignity.org

IFLA. (2017). IFLA guidelines for library services to people experiencing homelessness. *IFLA Library Services to People With Special Needs.* https://
www.ifla.org/publications/node/12642

INN Between. (2020). *What we do.* https://www.tibhospice.org

Johnson, J. (2020). Emergency flyer. *AmeriCorp Member 2019–2020, Central
Arkansas Library System.*

Jones, N. (2018, July 7). Richland County Library helps homeless find hope.
WLTX19. https://www.wltx.com/article/news/local/richland-county-library
-helps-homeless-find-hope/101-571513234

Kansas City Public Library. (n.d.). *Outreach services: Boots on the ground (BOG).*
https://www.kclibrary.org/community-services/outreach-services

King County Library. (2017). *Stories and experiences of homelessness.* https://
kcls.bibliocommons.com/events/59d265ed3e46b13500936c50

LA County Library. (n.d.). *Earn your diploma: Free diploma & career certificate for adults.* https://lacountylibrary.org/diploma

Larkin Street Youth Services (LSYS). (n.d.). *Education and employment.* https://
larkinstreetyouth.org/get-help/#section-education-employment

Let Me Vote. (2020). *Jail voting toolkit.* https://www.letmevoteca.org/toolkit

Lissau, R. (2020, April 13). Libraries joining fight against COVID-19 virus with
3-D printers. *Daily Herald.* https://www.dailyherald.com/news/20200413
/libraries-joining-fight-against-covid-19-virus-with-3-d-printers

Lutheran Social Service of Minnesota. (n.d.). *Available host home providers.*
https://www.lssmn.org/services/people-with-disabilities/residential
-support/host-homes/available-families

Marks, M. (2016, March 30). Inside the push to house San Antonio's homeless vets. *San Antonio Current.* https://www.sacurrent.com/sanantonio/inside -the-push-to-house-san-antonios-homeless-vets/Content?oid=2516812

May, L. (2019, May 9). The public library of Cincinnati and Hamilton County connects people to help, not just books. *WCPO/abc Cincinnati.* https:// www.wcpo.com/news/our-community/the-public-library-of-cincinnati -and-hamilton-county-connects-people-to-help-not-just-books

McGivney, J. T. (2019, December 15). Inside Charlotte's reimagining of what a library is supposed to be. *Charlotte Magazine.* https://www.charlotte magazine.com/inside-charlottes-reimagining-of-what-a-library-is-supp osed-to-be

Melko, E. (2020, January 23). Outreach programming: Serving hidden patrons. *WebJunction.* https://www.webjunction.org/news/webjunction/serving -hidden-patrons.html

National Alliance to End Homelessness (NAEH). (2020a). *Events: Upcoming events. COVID-19 webinar series.* https://endhomelessness.org/events /upcoming-events

National Alliance to End Homelessness (NAEH). (2020b, April 2). *NAEH COVID-19 webinar series: Protocols for addressing sheltered and unsheltered homelessness.* Live webinar.

National Association of Counties (NAC). (n.d.). *Coffee and conversation with a librarian.* https://www.naco.org/brilliant-ideas/coffee-and-conversation -librarian

National Coalition for the Homeless. (2019). *Homeless Persons' Memorial Day.* https://nationalhomeless.org/about-us/projects/memorial-day

A New Way of Life Reentry Project (2017, May 1). *Mothers talk—Breaking Free Living Library gives formerly incarcerated women their voice.* http:// anewwayoflife.org/pressrelease/mothers-talk-breaking-free-living -library-gives-formerly-incarcerated-women-their-voice

Nonprofit VOTE. (n.d.). *Voting and homelessness.* https://www.nonprofitvote.org /voting-in-your-state/special-circumstances/voting-and-homelessness

Nordstrom. (2020). *Nordstrom now: Working together in our communities.* https://investor.nordstrom.com/news-releases/news-release-details/work ing-together-our-communities?&utm_source=email&utm_medium=mark eting&utm_term=322490_20200327_142511_body8&utm_channel=email _mark_ret_p&sp_source=email&cm_em=BB481430689FBAAFCB043 ACFA3EDCBA09E4D51E9

Palm Beach State College. (2019, December 4). *Community resources: Housing insecurity/homelessness & more: Home.* https://palmbeachstate.libguides .com/HousingInsecurity2019-2030

Pankrat, C. (2017, June 8). 5 ways the Denver Public Library supports the home-less population. *Shareable.* https://www.shareable.net/5-ways-the-denver -public-library-supports-the-citys-homeless-population

Peterson, J. (2016, November 16). Three ways libraries can channel understand-ing in confusing times. *OCLC/WebJunction.* https://www.webjunction .org/news/webjunction/3-ways-libraries-can-channel-understanding-in -confusing-times.html

Point Source Youth. (n.d.). *Host homes: Empowering youth through the housing they need.* https://www.pointsourceyouth.org/host-homes

Point Source Youth. (2020). *Register for our free COVID-19 weekly webinars.* https://www.pointsourceyouth.org/psy-covid19-resources/#registerwebinar

Public Library Association. (2020). *Public libraries respond to COVID-19: Survey of response and activities.* http://www.ala.org/pla/issues/covid-19/surveyoverview

Queensborough Community College, CUNY. (2020, August 28). *Student basic needs supports: Home.* https://qcc.libguides.com/studentneeds

Richland Library and United Way of the Midlands. (2020). *COVID-19 updates.* https://drive.google.com/file/d/1Uqryy5ervRQ_Hw2Nuu8torSZZm_f9QwW/view

Rockingham Now. (2020, March 19). *Rockingham Public Library closed but special services for patrons.* https://www.greensboro.com/rockingham_now/news/rockingham-public-library-closed-but-special-services-for-patrons/article_1e7533cf-cdf3-5f72-a23c-74fe29fa0f79.html

Romero, F. J. (2016, February 16). Teen health care van delivers more than medical care to homeless youth. *NPR.* https://www.npr.org/sections/health-shots/2016/02/17/466945298/teen-health-van-delivers-more-than-medical-care-to-homeless-youth

Rossen, J. (2019, May 9). This Cincinnati library is lending help to the homeless. *Mental Floss.* https://www.mentalfloss.com/article/582849/cincinnati-public-library-lends-help-to-homeless

SAMHSA_HRA Center for Integrated Health Solutions. (n.d.). *Peer providers.* https://www.integration.samhsa.gov/workforce/team-members/peer-providers

Scott, E. (2020, April 10). 4 reasons coronavirus is hitting black communities so hard. *Washington Post.* https://www.washingtonpost.com/politics/2020/04/10/4-reasons-coronavirus-is-hitting-black-communities-so-hard

Seattle Public Library. (2020). *Impact on people in need.* https://www.spl.org/about-us/library-impact/2018-impact-report/2018-impact-on-people-in-need

SF LGBT Center. (n.d.). *What is host homes?* https://www.sfcenter.org/host-homes

Silva, D. (2016, December 28). One city in Portugal is offering "solidarity lockers" to the homeless to help them get back on track. *Business Insider.* https://www.businessinsider.com/afp-lockers-lighten-load-for-lisbons-homeless-2016-12?op=1

Sonoma County Library. (n.d.). *Seen and heard: Visual histories of homelessness in Sonoma.* https://sonomalibrary.org/node/21597

Spokane Public Library. (n.d.). *Community Court.* https://www.spokanelibrary.org/community-court

SSW Communications. (2018, October 3). Social work students to serve in three more libraries. *University of Maryland School of Social Work.* https://www.ssw.umaryland.edu/about-the-ssw/ssw-news/social-work-students-to-serve-in-three-more-libraries.php

Stanford Children's Health/Lucile Packard Children's Hospital Stanford. (n.d.). *Mobile adolescent health services program—teen van.* https://www.stanfordchildrens.org/en/service/teen-van

State Library of North Carolina. (2014, January 29). LSTA highlights: Charlotte's job-help for the homeless. *Library Development.* http://statelibrarync.org/ldblog/2014/01/29/lsta-highlights-charlottes-job-help-homeless

Stuart, G. (2017). What is asset-based community development? *Sustaining community.* https://sustainingcommunity.wordpress.com/2013/08/15/what-is-abcd

Sturgeon, N. (2017, October 11). "Homeless is not a disease": Living library offers stories from the street. *CBC.* https://www.cbc.ca/news/canada/new-brunswick/homelessness-living-library-fredericton-1.4349627

Taylor, D. (2014, December 31). Santa Rose library offering art workshops to homeless. *The Press Democrat.* https://www.pressdemocrat.com/lifestyle/3291543-181/santa-rosa-library-offering-art?sba=AAS

Tempe Public Library. (n.d.). *Tempe book bike.* https://www.tempepubliclibrary.org/how-do-i/use-the-library/learn-about-tempe-book-bike

Terrile, V. C., & Vilardell, S. (2017). Libraries here and in the community: NYC's shelter library pilot project. *National Youth-at-Risk Conference.* https://digitalcommons.georgiasouthern.edu/nyar_vegas/2017/2017/9

Troy University. (n.d.). *What is food insecurity?* https://troy.libguides.com/c.php?g=979456

United States Interagency Council on Homelessness (USICH). (2017a). *Criteria and benchmarks for achieving the goal of ending veteran homelessness.* https://www.usich.gov/tools-for-action/criteria-for-ending-veteran-homelessness

United States Interagency Council on Homelessness (USICH). (2017b). *10 strategies to end veteran homelessness.* https://www.usich.gov/tools-for-action/10-strategies-to-end-veteran-homelessness

University of Pittsburgh. (2020, May 21). Pitt and community assistance resources. *University of Pittsburgh Library.* https://pitt.libguides.com/assistanceresources

Urban Libraries Council (ULC). (2020). *Fine free map.* https://www.urbanlibraries.org/member-resources/fine-free-map

VoteRiders. (2020). *Do you need an ID to vote?* https://www.voteriders.org

Warth, G. (2015, December 30). Libraries pitch in with homeless count. *The San Diego Union-Tribune.* https://www.sandiegouniontribune.com/lifestyle/people/sdut-homeless-count-county-libraries-2015dec30-story.html

Whole Person Librarianship (WPL). (n.d.). *Whole Person Librarianship: The hub for library–social work collaboration.* https://wholepersonlibrarianship.com/about-2

Whole Person Librarianship (WPL). (2020). *Whole Person Librarianship community of practice.* https://groups.google.com/forum/#!forum/wpl-cop

Willams, C. & Zhao, J. (2020, November 15). Do direct cash transfers work? *Brink.* https://www.brinknews.com/do-direct-cash-transfers-work/

WRAP (Western Regional Advocacy Project). (n.d.). *Legal research.* https://wraphome.org/research-landing-page/legalresearch

YALSA. (2020, April 13). Serving teens during COVID-19. *YALSA Blog.* http://yalsa.ala.org/blog/2020/04/13/serving-teens-during-covid-19/#comments

Youth Spirit Artworks. (n.d.). *About YSA.* http://youthspiritartworks.org/about-ysa

Youth Spirit Artworks. (2020). *Tiny house village.* http://youthspiritartworks.org/programs/tiny-house-village

Conclusion

LOOKING TOWARD THE FUTURE

If you are just entering the library profession, I hope this book will provide you with relevant information and support in your journey. In the library school classes I teach on homelessness and libraries, I've found the two most powerful ways to approach addressing homelessness are through partnerships and hearing from those who are most impacted. I highly recommend both.

If you are an LIS teacher, I encourage you to take advantage of the passionate professionals who are doing the work in myriad ways by inviting them to speak to your class. Hearing from those who are using trauma-informed and person-centered approaches as they are engaged in addressing homelessness and poverty in their daily work lives provides critical insights and observations that will inform and inspire your students. My heartfelt thanks to all the guest speakers who have taken the time from their work to share their thoughts and experiences with the class and for the work they do. There are so many amazing organizations, many of which are listed in Appendix G, Recommended Resources, as well as throughout this book.

These professionals, in turn, may be able to connect you with people who have the lived experience of homelessness and are comfortable sharing their stories with your students.

I also want to acknowledge here how grateful I am for every one of my students, who brought to my classes their hearts, compassion, and determination to make a difference. I learn so much from you.

If you work in a library, whatever your role, I hope this book has helped you think of ways your library can address homelessness among your community members. However you move forward, whatever actions you take—large or small—you will make a difference. Because as library staff, that's what we do.

I look forward to the day when homelessness returns to being an adjective, when it is rare and fleeting, and to a time when we no longer define people by where they lay their heads at night. I look forward to seeing more and more libraries be part of the change that is needed, as we hold firmly to the belief that none of our community members should be stigmatized or disenfranchised and as we become active partners in addressing the range of intersectional challenges that currently produce homelessness.

If you create a program, a training, a partnership, a resource, a display, a statement—whatever you do—it would be great to know about it. Please feel free to contact me, with ideas, examples, actions, questions, comments, suggestions. I'd love to hear from you.

—Julie Ann Winkelstein

Appendix A: Glossary and Related Terms

With any community members you serve at your library, it's important to use respectful and appropriate vocabulary. It is hoped this Glossary will help.

GENERAL TERMS RELATED TO HOMELESSNESS

Experiencing Homelessness

According to the U.S. Department of Housing and Urban Development (HUD), homelessness can be divided into four categories:

- People who are living in a place not designed for human habitation, or who are in emergency or transitional housing.
- People who are about to lose their primary nighttime residence.
- Families with children or unaccompanied youth who are unstably housed.
- People who are fleeing or are attempting to flee domestic violence (NAEH, 2012).

Chronic Homelessness (as Defined by HUD)

- A homeless individual with a disability who lives either in a place not meant for human habitation, a safe haven, or in an emergency shelter.
- Has lived as described continuously for at least 12 months or on at least four occasions in the last 3 years, and this time totals at least 12 months.

Invisible Homelessness

- No accurate count.
- Includes couch surfing, sleeping outside, or sleeping in vehicles.
- Nighttime shelter can be more fluid for young people than for adults—couch surfing one day, shelter the next, a friend's floor the next, the streets the next, and so on.

Point-in-Time Counts (PIT) (HUD)

- Unduplicated one-night estimates of both sheltered and unsheltered homeless populations.
- The one-night counts are conducted by CoCs (Continua of Care) nationwide and occur during the last week in January of each year.

Housing Inventory Count (HIC) (HUD)

- From each Continuum of Care (CoC).
- Provides an annual inventory of beds.
- Assists people in the CoC who are experiencing homelessness.

Homelessness and Youth

McKinney-Vento Homeless Assistance Act

- Subtitle VII-B of the McKinney-Vento Homeless Assistance Act authorizes the federal Education for Homeless Children and Youth (EHCY) Program and is the primary piece of federal legislation related to the education of children and youth experiencing homelessness. It was reauthorized in December 2015 by Title IX, Part A, of the Every Student Succeeds Act (ESSA) (NCHE, n.d.).
- Includes homeless liaisons in schools, who ensure that unhoused or unstably housed children are identified, and homeless children and youths are enrolled in, and have a full and equal opportunity to succeed in, schools of that local educational agency.
- "Homeless families and homeless children and youths have access to and receive educational services for which such families, children, and youths are eligible.
- Homeless families and homeless children and youths receive referrals to health care services, dental services, mental health and substance abuse services, housing services, and other appropriate services.

- The parents or guardians of homeless children and youths are informed of the educational and related opportunities available to their children and are provided with meaningful opportunities to participate in the education of their children" (NCHE, 2017).

RHY

- Runaway and Homeless Youth.

Youth Experiencing Homelessness (or Unhoused Youth)

- Ages 12 to 24.
- Unaccompanied youth—youth who are not with family or guardians.
- They may be or may have been part of the juvenile carceral system.
- Youth experience homelessness for many reasons, including:
  - Family poverty or homelessness.
  - Family conflict.
  - Parental or sibling alcohol and/or drug abuse.
  - Physical and/or sexual abuse at home.
  - Leaving the foster system.

LGBTGQ+ (Lesbian, Gay, Bisexual, Transgender, Gender-Expansive, and Queer/Questioning) Youth Experiencing Homelessness

- Same bullet points as youth experiencing homelessness.
- Frequently caused by conflicts over sexual orientation or gender identity.

Throwaway Youth

- Youth who
  - Are abandoned/deserted.
  - Are told to leave home by a parent or other adult in the household.
  - Leave and are prevented from returning home.
  - Run away and whose parents/caretakers make no effort to recover them/do not care if they return (Foster, 2010).

Runaway Youth

- Minors age 14 years or younger who have left home for one or more nights without parental permission.
- Age 15 and older who have left home for two or more nights (Foster, 2010).

System Youth

- Youth who have been involved in the foster, mental health, and/or juvenile carceral systems (Foster, 2010).

Street Youth

- Youth who spend a significant amount of time on the street and in other areas (such as abandoned buildings), which increases their risk for sexual abuse, sexual exploitation, and drug overuse (Foster, 2010).

TAY (Transitional Age Youth)

- Usually defined as youth ages 18 to 24, although sometimes includes ages 16 to 24.
- Transitioning out of the state system, the foster system—"aging out."
- A vulnerable time when many young people end up unstably housed.

HOUSING

United States Interagency Council on Homelessness (USICH)

- Charged with coordinating the federal response to homelessness.
- Creates a national partnership at every level of government and with the private sector (United States Interagency Council on Homelessness, n.d.).

Sheltered Homelessness (HUD)

- Refers to people who are staying in emergency housing, shelters, motels, and hotels.
- Not considered housed because the housing is temporary/short-lived.

Unsheltered Homelessness (HUD)

- People whose primary nighttime location is a public or private place not designated for, or ordinarily used as, a regular sleeping accommodation for people (e.g., the streets, vehicles, parks, abandoned buildings, under bridges).

Emergency Housing/Shelter

- Temporary.
- Emergency basis.
- Limited time.
- Can be a first step in housing.

Transitional Housing

- More stable.
- Specific period—can be 1 to 2 years.
- More predictable than emergency housing.

Supportive Housing

- Can be transitional or permanent.
- Tied to supportive services, such as having a case worker.

Shelter Plus Care (S+C)

- Includes grants from HUD for rental assistance for people with chronic disabilities.
- Eligible recipients are state and local government units, and public housing agencies.
- Rental assistance grants must be matched in the aggregate by supportive services that are equal in value to the amount of rental assistance and appropriate to the needs of the population to be served. Recipients are chosen on a competitive basis nationwide (HUD, n.d.).

Permanent Supportive Housing (HUD)

- A housing model designed to provide housing assistance and supportive services on a long-term basis for people who were experiencing homelessness. Clients are required to also have a disability.

Permanent Housing
- No limit on stay.
- Own or abide by lease.

Community Land Trusts (CLTs)
- "Non-profit, community-based organizations designed to ensure community stewardship of land."
- "Primarily used to ensure long-term housing affordability" (Community -Wealth.org, n.d.).

SRO
- Single resident/room occupancy.
- Can get rental assistance.
- Permanent housing within a Continuum of Care.

Housing First
- Different from past traditional approaches to homelessness.
- Focuses on providing people experiencing homelessness with housing as quickly as possible—and then providing services as needed.
- Pro: Provides a stable place to sleep.
- Con: Can be isolating.

Rapid Rehousing
- Intervention designed to help individuals and families to quickly exit homelessness and return to permanent housing.
- Three components: Housing identification, rent and move-in assistance, and rapid rehousing case management and services.
- Pro: Provides quick access to housing.
- Con: Is only subsidized for a specific amount of time, so people can end up back on the streets.

Section 8 Housing: Housing Choice Vouchers
- Federal government program.
- Administered locally by public housing agencies (PHA).

- Funds are paid by PHA directly to landlord.
- Tenants pay the difference.
- The housing voucher families pay 30% of their monthly adjusted gross income for rent and utilities, but must pay additional amount of rent, up to 40% if rent is higher.
- The national average wait time for a voucher is 2 years and much longer in larger cities like New York City and Los Angeles.

Low-Threshold Housing

- Low occupancy requirements, including sobriety and background checks.
- Related to harm reduction approach.
- Applies to all kinds of housing.

GOVERNMENT BENEFITS

Supplemental Security Income (SSI)

- A monthly benefit for people with limited income and resources.
- Must be blind, have disabilities, or be 65 or older.
- Is not part of Social Security funds—money comes from U.S. Treasury general funds (Social Security, 2019).

Social Security Disability Insurance (SSDI)

- Offers monthly Social Security Disability Insurance payments to people under age 65 who have qualifying disabilities and sufficient work credits.
- Qualifying employment for SSDI means recipients paid into the Social Security system (Disability Benefits Help, n.d.).

Supplemental Nutrition Assistance Program (SNAP)

- Government-funded program, but must apply in the state of residence.
- Funds are loaded onto a debit card.
- SNAP pays for most household foods, including seeds and plants used to produce food (USDA Food and Nutrition Service, 2019).

Special Supplemental Nutrition Program for Women, Infants, and Children (WIC)

- Provides federal grants to states for supplemental foods, health care referrals.
- For low-income pregnant, breastfeeding, and nonbreastfeeding post-partum women.
- For infants and children up to age 5 who are found to be at nutritional risk (USDA Food and Nutrition Service, n.d.).

Temporary Assistance for Needy Families (TANF)

- Time-limited program that provides assistance to families with children when parents or other relatives are unable to meet the family's basic needs.
- Federal grants to states.
- States decide how to carry out programs (HHS.gov, n.d.).

SOCIAL SERVICES

Caseworker

- Helps a client locate and coordinate needed services, such as mental health, housing, and educational resources.
- Relationships are key: One of most important relationships a person experiencing homelessness can have is between themselves and their caseworker.

Case Management

- Arranges for provision of an array of services; addresses unique identified needs.
- Creates opportunities to be involved in the larger community.

Coordinated Entry

- "Process by which people experiencing homelessness are given access to housing and assistance based on their level of need and resources available" (Strategies to End Homelessness, n.d.).

Continuum of Care

- Continuum of Care (CoC) is a regional or local planning body that coordinates housing and services funding for homeless families and individuals.
- CoCs represent communities of all kinds, including major cities, suburbs, and rural areas (NAEH, 2010).

Kinship Care

- Formal or informal arrangements for children to be raised by a close relative or family friend.
- In 2017, nearly 141,000 children and teens were in kinship foster care, defined as living with relatives but remaining in the legal custody of the state (Annie E. Casey Foundation, 2019).

Harm Reduction

- Nonjudgmental philosophy.
- Allows the person to have input into their own treatment plan.
- Begins with the person—they set the pace.
- Syringe exchange is an excellent example of harm reduction.
  - Syringe exchange involves doctors or other social agents giving free clean needles to patients to help prevent the spreading of diseases like HIV.
- Related terms to avoid
  - "Resistant."
  - "Refusal of care/services."
  - These labels further stigmatize people who are experiencing homelessness and trauma.
  - The implication is that they're not interested, rather than taking into account trauma and past experiences.

Service Resistant/Resistant to Services

- Term commonly used by service providers/bureaucrats to indicate a person experiencing homelessness isn't following a plan or open to suggestions from social worker/social services.

- Belied by studies and interviews that show people aren't resistant, they are dealing with bureaucracies, unsafe environments, lack of permanent housing, and confusion over required documents (NYU, 2019).

Trauma-Informed Care

- An organizational structure and treatment framework that involves understanding, recognizing, and responding to the effects of all types of trauma.
  - A traumatic event can involve physical, emotional or sexual abuse, war, community violence, neglect, maltreatment, loss of a caregiver/loved one, natural disasters, terrorism, witnessing violence or experiencing violence vicariously; it can also result from chronic adversity; chronic, severe, or life-threatening injuries, illness, and accidents (Evans, 2013).
- Trauma interferes with one's ability to cope (Evans, 2013).
- Trauma affects youth development.
- People respond to trauma in multiple ways—it's helpful to be familiar with possibilities for how a library user and library staff may react.

Warm Handoff

"A warm handoff is a transition conducted between two members of the support team in the provision of homelessness and housing services" (De Jong, 2018). For library staff, the goal of a warm handoff is to create a direct and personal connection between the community member you're working with at the library and a contact at an agency or organization. A warm handoff increases the chances the community member will be able to take advantage of the connection you've provided.

Wraparound Services

- "Intensive individualized care planning and management process."
- With wraparound services, all aspects of a person's life are considered and coordinated: housing, education, health, and so on (National Wraparound Initiative, 2013).

HEALTH-RELATED TERMINOLOGY

Mental Health and Homelessness

- In the general population about 1 in 5 people experience some sort of mental health condition.
- For those experiencing homelessness, that number is generally larger, depending on the location. Some people experience homelessness due to their mental health status, while with others their mental health is affected by homelessness.

People-First/Person-First Language

- An objective way of acknowledging, communicating, and reporting on disabilities.
- Puts the person before the disability.
- Eliminates stereotypes and misrepresentations.
- Example: A person who has depression (not "who is depressed") or a person living with bipolar disorder (not "a bipolar person") or a person with mental health life experiences (not "the mentally ill").
- Is not always embraced, depending on the person. *Always listen and follow the lead of the person you're engaging with.*

Strengths-Based Language

- Language that emphasizes the strengths of the person.
- Example: "Person who has developed coping skills in adverse circumstances" instead of "homeless alcoholic."
- Using strengths-based language removes judgment and focuses on the person's ability to adapt and survive in a hostile or challenging situation.

Person- and Family-Centered Treatment Planning

- "A collaborative process where care recipients participate in the development of treatment goals and services provided, to the greatest extent possible.
- Is strength-based and focuses on individual capacities, preferences and goals" (SAMHSA, 2020).

Offensive or Negative Language

- Words or phrases that imply something is wrong or abnormal with the individual.
- Negative words that imply tragedy, such as afflicted with, suffers, victim, struggles.
- Do not use special to mean segregated.
- Avoid euphemisms such as physically challenged, inconvenienced, and differently abled.

Stigma

- The result of false ideas that people have when they describe someone they see as "different."
- Separates the individual from the rest of their community.
- People-first language helps a person feel respected rather than labeled as "abnormal" or "dysfunctional," eliminating the stigma of a mental health diagnosis (but keep in mind earlier comments about people-first language).
- Stigmatized words include:
  - Mentally ill, emotionally disturbed, insane, crazy, odd, abnormal, psycho, maniac, lunatic, loony, wacko, cuckoo, mental, deranged, mad, loopy, out of it, slow, nuts, disturbed, demented, screw loose, brain dead, delusional, issues, schizophrenic (Disability Rights California, n.d.).

LGBTGQ+ RELATED TERMS

Note: Many of these terms are evolving and changing and may be replaced or added to other terms. Just as gender and sexuality are fluid, so is the vocabulary used.

Thank you to GLAAD (GLAAD, n.d.), the Human Rights Campaign (n.d.), and the UC Davis LGBTQIA Resource Center (n.d.) for many of the following definitions.

LGBTGQIAA

- Lesbian.
- Gay.
- Bisexual.

- Transgender.
- Gender-expansive.
- Queer/questioning.
- Intersex.
- Asexual.
- Ally.

Gender Expression

- External appearance of one's gender identity, usually expressed through behavior, clothing, body characteristics or voice, and which may or may not conform to socially defined behaviors and characteristics typically associated with being either masculine or feminine (Human Rights Campaign, n.d.).

Binary Gender System

- An unspoken cultural system that defines and allows for two and only two distinct, natural, and opposite genders—male and female.
- Understood to represent mutually exclusive poles on a spectrum.
- Disregards any ambiguity or intermingling of gender traits.

PGP/Pronouns

- Personal gender pronoun or simply pronoun.
- Pronouns are linguistic tools used to refer to someone in the third person. Examples are they/them/theirs, ze/hir/hirs, she/her/hers, he/him/his. In English and some other languages, pronouns have been tied to gender and are a common site of misgendering (attributing a gender to someone that is incorrect).
- Sometimes called "preferred gender pronoun"—but this definition is becoming less popular, as people object to the idea of their pronoun being "preferred."
- Allows a person to state what pronoun they use and would like to be used when being referred to.

Sex

- The classification of people as male or female. At birth infants are assigned a sex, usually based on the appearance of their external anatomy. (This is what is written on the birth certificate.) However, a person's sex is actually a combination of bodily characteristics, including chromosomes, hormones, internal and external reproductive organs, and secondary sex characteristics.

Gender

- A social combination of identity, expression, and social elements classifying a person as a man, woman, or an identity that is not limited to this binary. Includes gender identity (self-identification), gender expression (self-expression), social gender (social expectations), gender roles (socialized actions), and gender attribution (social perception).

Gender Identity

- One's psychological sense of self; one's identity; who someone is intrinsically.
- One's internal, deeply held sense of one's gender.
- Unlike gender expression, gender identity is not visible to others.

Gender Fluid

- Being fluid between two or more genders.
- Shifting naturally in gender identity and/or gender expression/presentation.

Bigender

- Someone who identifies with two distinct genders, such as man/woman or woman/androgyne. Bigender people don't necessarily identify with each gender 50% of the time, and unlike gender fluid people, they don't exist on a spectrum, either (Borge, 2019).

Cisgender

- A gender identity that society considers to match the sex assigned at birth.
- The prefix "cis-" means on this side or not across from.
- A term used to call attention to the privilege of people who are not transgender or gender nonconforming, gender fluid, nonbinary, and gender expansive.

Transgender

- An umbrella term that describes people whose gender identity or gender expression differs from expectations associated with the sex assigned to them at birth.

- People who are transgender may or may not have gender-affirming surgery or other surgeries and may or may not use hormone therapy.

- Transgender people may be heterosexual, bisexual, gay, lesbian, or asexual, and so on. In other words, knowing a person is transgender doesn't tell you anything about that person's sexual orientation.

- You may see this written as trans*. "The asterisk placed after trans has been used in many different ways. Some folks think of it as being more inclusive towards gender non-conforming and non-binary folks. But others have offered critique that it feels exclusionary towards GNC and non-binary folks for enforcing a binary expectation to "fill in the blank" for trans man or trans woman" (UC Davis LGBTQIA Resource Center, n.d.).

Transsexual (adj.)

- An older term that originated in the medical and psychological communities. Still preferred by some people who have permanently changed—or seek to change—their bodies through medical interventions (including but not limited to hormones and/or surgeries). Unlike *transgender, transsexual* is *not* an umbrella term. Many transgender people do not identify as transsexual and prefer the word *transgender*. It is best to ask which term an individual prefers. If preferred, use as an adjective: transsexual woman or transsexual man.

Drag Queen

- A (usually cisgender) man who performs as a woman for an audience (Borge, 2019).

Gender-Affirming Surgery

- Surgical procedures that alter or change physical sex characteristics in order to better express a person's inner gender identity. May include removal or augmentation of breasts/chest or alteration or reconstruction of genitals. Also written as gender-confirming surgery or sex reassignment surgery (SRS). Preferred term to "sex change surgery."

Transwoman

- A person who was assigned male at birth, but it wasn't consistent with her sense of self.
- May describe themselves as a transwoman or simply a woman.

Transman

- A person who was assigned female at birth, but it wasn't consistent with his sense of self.
- May describe themselves as a transman or simply a man.

Gender Nonconforming

- A term used to describe some people whose gender expression is different from conventional expectations of masculinity and femininity.
- *Please note that not all gender nonconforming people identify as transgender; nor are all transgender people gender nonconforming.*
- Many people have gender expressions that are not entirely conventional—that fact alone does not make them transgender. Many transgender men and women have gender expressions that are conventionally masculine or feminine. Simply being transgender does not make someone gender nonconforming.
- The term is not a synonym for *transgender* or *transsexual* and should only be used if someone self-identifies as gender nonconforming.

Gender-Expansive

- An umbrella term used for individuals that broaden their own culture's commonly held definitions of gender, including expectations for its expression, identities, roles, and/or other perceived gender norms. Gender-expansive individuals include those with transgender and nonbinary identities, as well as those whose gender in some way is seen to be stretching society's notions of gender (Gender Spectrum, n.d.).

Genderqueer and/or Nonbinary

- A term used by some people who experience their gender identity and/or gender expression as falling outside the categories of man and woman. They may define their gender as falling somewhere in between masculine and feminine, or they may define it as wholly different from these terms. The term is not a synonym for *transgender* or *transsexual* and should only be used if someone self-identifies as genderqueer.

Queer

- Generally used to recognize someone on the LGBTGQIAA spectrum.
- Use cautiously! This term has different meanings to different people. Some still find it offensive, while others reclaim it to encompass a broader range of identities, politics, and histories.

Questioning

- Questioning sexual orientation.
- Experimenting.
- Questioning gender.

Intersex

- Born with a sexual or reproductive anatomy and/or chromosome pattern that is not typically male or female. There are many intersex anatomy variations.
- The outdated and offensive term for intersex is hermaphrodite.

Sexuality

- A person's exploration of sexual acts, sexual orientation, sexual pleasure, and desire.

Asexuality

- A sexual orientation generally characterized by not feeling sexual attraction or a desire for partnered sexuality. This does not eliminate the capability or desire for a romantic relationship.
- Asexuality is distinct from celibacy, which is the deliberate abstention from sexual activity.
- Some asexual people do have sex.

Sexual Orientation

- A pattern of emotional, romantic, and/or sexual attraction to men, women, both genders, neither gender, or another gender.

Heterosexual Privilege

- The fact that being a heterosexual in society carries with it power and privileges.

Homosexual

- Not a recommended term.
- A person primarily emotionally, physically, and/or sexually attracted to members of the same sex.
- An outmoded term used by "others" to define the LGBTGQ+ community.
- Places emphasis on sex, rather than culture or social interactions.

Bisexual

- A person whose primary sexual and affectional orientation is toward people of the same and other genders, or toward people regardless of their gender.

Gay

- A sexual and affectional orientation toward people of the same gender.

Lesbian

- "A woman whose enduring physical, romantic, and/or emotional attraction is to other women. Some lesbians may prefer to identify as gay (adj.) or as gay women. Avoid identifying lesbians as 'homosexuals,' a derogatory term" (Borge, 2019).

Omnisexual/Pansexual

- People who have romantic, sexual, or affectional desire for people of all genders and sexes. Used by many in place of bisexual, which implies that only two sexes or genders exist.

- Sometimes described as the capacity to love a person romantically, irrespective of gender.
- Some people who identify as pansexual also assert that gender and sex are meaningless to them.

Coming Out

- "The process of first recognizing and then acknowledging non-heterosexual orientation in oneself, and then disclosing it to others" (Mallon, 2010).
- Often in stages.
- Nonlinear.
- A time when supportive information is critical.

Ally

- Someone who advocates for and supports members of a community other than their own. Reaching across differences to achieve mutual goals.

LGBTGQ+ Ally

- Someone who confronts heterosexism, homophobia, biphobia, transphobia, heterosexual and gender-straight privilege in themselves and others.

OTHER TERMS

Civic Engagement

As Peter Levine points out, there are many definitions of civic engagement. Here's one he lists on his blog:

- "Engagement, then, is not merely a matter of being active, of deploying the rhetorical and cognitive skills necessary to make your case and press your point. To engage with others requires that we hear what they have to say, that we make space in our interaction for them to respond fully and genuinely, and that we are fully responsive to their responses and proposals."—Anthony Simon Laden, "Taking the Engagement in Civic Engagement Seriously" (manuscript paper).

Latinx

- "A gender-neutral term used to replace the gender-specific Latino or Latina. It can be used to refer to a group of people or to a single person of Latin-American descent" (Borge, 2019).

Social Capital

- "Social capital theory assumes that people acquire at birth and accumulate through their lives unequal shares of capital that incrementally alter and determine their life chances" (Rosenberg, 1975, p. 228).

Raising Awareness

- Aims to make a specific issue known to the wider public, addressing existing attitudes, social relationships, and power relations in order to initiate social change.

Advocacy

- "Relates to a process where individuals, groups or communities try to influence policy and decision-makers. These groups aim to change policy, procedures and/or practice by focusing upon and minimizing the structural causes of poverty and disadvantage. . . . Advocacy activities typically cover a broad range of activities such as awareness-raising, lobbying, public relations and influencing specific legislation" (Source, n.d.).

Communication

- "A process by which information is exchanged between individuals through a common system of symbols, signs and behavior" (Merriam-Webster, n.d.).

Culture

- A learned set of values, beliefs, customs, norms, and perceptions shared by a group of people that provide a general design for living and a pattern for interpreting life. "Culture is those deep, common, unstated, learned experiences which members of a given culture share, which they communicate without knowing, and which form the backdrop against which all other events are judged (E. Hall)" (UC Davis LGBTQIA Resource Center, n.d.).

Cultural Humility

- Includes:
  - ◦ Lifelong learning and critical self-reflection.
  - ◦ Recognizing and challenging power imbalances.
  - ◦ Institutional accountability.
- No end point—there is no point at which we are "competent" and now know everything we need to know about a culture different from our own.
- Library staff need to be aware of their own personal culture and life experiences as well as the culture of libraries.
- Cultural humility helps us create a *professional* sense of self that may be different from our *personal* sense of self (Murray-Garcia & Tervalon, 2012).

Community

- "A group of people with diverse characteristics who are linked by social ties, share common perspectives, and engage in joint action in geographical locations or settings" (MacQueen et al., 2001).
- "Community is a body of people living in the same locality. . . . Alternatively, a sense of identity and belonging shared among people living in the same locality. . . . Also, the set of social relations found in a particular bounded area" (Dale, 1990, p. 562).

RESTORATIVE JUSTICE

- "Asks not 'who dunnit' and how to punish, but rather what and/or who was harmed and how do we repair it?
- Provides the conditions and possibility for lives to move beyond the conflict and pain associated with it.
- Recognizes that there is more than an absolute identity or role that someone is playing when crime and conflict occur, and that individuals and communities can play a proactive part in uncovering patterns

that have potential to be healed or in turn to further wounding and conflict.

- Separates the person from the action and values human life while maintaining accountability, safety, and restitution" (Restorative Justice on the Rise, n.d.).

REFERENCES

Annie E. Casey Foundation. (2019, August 7). *What is kinship care?* https://www.aecf.org/blog/what-is-kinship-care

Borge, J. & GLAAD (2019, June 5). The ultimate glossary of LGBTQ terms you need to know. *The Oprah Magazine.* https://www.oprahmag.com/life/relationships-love/g27629860/glossary-of-lgbtq-terms/

Community-Wealth.org. (n.d.). *Community Land Trusts (CLTs).* https://community-wealth.org/strategies/panel/clts/index.html

Dale, S. (1990). *Controversies in sociology. A Canadian introduction* (p. 562). Copp, Clark and Pitman.

De Jong, I. (2018, November 26). Making warm handoffs work. *OrgCode.* https://www.orgcode.com/making_warm_handoffs_work

Disability Benefits Help. (n.d.). *Social Security Disability Insurance.* https://www.disability-benefits-help.org/glossary/social-security-disability-insurance-ssdi

Disability Rights California. (n.d.). *People first language in mental health.* https://emmresourcecenter.org/resources/people-first-language-mental-health

Evans, J. K. (2013). What does trauma informed care really mean? *The Up Center.* www.cpe.vt.edu/ocs/sessions/csa-trauma.pdf

Foster, L. K. (2010). *Estimating California's homeless youth population.* California Homeless Youth Project/California Research Bureau.

Gender Spectrum. (n.d.). *Gender-expansive.* https://www.genderspectrum.org/glossary/gender-expansive

GLAAD. (n.d.). *GLAAD media reference guide—Transgender issues.* www.glaad.org/reference/transgender

HHS.gov. (n.d.). *What is TANF?* https://www.hhs.gov/answers/programs-for-families-and-children/what-is-tanf/index.html

HUD. (n.d.). Shelter Plus Care (S+C). *HUD.gov.* https://www.hud.gov/hudprograms/spc

Human Rights Campaign. (n.d.). *Glossary of terms.* https://www.hrc.org/resources/glossary-of-terms

MacQueen, K. M., McLellan, E., Metzger, D. S., Kegeles, S., Strauss, R. P., Scotti, R., Blanchard, L., & Trotter, R. T. (2001). What is community? An evidence-based definition for participatory public health. *American Journal of Public Health, 91*(12), 1929–1938.

Mallon, G. P. (2010). *LGBTQ youth issues.* CWLA Press.

Merriam-Webster. (n.d.). *Communication.* https://www.merriam-webster.com/dictionary/communication

Murray-Garcia, J., & Tervalon, M. (2012). *Cultural humility: People, principles and practices.* www.youtube.com/watch?v=_Mbu8bvKb_U

National Alliance to End Homelessness (NAEH). (2010, January 14). *Fact sheet: What is a Continuum of Care?* www.endhomelessness.org/library/entry/fact-sheet-what-is-a-continuum-of-care

National Alliance to End Homelessness (NAEH). (2012, January 18). *Changes in the HUD definition of homeless: Federal policy brief.* Retrieved January 1, 2016, from www.endhomelessness.org/library/entry/changes-in-the-hud-definition-of-homeless

National Center for Homeless Education (NCHE). (n.d.). *The McKinney-Vento Homeless Assistance Act.* https://nche.ed.gov/mckinney-vento

National Center for Homeless Education (NCHE). (2017). *Homeless liaison toolkit 2017 edition.* https://nche.ed.gov/homeless-liaison-toolkit

National Wraparound Initiative. (2013). *Wraparound basics.* nwi.pdx.edu/wraparoundbasics.shtml

NYU. (2019, June 10). *NYU Silver Study counters narrative that street homeless are service resistant.* https://www.nyu.edu/about/news-publications/news/2019/june/StreetHomelessReport.html

Restorative Justice on the Rise (n.d.). What is Restorative Justice? https://restorativejusticeontherise.org/resource-hub/faqs/

Rosenberg, M. (1975). The dissonant context and the adolescent self-concept. In S. Dragastin & G. Elder Jr. (Eds.), *Adolescence in the life cycle: Psychological change and social context.* Halstead Press.

SAMHSA. (2020). *Person- and family-centered care and peer support.* https://www.samhsa.gov/section-223/care-coordination/person-family-centered

Social Security. (2019). Understanding Supplemental Security Income overview. *Social Security Administration.* https://www.ssa.gov/ssi/text-over-ussi.htm

Source. (n.d.). *Advocacy for inclusion.* https://asksource.info/topics/cross-cutting-issues/advocacy-inclusion

Strategies to End Homelessness. (n.d.). *Coordinated entry.* https://www.strategiestoendhomelessness.org/what-we-do/coordinated-entry

UC Davis LGBTQIA Resource Center. (n.d.). *LGBTQIA resource center glossary.* https://lgbtqia.ucdavis.edu/educated/glossary

United States Interagency Council on Homelessness. (n.d.). *USICH.* https://www.usich.gov/about-usich

USDA Food and Nutrition Service. (n.d.). Am I eligible for WIC? *U.S. Department of Agriculture.* https://www.fns.usda.gov/wic

USDA Food and Nutrition Service. (2019, August 14). SNAP eligibility. *U.S. Department of Agriculture.* https://www.fns.usda.gov/snap/recipient/eligibility

Appendix B:
Action Planning Tool

Need	
Your Action	
Library Assets	
Steps	1. 2. 3.
Potential Barriers	1. 2. 3.
Strategies	1. 2. 3.
Time Line	
Budget	
Evaluation	1. 2. 3.

Appendix C: Library Staff Survey

One way to better understand library staff concerns related to homelessness and poverty is to do a brief survey. Below are examples of survey questions. Some of these questions are drawn from a survey done of academic and public libraries.

1. What do you see as the three biggest challenges to our library in addressing homelessness?

2. From your experience working in the library, what do you think are the three biggest needs for your community members who are experiencing homelessness?

3. What would be most helpful to you? Indicate order of importance, number 1 being most important.

   Related to homelessness, I'd like to know more about:

   a. What other libraries are doing.

   b. Staff training related to homelessness.

   c. Staff training related to mental health challenges.

   d. Justification to our funders/taxpayers for providing services/ resources related to homelessness.

   e. Creating community partnerships.

   f. How to balance the needs of all my library users.

   g. Tips on how to address the barriers to service, such as library policies, rules, and procedures.

   h. Staff burnout/compassion fatigue and what to do about it.

   i. Youth homelessness.

   j. Veteran homelessness.

    k.   Families with children and homelessness/food insecurity.

    l.   College students and homelessness/food insecurity.

    m. Other _____ .

4. Where do you find information about homelessness in the community? Please check all that apply.

    a.   Local print and online newspapers

    b.   National print and online newspapers

    c.   Local radio/television

    d.   Social media

    e.   Blogs

    f.   Listservs

    g.   Professional associations/networks

    h.   Friends/community members experiencing homelessness

    i.   National advocacy organizations

    j.   Local community organizations

    k.   Local social services agencies

    l.   Local schools

    m. Library users

    n. Other _____

5. What homelessness-related services would you like to see the library offer?

6. What would help you better understand homelessness in the community?

7. Do you think it's appropriate for the library to provide support/services/resources for community members who are experiencing homelessness? Why or why not?

8. Do you feel safe at work?

    a.   If no, why not?

    b.   If no, what would help you feel safe?

    c.   What does safety mean to you?

9. How successful do you feel working with unhoused community members?

10. How do you describe homelessness?

    a.   It's a personal problem and caused by a lack of initiative and perseverance.

b. It's a personal problem and caused by mental health challenges, including substance use disorders.

c. It's a societal problem.

d. It's a systemic issue.

e. Other _____.

11. What would you like to know or have help with or understand or get funding for? That is, what would be most helpful to you and the library work you do?

12. Is there anything else you'd like to add?

Appendix D: Creating a Dream Plan to Address Community Homelessness

Sometimes it's important to put together your ideas and create a "dream plan," even if you don't think it's attainable. A dream plan helps you understand where you'd like your library to go, what you'd really like to accomplish or change or create or even just imagine. Because sometimes being practical can get in the way of some of our best ideas. Instead of starting with limitations, start with your biggest ideas.

CREATING YOUR DREAM PLAN

Ask yourself: What is the most frustrating part of doing this work? For instance, if you only had more staff, plenty of money, support from the housed community, administrative support, a larger building? Ask other staff members: What would they like to see? You could make it a joint dream plan—work with staff, housed and unhoused community members, city officials, local organizations. Invite suggestions—out of the box, even out of the ball park suggestions. Huge ideas. Say: If money, space, staff, and support were all there, what would a dream plan look like?

EXAMPLE

For a class on libraries and homelessness and poverty, students were asked for their dream plans in relation to addressing youth homelessness. Their assignment was:

Imagine that you have an unlimited budget and universal support from the administration and community. What would be your dream program?

Describe what it would be, what you would call it, what specific challenge it would address, and how you would implement it. Then discuss how you think it would affect the library staff, the housed library users, and the unhoused library users. What would be your goal?

Student responses included a range of ideas from tutoring, meals, building a wing onto the library just for youth services (and it would include enough library staff members), to supplying connections to basic necessities, rerouting the school buses so students can come to the library, providing laundry services, hosting art events, and more. Each idea was well thought out and supported by accurate information about local needs.

Dream plans can be inspiring and offer insight into what is needed and what would be a significant contribution to your library. No matter how huge the plan, it can be a great place to start, especially if done cooperatively with the community. Sometimes people can be reluctant to give voice to their needs or dreams. Working on this project could help everyone feel connected, listened to, and who knows, it might lead to a concrete plan that you are able to put in place.

Appendix D   Dream Plan

Name of the Plan	
Description	
What Challenge It Addresses	
Goal of the Plan	
How You Would Implement It	
Possible Reactions: Staff, Housed Library Users, Unhoused Library Users, Others	

Appendix E: Planning a Fair

Whether you are planning a social services resource fair, a health fair, a jobs fair, or another kind of fair related to homelessness, it helps to have some guidelines. The following suggestions are based on the experiences of organizers from both inside and outside the library world:

- **Decide what you want to offer, who the audience will be, and why you're holding the fair. What are your goals and objectives?** For example: For a health fair, do you want to provide only resources, or will there be more interactive opportunities? Do you want to reach out to all community members who are unhoused, or do you have a particular population in mind? Or maybe your fair will be for all community members and so will include resources and activities related to experiencing poverty and homelessness. Make a list of what you'd like to include, and ask local service providers, unhoused community members, health professionals, and other local experts for suggestions. Reach out to other organizations/libraries who have sponsored a similar fair and ask for suggestions.

- **Establish a budget:** What funds will you need? Where will they come from? If the fair is held at your library and you don't need to rent furniture, the budget may be small. If you're going to offer refreshments, could a local restaurant/bakery/café/cooking school provide them? Do you already have the materials for flyers? A fair doesn't have to be expensive—the most important part is providing the information in an engaging way and offering a range of resources.

- **Set a date, time, and location at least 3 months in advance, ideally 6 months:** This allows for bringing in agencies, organizations, and volunteers who may have busy schedules. It also allows plenty of time to publicize your event.

- **Create a time line/schedule**: When do you need to get confirmation from potential partners? When will you set up for the event? How long will the fair be?

- If you're going to need to **borrow or rent extra furniture, like tables and chairs**, also make those arrangements at least 3 months in advance or more.

- Will there be a **theme** or a **catchy title** to draw attention to your event? Again, decide in advance so you can get the word out.

- **Make a list of potential partners:** For example, is there a free health clinic in town who would be willing to have a table at your fair? A yoga or meditation teacher or studio? The local YMCA? Not sure who to partner with? Ask the people you want to serve: What would be helpful to them? If you already have community partners, ask them if they can connect you to their other partners.

- Create a **script** for yourself and **reach out** to potential partners. Keep it simple. For instance: "The X Public Library is committed to being part of the supportive community for unhoused community members. We're going to host a health fair on [this date] and would like to know if you would be interested in participating? We're planning to provide a range of health-related services and activities." If possible, reach out in person. If not, try a telephone call before e-mail.

- Once you've finalized the participants, **publicize** the fair. Use a variety of ways, including: posters, flyers, the library's website, through the library's newsletter, announcements at library events, through social media, on the library's Facebook page, through local media outlets, bookmarks inserted into books that are checked out, through the partner agencies, e-mail, text, flyers posted at local businesses, through the schools, the local YMCA, and the faith community.

- **Create an evaluation tool:** A paper survey, a head count, anecdotal responses from fair attendees and community partners, an online survey link on the library's website—all of these will help you understand the impact of your event and help with planning the library's next fair. Be sure to ask for suggestions for future events. What was missing? What was particularly appreciated? How will people use the information?

- **Send thank you letters to the partners:** Let them know you appreciate partnering with them. Ask for their feedback on the event.

Appendix F: Tips for Community Service Providers/Social Workers

This document offers tips for community service providers on reaching out to their local public libraries and some suggestions for how to do so. *Please feel free to adapt it for your particular library and community.*

WHY REACH OUT TO YOUR PUBLIC LIBRARY?

- Many of your clients are most likely spending time there.
  - They may not be interacting directly with library staff.
  - They may or may not feel welcome there.
  - Public libraries can act as sanctuaries, out of the elements and away from the constant pressure of being in public and feeling judged.
  - Public libraries can be safe spaces.
- Public libraries have resources.
  - Internet access: which is critical for staying in touch with family and friends, as well as accessing the many services and programs that could provide support in the lives of your clients.
  - Legal information: how to find out about legal rights, how to obtain legal documents.
  - Computers: for word processing, résumés, writing, and so on.
  - Lists: such as low-cost or free doctors or clinics, LGBTGQ+-friendly housing.
  - Education: GED, FAFSA, colleges, local programs, lists of schools.
  - Housing: fact sheets (e.g., Section 8, local housing policies and so on), websites.

- ○ Employment: websites, fliers, other resources.
- ○ Health: information about local free/low-cost clinics.
- ○ Literacy resources, classes.
- Public libraries have services.
  - ○ Reference staff who can answer questions.
  - ○ Bathrooms—and possibly even gender-neutral bathrooms, which would mean a safe facility for all people.
  - ○ Photocopying/scanning: A good example of scanning would be scanning important documents and saving them to an e-mail account as attachments. Some libraries may be able to help with this.
- Public libraries have programs/opportunities.
  - ○ They could showcase the work of your clients: photos, writings, artwork.
  - ○ Workshops/book groups/speaker series: On parenting; on job and interview skills; on applying to colleges or for financial aid; on staying healthy on the streets.
  - ○ You, as a service provider, could offer to host or cohost programs at the library.
  - ○ Volunteers, for adults as well as youth.
- Public libraries may have meetings rooms.
  - ○ For interviewing.
  - ○ For small groups.
- Public libraries are committed to equal access to information.
  - ○ This is a priority for libraries.
  - ○ Information may be what your clients need.
  - ○ Library staff are nonjudgmental and there to help.
- Public librarians can be allies.
  - ○ For service providers.
  - ○ For all who are experiencing homelessness in their communities: youth, families, individuals experiencing homelessness.
  - ○ They are caring adults who can provide personal connections.
- Public libraries could use your expertise.
  - ○ With trauma-informed care.
  - ○ With mental health challenges.
  - ○ For staff trainings.
  - ○ For creating person-centered and trauma-informed library policies and procedures.

REACHING OUT TO YOUR LOCAL PUBLIC LIBRARY

- In person.
  - ○ Ask any *staff person* who you should talk to.
- By telephone.
  - ○ Start by calling the *reference desk* or *reference line.*
  - ○ For a small library, look for the telephone number of the *library director.*
- By e-mail.
  - ○ Look on the library's website for an e-mail address for reference questions. This may be an online form to be filled out and submitted.
  - ○ For a small library, look for the e-mail address of the *library director.*
- Attend a *library trustee* or *library board* meeting.
  - ○ The schedule for these should be on the library's website.

WHAT TO SAY

- You are interested in working *with* the library on serving your clients.
- You'd like to meet.
  - ○ To talk about ways you can partner.
  - ○ To talk about your clients and what they need.
  - ○ To exchange information about each other.
  - ○ To find out what they are already doing.
- You'd like to invite a library representative to your meetings.
- If possible, you'd like to attend their meetings.
- You'd like to send them fliers.
- You'd like to post their fliers.

POSSIBLE BARRIERS AND SOLUTIONS

- Public librarians may not understand the needs of your clients.
  - ○ They may have little information about those who are experiencing homelessness.
  - ○ They are interested in knowing more.

- Your clients may be confused or discouraged by the library's rules, policies, and procedures, such as:
    - ID requirements.
    - Confusion about the rules and when they are flexible.
    - Permanent address requirements.
    - Baggage limitations.
    - No-sleeping policies.
    - Other public conduct policies.
    - Confusion about how to use catalog and other library resources.

  By working with the library staff, you can help them create policies, rules, and instructions that will facilitate creating a safe and supportive space for all.
- Stereotypes.
    - Stereotypes of all of us get in the way, and dispelling these stereotypes is one of the challenges in providing relevant services to your clients.
    - These include stereotypes of library staff, people experiencing homelessness, and social workers/service providers.
    - Creating relationships with the library staff can help break down these stereotypes.
- Library staff are too busy.
    - They are busy, but they are also willing to listen.
- You are too busy.
    - Librarians make good allies and partners.
- You or your clients have had negative experiences with the library.
    - Library staff may need more information about the work you do.
- Library staff are not aware of unhoused youth in their libraries.
    - They need specific information about the young people and how to create a welcoming environment.
- Library staff may not see the connection between their work and yours.
    - A conversation with them may help.
    - Their work directly overlaps with yours: Their resources and services are needed by all library users.
- Library staff may be intimidated by people experiencing homelessness, especially those they don't know.
    - Meetings, conversations, and information can all help.

EXAMPLES OF WHAT LIBRARIES HAVE DONE

- Hosted a job fair at the library.
- Hosted a monthly social services fair at the library.
- Took a laptop to a shelter and helped shelter residents get library cards and clear their library records of fines and fees.
- Provided a library tour to youth and staff at a shelter.
- Maintained a small library at a youth shelter and talked about books with the youth.
- Invited youth to join library's Teen Advisory Board.
- Hired social workers.
- Hired public health nurses.
- Created opportunities for ongoing conversations at the library between housed and unhoused library users.
- Showcased work of unhoused community members.
- Provided connections to local mobile shower and laundry units.
- Co-created a community garden.
- Hosted a Community Court to address minor citations.
- Provided a storytime at a local shelter for families with children.

Appendix G: Recommended Resources

Note: This brief list of resources offers a look at the kinds of resources that are available. The references at the end of each chapter are also recommended and some are duplicated here.

You can subscribe to the newsletters from many of the organizations listed here, and that is a great way to stay informed and current on the topic of homelessness.

LIBRARY RESOURCES

American Library Association Policy B.8.10: "Addressing Poverty, Inequality and the Responsibilities of Libraries." http://www.ala.org/aboutala/governance/policymanual/updatedpolicymanual/section2/52libsvcsandrespon#B.8.10

> *This is the latest version of this policy, which has evolved over the years to be more inclusive and respectful.*

Hunger, Homelessness and Poverty Task Force (HHPTF) (ALA) http://www.ala.org/rt/srrt/hunger-homelessness-and-poverty-task-force-hhptf http://hhptf.org

> *A task force of the ALA Social Responsibilities Round Table.*

> *Charge: "Fosters greater awareness of the dimensions, causes, and ways to end hunger, homelessness, and poverty."*

> *Includes resources and the opportunity for library staff to be involved in addressing homelessness and poverty, through online and face-to-face conversations.*

"Veterans Connect @ the Library" https://calibrariesforveterans.org

> *California library program for veterans.*

"Community-Led Libraries Toolkit" from the "Working Together Project" http://
www.librariesincommunities.ca/resources/Community-Led_Libraries_Toolkit.pdf

*Highly recommended for gaining insight into how to serve all community
members well.*

IFLA Guidelines for Library Services to People Experiencing Homelessness
www.ifla.org/publications/node/12642

*This thorough international guide covers a range of topics, including
adults, families with children, unaccompanied youth, refugees, and more.
It also includes an Executive Summary, as well as a checklist.*

NATIONAL ORGANIZATIONS

National Alliance to End Homelessness (NAEH) https://endhomelessness.org

*Excellent organization with extensive resources, including webinars, vid-
eos, and publications. Can subscribe for e-mail updates.*

National Center for Homeless Education https://nche.ed.gov

*Includes a range of excellent resources on education and homelessness.
Good for public and school librarians. Their video links are good, too.*

National Law Center on Homelessness and Poverty: "News Coverage" www
.nlchp.org/news

*Includes a range of articles related to laws and homelessness. Extensive
insight into various topics, such as tent communities, McKinney-Vento awards,
the criminalization of sleeping in public, antipanhandling laws, and more.*

ACLU: Tips for Homeless Individuals on Interacting with Law Enforcement
https://www.aclunv.org/en/tips-homeless-individuals-interacting-law-enforcement

*This article offers practical tips to unhoused community members in
Nevada when interacting with police officers. While it is not legal advice,
it provides excellent information.*

ACLU App Puts Power to Hold Police Accountable in Public's Hands https://www
.santafenewmexican.com/news/local_news/aclu-app-puts-power-to-hold-police
-accountable-in-public/article_3c7f59b2-627a-59be-b22f-fc0ad78b5c7e.html

*Article about the ACLU "Mobile Justice" app and how one unhoused per-
son used it.*

Homeless Hub https://www.homelesshub.ca

*Outstanding Canadian organization that addresses homelessness in its
many forms. Includes extensive resources and research for homelessness
among all ages. Although Canadian, resources are applicable for the
United States. Highly recommended.*

United States Interagency Council on Homelessness (USICH) https://www.usich
.gov

"The U.S. Interagency Council on Homelessness leads the national effort to prevent and end homelessness in America. We drive action among our 19 federal member agencies and foster partnerships at every level of government and with the private sector."

Website includes tools, webinars, resources, and information.

Western Regional Advocacy Project (WRAP) https://wraphome.org

Advocacy organization centered in the western United States. Very action-oriented and passionate about their work.

The National Coalition for the Homeless https://nationalhomeless.org

"The National Coalition for the Homeless is a national network of people who are currently experiencing or who have experienced homelessness, activists and advocates, community-based and faith-based service providers, and others committed to a single mission: To end and prevent homelessness while ensuring the immediate needs of those experiencing homelessness are met and their civil rights are respected and protected."

Provides passionate, informed information, resources, suggestions, and ideas for addressing homelessness in the United States.

lavamae[x] https://lavamaex.org

"Lavamae[x] is a nonprofit accelerator changing the way the world sees and serves our unhoused neighbors."

Outstanding organization, dedicated to providing mobile shower services, but also extending their reach to provide "real-world training while expanding local access." The tone of their website and vision is a great model for libraries.

Justice in Aging https://justiceinaging.org

"We focus our advocacy, training, and litigation on the two areas where we can have the most impact on the lives of low-income seniors—Health Care and Economic Security."

Provides great resources, including trainings, publications, and webinars.

National Low Income Housing Coalition (n.d.). *Explore issues.* https://nlihc.org/explore-issues

Includes a range of relevant and useful resources related to Native American housing, fair housing, rural housing, homelessness, racism, housing and criminal justice and more.

SOCIAL WORK

"Supporting autonomy while setting clear boundaries" by Elissa Hardy and Jean Badalamenti. http://publiclibrariesonline.org/2019/02/supporting-autonomy-while-setting-clear-boundaries

Excellent article by two social workers in libraries.

"Implementing a Trauma-Informed Care Approach" by Rhiannon B. Eades
http://publiclibrariesonline.org/2020/04/implementing-a-trauma-informed-approach

Inspiring article about the Athens-Clarke County (GA) Library's commitment to providing a trauma-informed approach at the library.

"What Is Trauma-Informed Care?" http://socialwork.buffalo.edu/social-research
/institutes-centers/institute-on-trauma-and-trauma-informed-care/what-is-trauma
-informed-care.html

Good basic information about trauma-informed care.

PLA Social Work Interest Group/PLA Social Work Interest Group Virtual
Forum Series https://connect.ala.org/pla/communities/community-home?Commu
nityKey=5c2df085-e960-4608-87e7-fc132b3a43d9

"This community is for anyone interested in learning more about social work in public libraries. The PLA Social Worker Task Force will use this space to discuss issues facing public libraries, provide a space to connect with others, generate and share best practices and resources."

"Vulnerable to Hate: A Survey of Bias-Motivated Violence Against People
Experiencing Homelessness." From the National Alliance to End Homelessness.
https://nationalhomeless.org/vulnerable-to-hate-2016-2017

Disturbing and important report on violence against people experiencing homelessness.

HOUSING

FAHE: "Summary of Issues Facing Rural Housing" https://fahe.org/wp-content
/uploads/Summary-of-Issues-Facing-Rural-Housing-V1.2.pdf

As the title indicates, this is an excellent overview of housing issues in rural areas.

Homebase https://www.homebaseccc.org

A great example of an organization dedicated to "building community capacity to prevent and end homelessness."

Maharidge, D. (2021 January 25). "How America chose homelessness." *The Nation*, 312, 16.

LGBTGQ+ (LESBIAN, GAY, BISEXUAL, TRANSGENDER, GENDER-EXPANSIVE, QUEER/QUESTIONING) RESOURCES

Note: There are many, many excellent LGBTGQ+ organizations—these are just a few.

Transgender Law Center https://transgenderlawcenter.org

"Largest national trans-led organization advocating self-determination for all people."

National LGBTQ Task Force https://www.thetaskforce.org

"The National LGBTQ Task Force advances full freedom, justice and equality for LGBTQ people."

Human Rights Campaign https://www.hrc.org

"As the largest national lesbian, gay, bisexual, transgender and queer civil rights organization, HRC envisions a world where LGBTQ people are ensured of their basic equal rights, and can be open, honest and safe at home, at work and in the community." Provides extensive, thorough, and up-to-date resources. Highly recommended.

PFLAG https://pflag.org

"PFLAG is the first and largest organization for lesbian, gay, bisexual, transgender, and queer (LGBTQ+) people, their parents and families, and allies."

True Colors United https://truecolorsunited.org

"True Colors United implements innovative solutions to youth homelessness that focus on the unique experiences of LGBTQ young people." Website includes excellent research and reports, including "The State Index on Youth Homelessness" (https://truecolorsunited.org/index).

"Centering the Marginalized: Symphony and Triptych" medium.com/@jpc_cb /centering-the-marginalized-symphony-and-triptych-9dabc93cd461 By CB Beal.

Beautifully written, personal, and informative posting written in response to an article about trans people. Highly recommended!

VOTING RESOURCES

Politico Magazine: "The Income Gap at the Polls." https://www.politico.com /magazine/story/2015/01/income-gap-at-the-polls-113997

Interesting article about the economic divide and voting.

TurboVote https://turbovote.org

National organization dedicated to making voting easy for everyone.

VoteRiders https://www.voteriders.org

Answers questions and provides free services related to obtaining necessary documents for being able to vote.

GODORT (ALA) Voting and Election Toolkits https://godort.libguides.com/votingtoolkit

Provides general and specific voting information "for librarians, by librarians."

Rigged: The Voter Suppression Playbook https://www.riggedthefilm.com

Film and website about the history of voter suppression in the United States. The website also includes information about checking your voter registration status. Outstanding and powerful film. At this writing, the producers were offering free copies of the film to libraries across the United States.

NonprofitVOTE https://www.nonprofitvote.org

"We help non-profits engage the people they serve in voting and elections."

Includes webinars, articles, and resources. A great resource for libraries that want to address voting inequities.

Restore Your Vote: I have a felony conviction. Can I vote? https://campaignlegal.org/restoreyourvote

Provides an anonymous questionnaire that helps people with a felony conviction find out if they are allowed to vote.

OLDER ADULTS

Justice in Aging: Fighting Senior Poverty Through Law https://justiceinaging.org

Excellent organization that provides resources and information addressing multiple aspects of aging, including homelessness. One publication, called "How to Prevent and End Homelessness Among Older Adults," offers outstanding insights and suggestions and a moving video about Bill (https://vimeo.com/162403308).

CHILDREN/YOUTH/STUDENT HOMELESSNESS

Point Source Youth https://www.pointsourceyouth.org

Outstanding organization addressing youth homelessness, with extensive resources and youth videos. Highly recommended.

Point Source Youth: Indigenous Youth
"Advocacy and Liberation: Prioritizing Indigenous Youth Voice in Ending the Youth Homelessness Crisis in the West" https://www.pointsourceyouth.org/western-symposium-library/my3rye6ybxzjpmr26wat4sbwym4wk8

Thoughtful and insightful conversation between two leaders who are addressing Indigenous youth homelessness. Excellent.

"Voices of Youth Count" https://voicesofyouthcount.org

"*Voices of Youth Count (VoYC) is a national initiative designed to fill gaps in the nation's knowledge about the scope and scale of youth homelessness, as well as the life circumstances and experiences of runaway, unaccompanied homeless and unstably housed youth between the ages of 13 and 25 years old.*"

Humboldt State University: "Homeless Students' Photography to Show Life and Strength." http://now.humboldt.edu/news/homeless-students-photography-to-show -life-and-strength

Brief and excellent article about photographs taken by unstably housed college students.

"The Hope Center for College, Community and Justice" https://hope4college.com

Dedicated to making sure all students have their basic needs met, so they can attend and graduate from college.

"What Do Asthma, Heart Disease and Cancer Have in Common? Maybe Childhood Trauma." www.npr.org/sections/ed/2018/01/23/578280721/what-do-asthma -heart-disease-and-cancer-have-in-common-maybe-childhood-trauma

Excellent article on the health effects of trauma, with a great explanation of toxic stress.

New York State Technical & Education Assistance Center for Homeless Students www.nysteachs.org/afc/?number=1

Simulation of how to interact with parents/children who are experiencing homelessness and enrolling in school. Excellent model for librarians! Try making all the choices for responses so you can see how the conversation is affected by different responses.

Advocates for Youth https://advocatesforyouth.org

Has excellent resources. Use for resources and also for organizational ideas.

"Serving Our Youth 2015: The Needs and Experiences of Lesbian, Gay, Bisexual, Transgender and Questioning Youth Experiencing Homelessness" escholarship.org/uc/item/1pd9886n#page-1

Outstanding and thorough report from surveys done with 126 agencies that offer services to youth experiencing homelessness.

"The 'Hidden Crisis' of Rural Homelessness." https://www.thenation.com/article /archive/rural-homelessness-housing
Jake Bittle (2019). *The Nation.*

This excellent article provides much-needed insights into ongoing challenges of rural homelessness.

"Public Library Support of Families Experiencing Homelessness." https://www .tandfonline.com/doi/full/10.1080/10796126.2016.1209166

Vikki C. Terrile (2016). *Journal of Children and Poverty, 22*(2), 133–146.

Excellent article on libraries and family homelessness. Includes insights into the causes of homelessness, as well as examples of what one library has done.

The Roadmap for the Prevention of Youth Homelessness https://www.home lesshub.ca/youthpreventionroadmap

This outstanding guide, drawn directly from the lived experience of young people, offers concrete suggestions for the critical prevention of youth homelessness.

MISCELLANEOUS

"15 Examples of 'Anti-Homeless' Hostile Architecture That You Probably Never Noticed Before." https://interestingengineering.com/15-examples-anti-homeless -hostile-architecture-that-you-probably-never-noticed-before

Examples of hostile architecture.

ACLU: "Know Your Rights" https://www.aclu.org/know-your-rights

In-depth information about legal rights. The ACLU offers wallet cards that can be ordered from them and given out at the library. They also offer them for free at their events. Inviting them to present at the library about people's rights on the streets would be a good program to offer at your library, in partnership with a local shelter or agency.

BOOKS

Beck, E., & Twiss, P. (2018). *The Homelessness industry: A critique of US social policy.* Lynne Rienner Publishers.

An outstanding look at the history of homelessness in the United States.

Eberhardt, J. (2019). *Biased: Uncovering the hidden prejudice that shapes what we see, think, and do.* Penguin Books.

Outstanding look at prejudice in its many forms.

Oluo, I. (2018). *So you want to talk about race.* Seal Press.

Straightforward, easy to read, thoughtful and thought-provoking includes conversations and actions.

Zettervall, S.K., & Nienow, M. C. (2019). *Whole person librarianship: A social work approach to patron services.* Libraries Unlimited.

A personal, in-depth and highly useful guide to social workers in libraries.

VIDEOS/AUDIO

Finding Solutions to Homelessness at Hennepin County Library (3 minutes)
www.youtube.com/watch?v=Trzg53UIlGU

Excellent 3-minute video on the program at Hennepin County Library (MN).

"In Their Own Words: Homeless Youth" (3 minutes) https://www.youtube.com
/watch?v=BQ14I89WEEQ

Video of unhoused youth in Hennepin County.

"Duluth Homeless Youth: Walking in Their Shoes" (7.5 minutes) https://www
.youtube.com/watch?v=IM95uk4hRIo

Video of unhoused youth in Duluth.

The Homestretch trailer (4 minutes) https://www.youtube.com/watch?v=5rN85Xwa
ZwQ

Trailer for outstanding film about youth homelessness.

Homestretch full film (90 minutes) https://www.youtube.com/watch?v=hSdYlA
uXUK0

Outstanding film about youth homelessness.

"Organization iDignity Promises to Help Homeless People in Central Florida."
(2.5 minutes) https://www.youtube.com/watch?v=Msvhs0qnrFU

*Short video about iDignity, which provides various forms of IDs, on the
spot. A good model for libraries and partners.*

"Non-Profit Provides Care for People's Pets" (6 minutes) www.youtube.com
/watch?v=sCHH_VmpgyM

*Moving video about a nonprofit that works with volunteer veterinarians
across the country to provide pet health services for the pets of people
experiencing homelessness.*

American University Radio: "After Being Homeless, Former Government
Worker Struggles to Maintain Identity." (4:48 minutes) wamu.org/programs/metro
_connection/15/02/20/after_years_of_homelessness_former_government
_worker_struggles_to_maintain_identity

*A government worker talks about losing first his job and then his home.
He makes some great points. For example, he didn't know how to be
homeless—where to go, who to contact; he feels like a different person
being on the streets. Interviewer met him at the public library. Very moving.*

TED Talk: Nadine Burke Harris. "How Childhood Trauma Affects Health Across
a Lifetime." (15 minutes) https://www.ted.com/talks/nadine_burke_harris_how
_childhood_trauma_affects_health_across_a_lifetime#t-187426

Outstanding talk about the lifetime impact of toxic stress on children.

"Homeless Campground in San Diego Providing Lifeline for 40 Children" https://www.youtube.com/watch?v=gFavGiHNUro

This moving video offers insights and comments from parents and children about homelessness and their lives at the campground.

"Employed but Homeless in the US: The 'Working Poor' Who Can't Afford to Rent" https://www.youtube.com/watch?v=B_UZyT0nShI

This short video tells the story of people who are employed, some full-time, but who live in their vehicles. It offers meaningful insights into the challenges of being unhoused.

Homeless at the End (57 minutes) www.pbs.org/video/homeless-at-the-end -o4vvdt

Emotional documentary about a hospice facility for people experiencing homelessness. Highly recommended as a film to show at a library, followed by a panel and conversation.

"Brenda." From Invisible People. https://invisiblepeople.tv/videos/brenda-home less-woman-new-york-city

Moving video about Brenda, who was living on the streets of Manhattan. Highly recommended—Brenda is blunt and honest and offers insights into her daily life. This video is part of the series of videos called "Invisible People." An update in October 2019 noted that Brenda eventually found housing.

Patrick, A. (2021 February 2). "Did you miss this week's panel on racism and homelessness? Here are some highlights." Project Homeless. *The Seattle Times.* https://www.seattletimes.com/seattle-news/homeless/did-you-miss-this-weeks -panel-on-racism-and-homelessness-here-are-some-highlights/

Excellent and honest video and article about racism and homelessness. Highly recommended.

Youth First (n.d.). *Jim Crow juvenile justice.* https://vimeo.com/252590913

Quick and powerful tour through the history of racism and the juvenile carceral system. Highly recommended.

Appendix H: Emergency Resource Guide (Central Arkansas Library System)

EMERGENCY RESOURCE GUIDE

C A L S — CENTRAL ARKANSAS LIBRARY SYSTEM

Little Rock Metro Area

Emergency Shelters

Salvation Army
1111 W. Markham Street
(501) 374-8656
Women and families only
Check in: 6:15 p.m.
Call after 4:30 p.m. for shelter availability
Length of stay: 7 free consecutive nights

Little Rock Compassion Center
3618 W. Roosevelt Road (men)
4210 Asher Ave (women)
(501) 296-9114
Check in: 3 p.m.–7 p.m.

Women and Children First
(501) 376-3219
Emergency shelter for women and children fleeing domestic violence.
Shelter intake available 24 hours a day.

PATH (Partners Against Trafficking Humans)
(501) 993-1641
24-hour emergency shelter for adult victims of sex trafficking.

A.B.B.A. House
1014 S Oak St
(501) 666-9718
Shelter for pregnant and homeless women
Length of stay: Non-pregnant women up to 3 weeks; pregnant women up to a month after birth

Our House
302 E Roosevelt Road
(501) 374-7383
Residents required to find and maintain full-time jobs soon after arriving
Length of stay: Up to 2 years
Call for shelter availability

Other Resources

The Van
(501) 955-3444
Mobile resource provider taking food, clothing, and other necessities to unsheltered individuals.
Works with area churches to open emergency shelters during extreme cold weather when the temperature is 32 and below with freezing precipitation or below 25.
Text THEVANALERT to 33222 for emergency messages from The Van.

Crisis Lines

Arkansas Crisis Line: (888) 274-7472
Domestic Violence: (800) 799-7233
LGBTQ Hotline: (800) 843-4564
Rape Crisis Hotline: (800) 813-5433
Veterans Crisis Hotline: (800) 273-8255
Human Trafficking Hotline: (888) 373-7888
Women and Children First: (800) 332-4443

Library Resources

Rebecca Beadle
Community Resource Specialist
Main Branch – First Floor
(501) 918-3005

Be Mighty
After-school and weekend meals
For locations, visit bemightylittlerock.org

BE MIGHTY
Eat. Play. Learn. LITTLE ROCK.

Meals

Friendly Chapel
116 S. Pine St. NLR
(501) 371-0912
Soup kitchen operational
June–August and
November–March 11 a.m.–12
p.m.

The Stewpot
First Presbyterian Church
800 Scott Street
(501) 372-1804
Monday–Friday 12–1 p.m.

**Little Rock Compassion
Center**
11558 W. Roosevelt Road
(501) 296-9114
Breakfast, lunch, and dinner
daily

Canvas Community Church
1111 West 7th Street
(479) 225-0242
Dinner and a Movie:
Wednesdays 5:30–7:30
(dinner served at 6)

Salvation Army
1111 W. Markham Street
(501) 374-9296
Breakfast 7 a.m. daily
Holiday meals served on
Thanksgiving and Christmas

**Quapaw Quarter United
Methodist Church**
11601 S. Louisiana St.
(501) 375-1600
Community Breakfast:
Sundays 9 a.m.
Stone Soup: Sundays 3 p.m.

River City Ministry
11021 Washington NLR
(501) 376-6694
Breakfast: Monday–Friday
7:30 a.m.
Lunch: Monday–Friday 12 p.m.
Sunday meal 2 p.m.

Immerse Arkansas
5300 Asher Avenue
(501) 404-9890
Monday, Tuesday, Thursday:
12–6 p.m.
Friday: 9 a.m.–5 p.m.
Youth ages 12–23

Clothing

The Stewpot
First Presbyterian Church
800 Scott Street
(501) 372-804
Thursdays 12–1 p.m.

**Greater Second Care
Center**
5615 Geyer Springs Road
(501) 352-7874
Third Thursday of the month
10 a.m.–12 p.m. ID required.

River City Ministry
11021 Washington NLR
(501) 376-6694
Clothing bus first and third
Wednesdays 8:30–11 a.m.

Salvation Army
1111 West Markham Street
(501) 374-1913
Monday – Thursday
8:30 a.m. to 4:00 p.m.

**St. John Missionary
Baptist Church**
2501 South Main Street
(501) 218-4224
Tuesdays and Thursdays
11 a.m.–5 p.m. ID required

Day Centers

Jericho Way Day Resource Center
3000 Springer Blvd
(501) 297-8904
Case management, showers, telephones,
computers, laundry services

Immerse Arkansas
5300 Asher Avenue
(501) 404-9890
Crisis Line: 501.507.2233
Monday, Tuesday, Thursday: 12–6 p.m.
Friday: 9 a.m.–5 p.m.
Skills classes, computer lab, hot meals, laundry,
showers for youth ages 12–23

Lucie's Place
300 S. Spring St., Suite 803
(501) 508-5005
Monday, Wednesday, Friday 9–noon, 1–5
Call Tuesday and Thursday
Center for LGBTQ+ homeless youth ages 18–25
Storage, cell phones, toiletries, case management

River City Ministry
11021 Washington NLR
(501) 376-6694
Monday–Friday 8:30–3
Case management, showers, toiletries, phones

Healthcare

Open Hands Clinic
Jericho Way Resource Center
3000 Springer Blvd.
Call (501) 244-2121 or 1-855-543-2560 to schedule an
appointment
Office Hours: Monday 8–7 p.m. Tues.– Fri. 8–5 p.m.
Walk-ins welcome.

Westside Free Medical Clinic
2415 N Tyler St.
(501) 664-0340
Limited primary care, diabetic eye exams and ear, nose
and throat, physical therapy, dermatology, pharmacy and
chiropractic services. Appointments required

Healthcare

Baptist Health Community Clinic
First Presbyterian Church
800 Scott Street
(501) 227-8478
Fridays 11 a.m.–2 p.m.
Blood pressure and blood sugar screenings, basic first
aid, flu shots (October and November), diabetes risk
assessment, and more

The Stewpot: Prescriptions and Free Medical Care
First Presbyterian Church
800 Scott Street
(501) 227-8478
Third Thursday of each month

River City Ministry
11021 Washington NLR
(501) 376-6694
Adult medical clinic for general medical services by
appointment. Call for appointment Mondays and
Wednesdays after 8:30 a.m.
Eligibility: Adults without insurance, Medicare, or VA
benefits & income below 200% poverty.
Dental services for Pulaski County residents. Call for
appointment Thursday at 10 a.m.
Eye clinic with full exam and prescription eyewear if
available. Call for appointment.

Clinic at Canvas
1111 West 7th Street
(479) 225-0242
Wednesdays starting at 5:30 p.m. HIV/SID screening,
OBGYN care, mental health care, podiatry care, and
general medical care

Harmony Health Clinic
201 East Roosevelt Road
(501) 375-4400
By appointment only. Outpatient preventive and acute
care, management of some chronic and long-term
medical conditions, dental care, health maintenance,
specialty referral, health education, limited optometry
services, and some prescription assistance.
Eligibility: Patients are required to be residents or work in
the Pulaski County, Arkansas for a minimum of 90 days,
and not be covered under Medicare, Medicaid, or any
other private medical insurance provider. Patients must
be able to show that their income is less than 200% of
the Federal Poverty Level.

Appendix I: Library Self-Assessment Checklist

Serving community members experiencing homelessness requires the entire library be behind the effort and that an awareness of the reality of homelessness be integrated into every aspect of the library's services and operations.

This checklist is adapted from the WebJunction "Serving Spanish Speaking Communities Checklist" (Cuesta, 2012) and used in the 2019 Infopeople class "Library Services for Patrons Experiencing Homelessness" (Winkelstein, 2019). (See reference list in Chapter 4.)

Planning: Services to community members experiencing homelessness should be an integral part of all library planning efforts. The library's mission, goals, and objectives should specifically address services to these folks.

☐ Library director and library board are involved and committed to serving community members experiencing homelessness.

☐ Services to community members experiencing homelessness are included in the library's long-range/strategic plan.

☐ Library management and staff understand why serving community members experiencing homelessness is important.

☐ Library staff are provided opportunities to learn more about the complex nature of homelessness, the challenges in addressing it, and library services to community members experiencing homelessness.

☐ Library staff across all departments and classifications are involved in planning services to community members experiencing homelessness.

☐ Library staff have revised existing policies and procedures that impact delivery of services to community members experiencing homelessness.

Community Involvement/Connections: Effective libraries are heavily involved with community members experiencing homelessness. They make sure that community representatives are involved in the design and evaluation of library activities.

☐ Library staff meet with key community leaders and groups that represent community members experiencing homelessness on a regular basis to review and revise the service plan.

☐ Library staff have identified public relations activities with which community leaders and groups from the community of those experiencing homelessness can assist.

☐ Library staff have participated in one or more events or programs related to homelessness.

☐ Library staff have developed a list of current and potential homelessness community partners and collaborators.

☐ Library staff have developed a process for tracking homelessness community connections made and a schedule for following up and staying in touch.

☐ A schedule/process is in place for library staff to participate in programs and services related to community members experiencing homelessness.

Facilitating Access and a Welcoming Environment: Access to library services by community members experiencing homelessness includes delivery systems and bibliographic processes that reflect the lives of all community members, including members who are experiencing homelessness.

☐ Signs directing people experiencing homelessness to the library can be found at shelters, food banks, free food services, churches, and other popular spots.

☐ Culturally sensitive posters, art, and displays help create a welcoming environment.

☐ Library is open at hours convenient to all segments of the community.

Collection: The library's collection should reflect the needs and lives of all community members, including members who are experiencing homelessness.

☐ A collection development policy related to homelessness and poverty has been written.

☐ Library has a schedule/process in place for ongoing community input to homelessness and poverty collection development.

☐ Relevant collection displays and materials are in areas where people gather in the library.

Programs/Services Offered: Effective services to community members experiencing homelessness must include a wide variety of programs that meet the specific needs and interests of the entire community.

☐ Programs/activities are offered in the library (e.g., finding and interviewing for a job; healthy eating on the streets; knowing your rights on the streets; how to apply for housing).

☐ Library programs/activities are offered in the community (e.g., library booth at a health or job fair for those experiencing homelessness, community events, visits to schools, speaking to concerned community groups).

☐ Staff are culturally responsive to those experiencing homelessness (e.g., eye contact, smiles, level of communications, respectful vocabulary).

☐ Additional activities of interest to those experiencing homelessness are available (other programs and/or grants).

☐ Methods for tracking programs and number of attendees are in place.

☐ Library delivers services in the community at local gathering spots for those experiencing homelessness (e.g., migrant camps, tent communities, public parks).

☐ Library coordinates/collaborates library services/programs with other agencies working with community members experiencing homelessness.

☐ Library programs encourage/facilitate participation by community members experiencing homelessness.

☐ Library has schedule/process in place for ongoing input from community members experiencing homelessness.

Internal Communications: Effective libraries make sure that staff, volunteers, Friends, and Trustees are informed and/or involved in the design and implementation of library plans to serve community members experiencing homelessness.

☐ Library staff, volunteers, Friends, and Trustees are aware of the plan and its impact on library services, staffing, promotion, and budget.

☐ Library staff, volunteers, Friends, and Trustees have been asked for input on how to best to implement the plan.

□ Contributions and achievements of staff and volunteers in helping to establish and implement the plan have been recognized.

Staff Recruitment and Development: Effective libraries actively recruit staff at all levels that mirror the demographics of the homelessness community. They provide encouragement and opportunities for staff to develop and update skills in serving community members experiencing homelessness.

□ A schedule/process for providing cultural humility, person-centered, and trauma-informed training for all staff is in place.

□ A schedule/process for encouraging staff to participate in activities in the homelessness community is in place.

Board Recruitment and Development: Effective libraries actively recruit board members who mirror the demographics of community members experiencing homelessness. They provide encouragement and opportunities for board members to develop and update skills in representing and serving community members experiencing homelessness.

□ A process for recruiting board members who mirror the demographics of unhoused community members is in place.

□ A schedule for providing training that includes cultural humility, person-centered interactions, and trauma-informed care is in place.

Publicity and Media Relations: Effective libraries develop and maintain connections with media contacts in organizations and agencies that work with community members experiencing homelessness, as well as the community members themselves. They monitor the impact of their marketing activities to unhoused community members.

□ Library staff have developed a thorough list of social services and homelessness media contacts.

□ Library staff have met with each homelessness media contact at least once to begin the relationship.

□ Library staff, volunteers, Friends, and Trustees are aware of homelessness promotional strategies.

□ The library website includes content appropriate to the lives of those experiencing homelessness.

Appendix J: Lavamae˟ COVID-19 Prevention Kits

lavamaex.org

COVID-19 Prevention Kits

We're handing out COVID-19 prevention kits to our unhoused neighbors and service partners.

● Plan how many hygiene kits you'd like to make with your group.

Estimate 100 kits/an hour for a group of 15 people. Purchase or get donations for the items listed... Please note, regular sized items, especially shampoo/conditioner and lotion is hard for people to carry around. Travel size and unused items only please.

● Assemble hygiene kits; begin by separating hygiene items by type.

Once the items are separated by type, create an assembly line and package each item into gallon sized plastic bags, or re-usable totes and *package them into boxes.

*Pro Tip: Seal up the plastic bags 2/3 of the way, and roll the items over to rid the air and seal immediately. You'll be able to package more kits into each box!

● Schedule drop-off, or ship to any of our office/ warehouse locations.

LavaMaex has drop-off and shipping locations in San Francisco, Alameda, and Los Angeles. Shipping and drop-off location depends on the size of the donation. Contact us to schedule a drop-off/ shipping.

Contact us at info@lavamaex.org

COVID-19 Kit Essentials
Travel sized only, not all required

- Hand Sanitizer (60%+ Alcohol)
- Sanitizer Wipes
- Body Wipes
- Socks
- Underwear
- Shampoo
- Liquid Body Wash
- Conditioner
- Lotion
- Razors
- Deodorant
- Toothbrush + Toothpaste
- Floss + Mouthwash
- Q-Tips
- Nail Filers
- Hairbrushes/ Combs
- Mini Sewing Kits
- Sunscreen
- Emergency Blankets

Appendix K: American Library Association Policy B.8.10 and Policy B.8.10.1 (Old 61 and 61.1)

POLICY B.8.10 ADDRESSING POVERTY, ECONOMIC INEQUALITY, AND THE RESPONSIBILITIES OF LIBRARIES (OLD NUMBER 61)

The American Library Association promotes equal access to information for all persons and recognizes the need to respond to people experiencing poverty, which include people experiencing homelessness, in the United States. Therefore, it is crucial that libraries recognize their role in supporting these communities, so they may participate fully in a democratic society, by utilizing a wide variety of available resources and strategies. Concrete programs of training and development are needed to prepare library staff to identify needs and deliver relevant services to people experiencing poverty. In addition, the American Library Association (divisions, offices, and units) should be strengthened to support low-income neighborhoods and people experiencing poverty through programs, services, and resources.

POLICY B.8.10.1 POLICY OBJECTIVES (OLD NUMBER 61.1)

The American Library Association shall implement these objectives by:

1. Promoting the removal of barriers to library and information services, particularly fees and overdue charges.

2. Promoting the publication, production, purchase, and ready accessibility of print and nonprint materials that focus directly on the issues of poverty, that engage people respectfully, and are practical and responsive to low-income library users and their needs.

3. Promoting full, stable, and ongoing funding for existing legislative programs and services in support of people experiencing poverty and for proactive library programs that reach beyond traditional service sites.

4. Promoting training opportunities for librarians and library staff to learn effective funding techniques to improve accessibility for library users experiencing poverty.

5. Acknowledging economic equity in funding by promoting the incorporation of programs, services, and resources for people experiencing poverty into regular budgets in all types of libraries, regardless of the availability of "soft money" like private or federal grants to support these programs.

6. Promoting supplemental support for library resources for and about low-income populations by urging local, state, and federal governments, and the private sector to provide adequate funding.

7. Promoting increased public awareness through program displays, bibliographies, and publicity related to libraries' responsibilities in addressing economic barriers to service.

8. Promoting the determination of service outcomes through the active support of community needs assessments that directly involve community members who are experiencing poverty.

9. Promoting direct representation and support of community members who are experiencing, have experienced, or advocate for people experiencing poverty on local boards and advisory committees.

10. Promoting library staff training that raises awareness; relates to issues affecting the daily realities of people experiencing poverty; and recognizes and addresses attitudinal and other barriers that hinder equal access to library services and resources.

11. Promoting networking and cooperation between libraries and other agencies, organizations, and advocacy groups to develop programs and services that are useful and relevant for people experiencing poverty.

12. Promoting the implementation of expanded federal programs that acknowledge and address poverty.

13. Promoting, supporting and facilitating local community efforts to meet the needs of all community members, especially those experiencing poverty.

14. Acknowledging the disproportionate rate at which poverty affects underserved populations, including but not limited to women, people of color, LGBTQ+ people, non-Native English speakers, formerly incarcerated people, and people with disabilities.

15. Encouraging the use of respectful, inclusive, and person-first language, such as "community members experiencing poverty."

16. Encouraging a parity of library services, hours resources, and facilities between affluent and low-income library neighborhoods.

17. Promoting an attractive and inviting environment in all libraries including low-income neighborhoods.

18. Promoting the development of collections, programs, and services to help bridge the literacy gap for non-English speakers and new readers in all libraries, including low-income neighborhoods.

19. Promoting publications, outreach, and marketing in the native language for Speakers of Other Languages in all libraries, including low-income neighborhoods.

20. Promoting the review of public conduct policies and administrative procedures to ensure they are not creating unintentional barriers to people experiencing poverty.

Appendix L: Responses from Social Workers

These are examples of answers from library social workers in response to a list of questions.

Some questions and responses follow:

1. *What would you like library staff to know about serving people experiencing homelessness?*

   a. People experiencing homelessness are just like everyone else. They have good and bad days, but they could really use compassion and support during a very difficult time. They didn't become homeless overnight, and it will likely take a long time to transition. Change can happen slowly, but you are in a position at the library to change someone's day and potentially their life with just a slightly open and welcoming approach. Every single person experiencing homelessness is different just like every human.

   b. I wish people understood that there is no particular "look" to people experiencing homelessness—that you can't tell if someone does not have housing based on what they are wearing or what they carry with them. If staff knew who was connecting with me for housing needs, they would likely be really surprised.

   c. It's important for staff to understand that people who are experiencing homelessness are unique individuals and none are the same. I sometimes hear our society refer to people in a lockstep manner as if all people with similar circumstances think and act in the same way. People who are unhoused are not any more similar to each other than people who are housed may be to each other. So I encourage staff to refrain from phrases such as "homeless people think or do or need x." Instead, I encourage staff to get to know their patrons over time and understand their individual needs and preferences. It's also important for staff to understand the role of trauma in people's lives. Someone who has been through significant trauma in the past (i.e., childhood abuse, violence on the street, or even chronic homelessness) may not respond to instructions in the same way as others who have not encountered such trauma. Trauma can affect brain development in profound ways and can inhibit one's ability to cope with stress well. Therefore, if a patron is not understanding staff directions or not responding in a way staff would prefer, more patience and compassion may be needed. In the end, most people don't desire to be behaviorally difficult, but are doing the best they can with the tools they have. I recommend all library staff seek training in trauma-informed care to better understand this dynamic.

2. *What do you see as the biggest barriers for you and library staff to serve these folks?*

   a. A lack of streamlined community resources. My community has an array of services, but they are spread out and fragmented. One must travel back and forth across the city to access everything they need with little collaboration happening between agencies or services. I spend a lot of time helping patrons wade through this. A severe lack of affordable housing and emergency shelters is another issue. This city has had a great increase in homelessness in the last few years due to an incredible rise in housing prices. For many patrons I know, I see no mechanism for them to eventually obtain housing—even with an income. And without enough emergency shelter beds available in the winter, many of them are stuck on the streets with few options. Since my role is so public and I'm easily accessed, people from the community walk in and share their frustrations with me about this fragmented system often. I think library staff experience this as well. Libraries are one of the few completely public spaces that allow citizens to walk in and share about their experiences. But libraries have a limited ability to improve the system or add more services in the community. We can only tell people about what does exist and try to connect them to resources when possible.

   b. The biggest barrier can be lack of support and networks, their family history of homelessness, prior bad experience with agencies that don't care or with limited resources, and lack of compassion and patience. Expectations and reality of available resources for housing. For library staff . . . probably fear. Being overwhelmed. Not knowing what to do. Wanting to "fix it." Feeling like there's an easy solution. Not wanting to deal with it. A general lack of concern from our society and systems of oppression. The history of our country. Policies. I mean . . . there's so many things. The library admin lack of support.

c. The system isn't set up to be easy to navigate. A lot of the people I connect with feel as though they have already tried everything and do not want to reengage with a system that has failed them so many times before. When a housing waitlist is several years long and you've got to call in once a month to keep your spot on the list for just one apartment building, and you're expected to juggle multiple of these locations, there isn't a lot of incentive to continue this labor-intensive work, especially if you need to focus on getting food and other immediate needs taken care of.

3. *What has been the most rewarding part of your job?*

a. The staff at my library are thoughtful and compassionate about the patrons we serve. And they are supportive in the work I do. That has made an important difference for me here.

b. Just being here is rewarding. It's a very interesting time to be a library social worker. Connecting with patrons is always overwhelming but can be rewarding. Seeing change in staff. Seeing someone get housing. Or overcome a challenge. This takes time so it's limited.

c. I love how creative social work in the library is. I get to do a lot of macro- and community-level work and try to shift some of the larger conversations that are happening, in addition to working with individuals. And then helping advise library leadership on important community issues is really rewarding as well. No two days look alike!

d. Despite the challenges, I love my job. I love being available for people in the place where they already spend their time—no barriers, no appointments, no extra travel, just right where they are. In that sense, my program operates from a "meet-you-where-you're-at" model. That makes a tremendous difference for people who have a lot of expectations placed on them by other agencies and systems that require intakes, screenings, scheduling, insurance, and so on. I love introducing myself to new people and seeing their delight that a social worker has walked up and offered help without requiring them to jump through hoops or take extra steps to get that help. And when a referral works and an important resource connection has been made, any challenges I face are worth it.

4. *What has been the most difficult part of your job?*

    a. Limited resources. Small team. No social work peers on-site. Supervision also off-site. Feeling isolated.

    b. People don't really have a sense of what social work is. There feels like an expectation that because the library has a social worker, all the patrons experiencing homelessness will become housed and the larger societal inequities will disappear. I really wish I had that magic wand that people think I have!

5. *What has been helpful?*

    a. Any support I can get. Other library social workers across the country are a huge support. Recognition of the work. Validation from the library. The new social work task force at PLA.

    b. Having a supportive supervisor who implicitly trusts my social work skills and believes in my vision for how social work can look in our library has been really helpful. Having someone in my corner who understands the boundaries I'm setting and why I'm setting them is amazing.

6. *What changes would you like to see in libraries for serving people experiencing homelessness?*

    a. I would like to see libraries offer more mental health services to their staff and to the community. The local library tends to be the place that people go to for assistance. Sometimes the staff feel inadequate to know how to talk and deal with the patrons that are coming to them for assistance.

    b. Staff trainings on trauma-informed care. Implement programming that is specifically designed for people experiencing homelessness. The staff of my library have implemented some extra programming that has been very enriching for our patrons. We hold a monthly get-together for staff and patrons to hang out together and talk. This has been a helpful way for staff to better know the patrons and developing important relationships. Our library also holds a writing group through which patrons can discuss and write about their experiences on the street. In the end, these writings are compiled into a booklet every few months and published—a point of pride for the group.

    Consider ways to change the milieu or layout of the library to reduce trauma and stress for patrons. One example: Do not have computers in close proximity to each other, but spread them out among public spaces. The use of library computers can be an important resource for people living on the street, but when people are crammed closely together (especially while taking care of personal business as is often done on computers), discomfort and arguments are bound to occur. I recommend computers be well dispersed instead. This may sound like a small issue, but it's not—believe me!

c. I would like to see all librarians include people experiencing homelessness in their view of active patrons. Patrons to create programs for and to help. Access—allowing exception for library cards to folks without proper documents. Not seeing patrons with needs as a problem but a person they want to serve or just know, connect with.

7. *What is the most important thing you've learned from working in a library?*

a. Working in the library, as opposed to a traditional social service setting, has opened my eyes to how much happiness there is in the world. Being able to walk by a children's area and see that there is a storytime happening and hear kids laughing is such a treat. I still see a lot of suffering on an individual level, and then being a part of the larger community conversations is depressing in its own way, but I also have access to a lot more joy than previously. Whenever I take a moment to look around at what's happening in the library—from the books on the shelves to a knitting class to a healthy cooking demonstration—it's a reminder that libraries are important for everyone in the community. It's really good for my soul to be a part of that.

b. The library is the only place where everyone is welcome. The mission and goal of libraries is to serve and welcome all. That's unlike anything else. You don't have to pay. You don't have to do anything. Buy anything. That's amazing! I didn't exactly realize that until I worked here.

c. Libraries are an incredible resource! They hold a vital role in our communities for a wide range of people, and this resource should be well-protected with adequate funding and support. For many of the patrons I serve, the library is one of the few places where they can simply sit without being harassed. And it's a place that offers access to important services that most housed Americans take for granted—such as computers, wall outlets, bathrooms, and a reprieve from the weather. Librarians should know the valuable difference they make in the lives of people who have very little.

Appendix M: Guidelines for Selecting Books for Young People

As you select books with unhoused characters for your children's and young adult collection, keep these questions in mind:

1. What assumptions does the text make about people experiencing homelessness?
2. How is homelessness represented through illustrations/text?
3. Whose voices are heard and whose aren't?
4. Whose interests might be best served by the text?
5. What kind of language is used, including adjectives?
6. What kinds of illustrations are used? What do unhoused people look like?
7. Who has the power in the story?
8. Who makes the decisions?
9. Who is "saved"?
10. Who does the saving?

Be aware of common themes:

1. **Benevolence:** The housed person saves/helps the unhoused person and then feels good about themselves.
2. **Homogeneity:** People experiencing homelessness can all be lumped together. Terms like "the homeless" are used.
3. **Infantilizing of adults:** The housed person treats the unhoused person, especially adults, as if they are children who can't care for themselves or have initiative or make decisions.

4. **Needing to be extraordinary:** The unhoused character has to have an extraordinary talent and is considered an exception to the "usual" unhoused people.

5. **Treated like "they're people/human":** The idea that one has to say that, implies the underlying assumption they aren't really "normal" people.

Examples:

1. The characters' teeth are mentioned (e.g., missing teeth, toothless).

2. The characters' clothes are described/illustrated (e.g., dirty, stained, torn, old).

3. The housed people (and their children) go to shelters to feed the unhoused people, who are portrayed as powerless and grateful.

Recommended children's picture books:

- *A Shelter in Our Car.* Author: Monica Gunning, illustrated by Elaine Pedlar. Children's Book Press, 2013.

- *The Old Man.* Author: Sarah V., illustrated by Claude K. Dubois. Gecko Press, 2018.

- *Stalebread Charlie and the Razzy Dazzy Spasm Band.* Author: Michael Mahin, illustrated by Don Tate. Clarion Books, 2018.

Appendix N: Example of Library Social Worker Proposal

PROJECT NARRATIVE

In general, it can be said that a library's mission is to better provide information and resources for our patrons, regardless of circumstance, to lead fuller lives. And one of the best things about the library is that all are welcome there. However, it should be understood that the library's welcoming vibe means that it can also be a gathering place for people facing a number of challenging life circumstances.

In recent years, the number of people living lives complicated by the impact of poverty and trauma that gather at libraries has grown. This trend doesn't have to be a problem in itself, but trauma and poverty can be accompanied by issues that cause difficulties for other patrons and library staff.

The increase in visitors with serious needs means that librarians are being asked to do things that they weren't trained for or weren't expecting. Staff wants to embrace the libraries' open-arms policy, but sometimes even helpful people can feel overwhelmed. Medical emergencies, abandoned children, vandalism—these incidents go beyond a librarian's normal day-to-day work.

Also, there are individuals and families facing homelessness. To them, the library is a safe place. We have friendly and helpful staff, air-conditioning in the summer, heat in the winter, and rest room facilities. Librarians are not looking to ban anyone from the library but to find a way to help them and get them the assistance they need.

Although the circumstances in Berlin, New Britain, and Plainville [Connecticut] aren't as dire as in large cities that have hired full-time library social workers to their staffs, our three libraries have noticed an uptick in challenging situations. A part-time social worker to rotate among the libraries would serve a twofold purpose. They would have the expertise needed to educate staff—as well as connect community members with resources that could address their larger concerns.

We envision the social worker to come one morning or afternoon a week, for 4 hours, to Berlin (est. 2017 pop. 20,505); Plainville (est. 2017 pop. 17,705) and to New Britain (est. 2017 pop. 72,710). Even though New Britain has seen a recent decrease of issues since municipal agencies have stepped up, the size of their city portends future situations. Having set hours in each library would be beneficial to our staffs who would know where to call in an emergency situation. We would expect the individual to build a more personal connection with a patron needing help. Instead of just handing them a referral phone number, the social worker could actually make the call and calm their fears. It's a little extra helping hand that people need and appreciate and that library staff don't have time to do. Although this sounds like something that could be done in a municipality's social services office, we feel that those offices, though staffed by helpful and sometimes overwhelmed town employees, can be more intimidating than the safer environment of the library.

Our hope is that the social worker will be able to assist individuals who are experiencing homelessness and those with mental health issues. According to the Connecticut Coordinated Access Network (CT CAN) data, the central region of our state, which includes Berlin, New Britain, and Plainville served approximately 820 homeless heads of households between emergency shelters, outreach, and rapid, supportive, and/or transitional rehousing. Assessing the number of individuals with mental health issues is a more complicated task, as many do not seek help. However, statistics from the Hospital of Central CT show that they alone treated approximately 7,500 people between the emergency room, outpatient, and inpatient settings.

We are very fortunate to partner with the Hospital of Central Connecticut (HOCC) in this project. It was a manager of Care Coordination and Social Work Services at Midstate Medical Center, Mary Beth Rolan, who saw an article in the *New Britain Herald* regarding the possibility of our applying for a social worker grant. She, in turn, passed the article to Jessica Collins, Regional Director, Behavioral Health at HOCC. Jessica was very excited because she and her team were looking for more ways to reach people who could use their services. We arranged a meeting, and she immediately offered to partner with us in this effort. The three libraries and Ms. Collins agree that there are many library patrons that struggle with mental health. A social worker can help make connections to other agencies, explaining their programs and the services they offer. They can be that middle person and help people understand what it means to have therapy, to walk through the process, help them fill out the referral form, and let them know that someone will call them in a day or two. They would help bridge that gap to services. Or perhaps people would just come by and talk to the social worker. They wouldn't have to give a lot of personal information. Social workers already working in libraries have discovered that many of the people they see prefer this nontraditional approach to mental health care. This is especially true for many cultures that have a stigma around these services.

The same is true for homelessness. Librarians may not know how to help someone beyond providing shelter phone numbers. A social worker understands the system and may be able to obtain help for the person right away.

On the other hand, our goal as libraries is to learn how to be more sensitive to the traumatic experiences our patrons may have gone through and to learn how to work with people a little bit better.

Throughout the first year of our program, the library directors will meet with the social worker to assess the progress of the project. Each of us will want an accounting of how things are going. In Berlin, I would request a written report that would be included in my own monthly report to the Board of Trustees and Town Manager. I would also request that the social worker attend our monthly staff meetings, so that everyone would have the opportunity to pose questions about specific patrons or behaviors in a private setting (our meetings take place before the library opens to the public).

Using funds obtained from the grant would not create any additional expenses for the libraries. In fact, we are only requesting enough money to pay for the social worker's salary. In speaking with our partner, HOCC, two scenarios were evaluated. In the first, a recent unlicensed graduate from the HOCC Social Work program would be hired at $22/hour for 12 hours per week, 4 hours at each library. In the second plan, an intern would be coming to each library, accompanied by a licensed supervisor. Although the supervisor would be paid more than $22 an hour, the intern receives no salary, only graduation credits. The HOCC would pick up the difference between our grant amount and the salary. The decision on which scenario we would choose will depend on the types of questions, meetings, and encounters our social worker will experience. Since the money amount stays the same, switching from one plan to another should not be too disruptive. However, we would ultimately leave that decision up to the HOCC team.

Another benefit of partnering with HOCC is that they will take care of all the payroll taxes and fringe benefits for our worker. That was one drawback that a few of our town managers and human resources staff brought up, as they didn't want the town budget to be affected by extra payroll costs.

No other sources of funds are being pursued at this point. Depending on the success of the program, we will determine if we will go forward after one year. Since the state and municipal budgets are so tight, and we have been requested to not request any new personnel, if we do continue this worthwhile project, we will continue to seek grant opportunities.

Helen Malinka
Library Director
Berlin-Peck Memorial Library

Index

About the Author

JULIE ANN WINKELSTEIN, MLIS, PhD, is a librarian, writer, activist, and teacher. She is the author of several book chapters as well as journal articles, and she was a contributing author as well as primary editor of the IFLA "Guidelines for Library Services to People Experiencing Homelessness." Winkelstein created and teaches a library school course on homelessness, poverty, and public libraries at the University of Tennessee, Knoxville, and a continuing education library course through the Infopeople Project, part of the Califa Group, a nonprofit library membership consortium. In 2021, she also cotaught a University of Washington library school class on unhoused youth and children and libraries. She has presented internationally on the topic of libraries and homelessness, including LGBTGQ+ youth homelessness, and through an IMLS grant provided trainings and workshops for library staff on this topic. She worked for 20 years as a public librarian, in a range of roles, from jail and prison librarian to family literacy coordinator to young adult and children's librarian. Her work focuses on the intersection of social justice and public libraries.